ADVANCED TAX STRATEGIES FOR LLCS AND PARTNERSHIPS

BY LARRY TUNNELL, PH.D., CPA;
ROBERT RICKETTS, PH.D., CPA

Notice to Readers

Advanced Tax Strategies for LLCs and Partnerships is intended solely for use in continuing professional education and not as a reference. It does not represent an official position of the Association of International Certified Professional Accountants, and it is distributed with the understanding that the author and publisher are not rendering legal, accounting, or other professional services in the publication. This course is intended to be an overview of the topics discussed within, and the author has made every attempt to verify the completeness and accuracy of the information herein. However, neither the author nor publisher can guarantee the applicability of the information found herein. If legal advice or other expert assistance is required, the services of a competent professional should be sought.

> **You can qualify to earn free CPE through our pilot testing program.**
> **If interested, please visit aicpa.org at http://apps.aicpa.org/secure/CPESurvey.aspx.**

Course Code: **745227**
DTT GS-0417-0A
Revised: **February 2017**

TABLE OF CONTENTS

Recent Developments

Users of this course material are encouraged to visit the AICPA website at www.aicpa.org/CPESupplements to access supplemental learning material reflecting recent developments that may be applicable to this course. The AICPA anticipates that supplemental materials will be made available on a quarterly basis. Also available on this site are links to the various "Standards Trackers" on the AICPA's Financial Reporting Center which include recent standard-setting activity in the areas of accounting and financial reporting, audit and attest, and compilation, review and preparation.

Chapter 1

ALLOCATION OF PARTNERSHIP AND LLC INCOME UNDER SECTION 704(b)

LEARNING OBJECTIVES

After completing this chapter, you should be able to do the following:

- Analyze a partnership or LLC agreement to determine whether any special allocations in the agreement will be allowed under the Title 26 *U.S. Code of Federal Regulations* (CFR) Section 704(b) regulations, and when they will not be recognized by the IRS).
- Identify the potential economic consequences of special allocations to a partner or LLC member.
- Recognize the sections of a partnership agreement that must exist in order for a special allocation to be valid.
- Identify the potential tax consequences when a partner or LLC member has a negative balance in his or her capital account.
- Recognize the relationship between partnership and LLC allocations of profit and loss and the allocation of the risks and rewards of entity operations.
- Distinguish between the requirements for substantiality and those for economic effect under the regulations and understand the importance of future expectations when determining whether a proposed allocation will be both appropriate to achieve the economic objectives of the partners or members and legitimate under the Section 704(b) regulations.

INTRODUCTION

Section 704 affords investors a wide degree of latitude in dividing partnership and LLC profits and losses. Section 704(a) allows the partners or members to divide items of entity income or loss in any manner they choose,[1] subject only to the constraints of Sections 704(b) and 704(c).[2] Section 704(c) requires special allocations with respect to contributed property. Section 704(b) requires that the partnership's tax allocations have substantial economic effect.

The criteria which must be satisfied before an allocation is considered to have substantial economic effect have been meticulously set forth in two sets of final regulations issued in September 1986 and December 1991. The basic premise of the regulations is very straightforward.

The tax consequences of partnership or LLC allocations must follow the economic consequences of those allocations. A partner or LLC member who receives the economic benefit of a partnership or LLC gain must be allocated the associated tax burden (the tax on the additional income). Conversely, an investor cannot be allocated the tax benefits of an entity loss unless he or she bears the economic burden of that loss. If an allocation has no significant economic consequence, it will be disregarded for tax purposes.

Allocations that are determined not to have substantial economic effect are disregarded and the investors' distributive shares of affected item(s) are determined according to their respective interests in the partnership.

The regulations establish the following two-part test to determine whether an allocation has substantial economic effect:

- First, the allocation must have economic effect.
- Second, the economic effect of the allocation on the partner or member must be substantial.

---

[1] Special allocations should be clearly stated in the partnership or LLC agreement.
[2] Further restraints have been laid out by the courts with respect to family partnerships. Allocations in family partnerships are governed by Section 704(e).

Economic Effect: The General Test

GENERAL REQUIREMENTS

For an allocation to have economic effect, it must affect the amount the partner or LLC member will receive upon liquidation of the entity. Thus, if an LLC member is allocated all of the LLC's depreciation expense, he or she must be entitled to a lesser share of the proceeds from an eventual liquidation of the LLC. That is, he or she must bear the economic burden of any depreciation in the value of LLC property.

This means that the entity must accurately record income or loss allocations in the investors' capital accounts and must tie the investors' rights at liquidation to the balances in those capital accounts. Accordingly, the regulations set forth three requirements for an allocation to have economic effect:[3]

1. The partnership or LLC agreement must provide for the proper determination and maintenance of partner or member capital accounts throughout the life of the entity;
2. The agreement must provide that upon liquidation of either the entity, or of an individual investor's interest, liquidating distributions must be made in accordance with the positive capital balances of the investors; and
3. The agreement must require investors with negative balances in their capital accounts at liquidation to restore the deficits in those accounts.

The third requirement above assures that sufficient funds will be available to the partnership or LLC to repay its creditors and to liquidate the interests of those partners or members with remaining positive capital balances.

Tax Planning Point: Note that under the substantial economic effect rules, tax losses allocated to partners and LLC members will generally be associated with real economic losses. Thus, practitioners whose clients receive so-called special allocations of losses from an LLC or partnership should take care to ensure that those clients understand the potential economic costs that may accompany those tax allocations. Indeed, investors in an LLC or partnership who receive disproportionate loss allocations will often be required to make additional contributions to capital if the entity is unsuccessful, particularly when the partnership is liquidated. The purpose of the regulations under Section 704(b) is to ensure that tax loss allocations are accompanied by real dollar costs to recipients.

MAINTENANCE OF CAPITAL ACCOUNTS

Because tax basis capital accounts seldom reflect fair market values, the regulations require the creation and maintenance of a separate set of investor capital accounts. These capital accounts are similar to the partnership's tax capital accounts with a few minor differences. They are intended to reflect as accurately as possible the economic relationship between the partners or members.

---

[3] Regulation Section 1.704-1(b)(2)(ii)(b).

The regulations require that capital accounts be increased by

- cash contributions (including increases in the partners' or members' shares of partnership or LLC liabilities);[4]
- the fair market value of property contributed to the partnership or LLC by the partners or members (net of liabilities assumed by the partnership or LLC); and
- allocated items of book income and gain as determined under Section 704(b) and the regulations thereunder, including non-taxable income and gain.

Capital accounts must be decreased by

- distributions of cash from the partnership or LLC to a partner or member (including partner or member liabilities assumed by the entity, but not including guaranteed payments made to the partner or member by the partnership or LLC);
- the fair market value of any property distributed to a partner or member (net of liabilities assumed by the distributee in connection with the distribution);
- allocated expenditures that are not deductible in computing partnership or LLC income under Sections 702 or 703 and are not properly chargeable to capital (for example, syndication costs, expenses incurred in generating tax-exempt income, and so on); and
- allocated items of book loss and deduction as determined under Section 704(b) and the regulations thereunder, including simulated oil and gas depletion.[5]

KNOWLEDGE CHECK

1. In 201X, J contributed $10,000 for a 10 percent interest in JDR Partners. On the 201X Schedule K-1 that J received from the partnership, the following items were reported:

- J's initial cash contribution of $10,000
- J's allocable share of partnership ordinary business income = $6,500
- J's allocable share of partnership rental loss = ($12,100)
- J's allocable share of partnership charitable contributions = $2,500
- J's allocable share of partnership nondeductible expenses = $800

J was unable to deduct the passive losses allocated to her by the partnership due to the passive loss limitations. Assuming there are no differences between book and tax income for the year, what will be the balance in J's capital account as of the first day of the next year?

a. $ 1,100.
b. $13,200.
c. $ 1,900.
d. $4,400.

---

[4] Regulation Section 1.704-1(b)(2)(iv)(c).
[5] Regulation Section 1.704-1(b)(2)(iv)(b).

Partnership Agreement: Maintenance of Capital Accounts

At times, accountants must go back to the partnership agreement to determine the correct tax treatment of partnership income and deduction items. The following is a sample paragraph from a partnership agreement addressing the maintenance of capital accounts in a manner consistent with the requirements of the regulations under Section704(b):

Section x.x. Capital Accounts

The Partnership shall establish and maintain a Capital Account for each Partner. A Partner's Capital Account shall be (i) increased by (a) the amount of such Partner's Capital Contributions, (b) such Partner's allocations of Operating Income and Investment Gain..., and (c) items of income or gain specially allocated to such Partner..., (ii) decreased by the amount of money and the fair market value of any property distributed to such Partner by the Partnership, such Partner's allocations of Operating Loss and Investment Loss..., and items of loss, deduction, or expenditure specially allocated to such Partner..., adjusted to reflect any liabilities that are assumed by such Partner or the Partnership or that are secured by property contributed by or distributed to such Partner, all in accordance with 26 CFR Sections 1.704-1(b)(2)(iv) and 1.704-2 of the Treasury Regulations. Except as otherwise provided in the Treasury Regulations, a transferee of an interest in the Partnership shall succeed to the Capital Account of its transferor to the extent allocable to the transferred interest.

Note that this is only an example of how one partnership agreement handled the capital account requirements, and the authors of this course make no representations as to its legality. You should always consult an attorney whenever you are involved in the drafting of a partnership agreement or other legal documents. The above reproduced section of the sample partnership agreement does address the capital account requirements concerning, for example, treatment of distributions of property at fair market value, treatment of liabilities contributed to the partnership, and the effect of partnership income on the capital accounts. All of these requirements must typically be contained in the partnership agreement in order to have a valid special allocation.

Section 704(b) Versus GAAP

It should be noted that Section 704(b) requires that partnership distributions be recorded at fair market value (FMV). As a result, the distribution of property by a partnership or LLC generally requires that either a gain or loss be recorded for Section 704(b) purposes.

Example 1-1

A and B form the AB partnership with equal cash contributions of $50,000. The partnership then borrows $200,000 and purchases several tracts of land at a total cost of $250,000. Immediately after the acquisition, the partnership's Section 704(b) balance sheet appears as follows:

Assets:	
Cash	$ 50,000
Tract 1	20,000
Tract 2	80,000
Tract 3	150,000
	$ 300,000
Liabilities	$ 200,000
Capital, A	50,000
Capital, B	50,000
	$ 300,000

Assume that Tract 1 is subsequently distributed to A in a nonliquidating distribution. If Tract 1 is valued at $40,000 at the date of distribution, A's Section 704(b) capital account must be reduced by $40,000. In order for the partnership's Section 704(b) books to remain in balance, the $20,000 appreciation in the value of Tract 1 at the date of distribution must first be recorded and the partners' capital accounts increased accordingly. Thus, assuming the partners share partnership profits and losses equally, their capital accounts will be adjusted as follows:

	Capital, A	Capital, B
Beginning balance	$ 50,000	$ 50,000
Gain on distribution of T1	10,000	10,000
Distribution of T1	(40,000)	—
Post-distribution balances	$ 20,000	$ 60,000

The Section 704(b) balance sheet would be as follows:

Assets:	
Cash	$ 50,000
Tract 2	80,000
Tract 3	150,000
	$ 280,000
Liabilities	$ 200,000
Capital, A	20,000
Capital, B	60,000
	$ 280,000

KNOWLEDGE CHECK

2. L and M form the LM partnership with equal cash contributions of $300,000. The partnership then borrows $1,400,000 and purchases several tracts of land at a total cost of $1,900,000. Immediately after the acquisition, the partnership's Section 704(b) balance sheet appears as follows:

Assets:	
Cash	$ 100,000
Tract 1	280,000
Tract 2	1,320,000
Tract 3	300,000
	$ 2,000,000
Liabilities	$ 1,400,000
Capital, L	300,000
Capital, M	300,000
	$ 2,000,000

Tract 1 is subsequently distributed to L in a non-liquidating distribution. If tract 1 is valued at $520,000 at the date of distribution, how much must L's Section 704(b) capital account be reduced by (after the book gain has already been allocated to the capital accounts)?

  a. $300,000.
  b. $520,000.
  c. $280,000.
  d. $240,000.

Some Section 704(b) departures from GAAP concern the recording of items that are treated differently for book and tax. For example, start-up expenses and organization costs are (at the taxpayer's election) deductible up to $5,000. The $5,000 limit for start-up or organizational expenses is reduced (but not below zero) by the amount by which the start-up or organizational expenses exceed $50,000, respectively. Any remaining start-up or organizational expenses are allowed as a deduction ratably over a 180-month period (Section 195(b) and Section 709(b)). These amortization expenses should be recorded in the partner capital accounts. Additionally, depreciation expense must generally be computed at the same rate both on the entity's tax return and in its Section 704(b) capital accounts.[6]

---

[6] Regulation Section 1.704-1(b)(2)(iv)(g)(3). The only exception to this rule applies when the partnership or LLC opts to use the remedial allocation method under Regs. Section 1.704-3(d)(2) to make allocations with respect to contributed property.

Example 1-2

On January 1, Y3, B contributes 5-year property to BCD Investors, a limited liability company that has chosen to be taxed as a partnership for federal income tax purposes.

The property, which B purchased in Y1 for $20,000, has an approximate value of $15,000 at the date of contribution.

B elected in Y1 to depreciate the property over 5 years using the statutory method under Section 168. Accordingly, its basis at the date of contribution is $9,600.

For tax purposes, the asset's basis to the LLC is also $9,600, and depreciation expense for Y3 will be $3,840 (19.2 percent of $20,000).

For purposes of Section 704(b), the asset will be recorded at its fair market value as of the date of contribution. Thus, in the LLC's Section 704(b) records, the property will be recorded at $15,000 and Section 704(b) book depreciation expense will be $6,000 ([3,840/9,600] × $15,000) in Y3.[7]

TREATMENT OF LIABILITIES

The treatment of liabilities under Section 704(b) is consistent with the general accounting treatment of debt. Direct transfers of liabilities between investors and a partnership or LLC are reflected in the investors' capital accounts, while mere increases or decreases in the investors' shares of partnership liabilities are not. Promissory notes between the partner or member and the partnership or LLC are not accounted for until converted into cash.

It is important to distinguish in this regard between the allocation of liabilities under Section 752, which determines a partner or member's basis in his or her partnership or LLC interest, and the method of accounting for those liabilities under Section 704(b), which is concerned merely with measuring his or her capital account. A partner's tax basis in the partnership interest represents the amount he or she stands to lose if the partnership becomes worthless. As such, it includes both the amounts the partner has previously invested in the partnership (less tax deductions claimed in connection with the partnership interest) plus amounts he or she will be required to pay should the partnership fail. Thus, a partner's tax basis includes the partner's share of partnership liabilities.

In contrast, the partner's capital account reflects how much the partner will be entitled to receive from (or contribute to) the partnership if the partnership were to sell all its assets for their book value and liquidate immediately. Tax basis thus reflects the net cost (unrecovered) paid, or to be paid, by the partner for the partnership interest. The capital account, in contrast, reflects the partner's legal claim against the partnership's assets in the event of a liquidation of either the partnership or the partner's interest therein.

---

[7] This example assumes that the partnership uses the traditional method or the traditional method with curative allocations to make allocations with respect to contributed property under Section 704(c).

Example 1-3

A and B form AB, a limited liability partnership, with the following contributions. A contributes $50,000 cash in exchange for a 50 percent interest in the entity. B receives the remaining 50 percent interest in exchange for a contribution of property with a basis and fair market value of $65,000, but encumbered by a nonrecourse liability of $15,000.

Under Section 704(b), the balance in A's capital account is $50,000 ($50,000 contributed, less 0 debt transferred to the partnership). Her basis in her partnership interest will be $50,000, plus her 50 percent share of the partnership's debt, $7,500.

Although the fair market value of the property contributed by B is $65,000, the balance in her Section 704(b) capital account will be only $50,000 ($65,000 contributed less $15,000 liability transferred); her basis in her partnership interest will be $50,000, plus her $7,500 share of the partnership's liabilities.

LIQUIDATING DISTRIBUTIONS

The economic effect of an allocation under the regulations is tied directly to the effect of that allocation on a partner or member's rights to the partnership's assets in the event of a liquidation of either the entity or the investor's interest therein. Thus, even if capital accounts have been established and properly maintained over the life of the partnership or LLC, allocations will not be considered to have economic effect unless the partners or members' rights in liquidation are tied to the balances in those capital accounts. Section 704(b) requires that liquidating distributions be made in accordance with the positive Section 704(b) capital account balances of the investors. Only in this way do special allocations affect the rights of the investors in liquidation.

 Example 1-4

A and B establish AB Co., a limited liability company choosing to be taxed as a partnership for federal income tax purposes. The two investors establish the company with equal contributions of $1,500 cash. The LLC borrows $12,000 and purchases video arcade equipment for $15,000. The equipment is placed in convenience stores in exchange for a share of the income from use of the machines. Income before depreciation in the first year of LLC operations is $3,000. Depreciation expense is $3,000. The agreement between A and B provides that depreciation expense will be allocated entirely to A. All other items of income and expense are shared equally. As a result, the balances in the members' capital accounts at the end of year 1 are as follows:

Example 1-4 (continued)

	A	B
Beginning balances	$ 1,500	$ 1,500
Income before depreciation	1,500	1,500
Depreciation expense	(3,000)	—
Ending balances	$ —	$ 3,000

If the members' rights in liquidation are tied to their capital accounts, a disposition of the equipment for its book value followed by liquidation of the LLC would entitle B to receive a payment of $3,000 while A receives nothing. Thus, the allocation of the depreciation expense entirely to A has economic effect and will be recognized under Section 704(b). If, on the other hand, the LLC agreement provides that liquidation proceeds will be split equally between the members (regardless of the balances in their capital accounts), the allocation of depreciation can be seen to have had no effect on A's economic rights in liquidation and therefore will not be recognized under Section 704(b).

KNOWLEDGE CHECK

3. Claire is a 50-percent partner in Elk Horn Partners. She acquired her partnership interest two years ago in exchange for a $150,000 cash contribution to the partnership. The partnership subsequently borrowed $700,000 on a nonrecourse note and purchased an office building. In its first two years of operations, the partnership reported net profits, of which Claire's share was $50,000 in year 1 and $64,000 in year 2. The allocations were recognized by the IRS under Section 704(b). Claire has received distributions totaling $30,000 over this two-year period. If the partnership were to sell all of its assets for their book values and liquidate at the end of year 2, how much of the liquidating proceeds would Claire be entitled to receive?

    a. $150,000.
    b. $234,000.
    c. $84,000.
    d. $264,000.

RESTORATION OF DEFICIT CAPITAL BALANCES

A corollary to the requirement that liquidating distributions be made in accordance with positive balances in the partner or members' capital accounts is that partners or members with deficit balances in their capital accounts must be obligated to restore those balances upon liquidation. The partnership or LLC agreement must require such restoration by the later of 90 days after the date of liquidation or the end of the partnership or LLC year in which the liquidation occurs.[8] Absent such a requirement, allocations to a partner or member of losses or deductions in excess of his or her capital contribution(s) would not affect his or her rights in a liquidation of the entity and thus could not have economic effect.

The regulations define liquidation very broadly. Deficit restoration is required upon the termination either of the partnership or LLC itself or of the individual partner or member's interest therein.[9] For this purpose, the term liquidation includes the unintended termination of a partnership or LLC resulting from the disposition of greater than 50 percent of the capital and profits interests, even if the remaining partner or members intend to continue operations.[10] Where the partners do intend to liquidate the partnership, but delay the distribution of liquidating payments in order to defer the required restoration of negative capital accounts, the regulations provide that liquidation will occur upon the termination of the partnership's primary business activity(ies).[11] Thus, a partner or LLC member will not be able to avoid satisfying his or her deficit restoration obligation by having the partnership or LLC enter into protracted liquidation proceedings.

KNOWLEDGE CHECK

4. Last year, Steve was trying to raise money to drill an oil well. He convinced Wendy to invest $200,000 in a newly formed drilling partnership. To convince her to invest, Steve agreed to assume responsibility for 75 percent of any losses which might be incurred by the partnership, while sharing in only 50 percent of any profits. The partnership agreement satisfied all the requirements of Section 704(b), so that these special loss allocations will be recognized by the IRS. Steve also invested $200,000 in the partnership so that, immediately after formation, he and Wendy each had balances of $200,000 in their capital accounts. Unfortunately, the partnership's drilling activities were not successful. It lost $360,000, and liquidated. How much will Wendy be entitled to receive at liquidation?

    a. Zero.
    b. $20,000.
    c. $110,000.
    d. $200,000.

---

[8] Regulation Section 1.704-1(b)(2)(ii)(c).

[9] Where a partner or member retires or otherwise terminates his/ her interest in the entity, and the departure of that partner or member does not terminate the partnership/ LLC under Section 708(b)(1), the departing partner/ member is obligated to restore any deficit balance in his/ her capital account; other partners or members who may have deficit capital balances do not have to restore those deficit balances to zero.

[10] Regulation Section 1.704-1(b)(2)(ii)(g).

[11] Id.

Partnership Agreement: Liquidating Distributions and Restoration of Negative Capital Account Balances

Below is a sample paragraph from a partnership agreement addressing liquidating distributions and the restoration of negative capital account balances:

Section x.x. Distributions Upon Liquidation

Upon the liquidation of the Partnership, the assets of the Partnership shall first be applied to the payment of, or the establishment of adequate reserves or other provision for the payment of, the debts and obligations of the Partnership. Thereafter, there shall be made a final allocation of Operating Income or Loss and Investment Gain or Loss, as the case may be, and other items to the Partners' Capital Accounts...If the General Partner has a negative balance in its Capital Account after such final allocation, it shall contribute to the Partnership an amount of cash equal to the excess of such negative balance over the amount that it is required to pay to the Partners...

The assets of the Partnership, including any Portfolio Securities, ...remaining after the payment or other provision for the Partnership's debts and obligations shall then be distributed to the Partners in proportion to the positive balances in their Capital Accounts, determined after the final allocation of Operating Income or Loss and Investment Gain or Loss, and of other items to Capital Accounts has been made.

Note again that this is only an example of how one partnership agreement handled the negative capital account restoration requirement, and the authors make no representations as to its legality. However, the above partnership agreement section does give the partnership directions concerning the steps it must take in the event that one or more partners have negative balances in their capital accounts upon liquidation. In order for a special allocation to be valid, the partnership agreement must include a paragraph to this effect, or state law must require deficit restoration upon liquidation of the partnership or a partner's interest therein.

Deemed Economic Effect

The regulations generally require that each of the three economic effect criteria,

1. capital account maintenance,
2. liquidating distributions according to capital accounts, and
3. deficit capital account restoration,

be clearly spelled out in the partnership or LLC agreement. Where the agreement is silent with regard to these issues, but the allocations are made in such a way that a liquidation of the partnership or LLC at the end of each taxable year would have the same consequences as if these requirements had been met, partnership allocations will be deemed to have economic effect.[12]

---

[12] Regulation Section 1.704-1(b)(2)(ii)(i).

Alternate Test for Economic Effect

RATIONALE

The regulations recognize that even if a partner or LLC member is not obligated to restore deficits in his or her capital account, the allocation of profits or losses to such partner or member will still have economic effect to the extent they do not create or enlarge a deficit in his or her capital account – assuming that the first two requirements of Section 704(b) are met. That is, as long as liquidation proceeds must be distributed in accordance with positive balances in the partners' or members' capital accounts, and as long as those capital accounts are properly maintained, allocations that do not reduce a partner's or member's capital account below zero will affect his or her rights at liquidation. Accordingly, the regulations provide an alternate test for economic effect.

REQUIREMENTS

Under the alternate test, allocations will be considered to have economic effect if the following requirements are met:[13]

1. The first two requirements of the general test for economic effect must be satisfied.
2. The partnership or LLC agreement must contain a qualified income offset provision.
3. The allocations must not cause or increase an excess deficit balance in any partner's or member's capital account after certain special adjustments are made.

QUALIFIED INCOME OFFSET: CORRECTING INADVERTENT ERRORS

A qualified income offset is a provision in the partnership or LLC agreement which requires that in the event a partner or member unexpectedly (outside of what would be considered normal operations) receives an allocation, a distribution, or some other capital adjustment which creates a deficit in his or her capital account in excess of the amount he or she is obligated to restore, he or she will be allocated sufficient income and/ or gain to eliminate the resulting excess deficit as quickly as possible.[14] This may require an allocation of gross income to the offending partner or LLC member if sufficient amounts of other income are not available.

Thus, under the alternate test, as long as capital accounts are properly maintained, liquidation proceeds are distributed in accordance with such capital accounts, and the partnership or LLC agreement contains a qualified income offset provision, allocations will have economic effect to the extent they do not create deficits in any investor's capital account in excess of the amount he or she is obligated to restore.

---

[13] Regulation Section 1.704-1(b)(2)(ii)(d).
[14] Regulation Section 1.704-1(b)(2)(ii)(e).

Partnership Agreement: Qualified Income Offset

Following is an example of how the qualified income offset was provided for in one partnership agreement:

Section x.x. Special Provisions

The following provisions shall be complied with notwithstanding any provision of this Agreement...:

A.   If any Partner unexpectedly receives any adjustment, allocation or distribution described in Section 1.704-1(b)(2) (ii)(d)(4), 1.704-1(b)(2)(ii)(d)(5), or 1.704-1(b)(2)(ii)(d)(6) of the Treasury Regulations which causes it to have an, or increases the amount of its, Adjusted Capital Account Deficit, items of Partnership income and gain shall be specially allocated to such Partner in an amount and manner sufficient to eliminate, to the extent required by the Treasury Regulations, such Partner's Adjusted Capital Account Deficit as quickly as possible, provided that an allocation... shall be made to a Partner only if and to the extent that such Partner would have an Adjusted Capital Account Deficit after all other allocations provided for...have been tentatively made... This Section...is intended to constitute a qualified income offset as defined in Section 1.704-1(b)(2)(ii)(d) of the Treasury Regulations.

B.   ...an allocation of Operating Loss or Investment Loss shall not be made to a Partner to the extent that such allocation would cause such Partner to have an Adjusted Capital Account Deficit. An allocation that would be made to a Partner... shall instead be made to the other Partners to the extent, and in the proportions, that they could then be made such allocation without causing them to have Adjusted Capital Account Deficits. Any excess allocation of Operating Loss or Investment Loss shall be made to the General Partner.

While no representation as to the legality of the above agreement section is intended here, the above sample language provides a representative illustration of how a qualified income offset provision might be written in a partnership agreement.

PARTIAL ECONOMIC EFFECT

It is important to note here that the regulations under Section 704(b) specifically provide that allocations may have partial economic effect.[15]Allocations under the alternative test for economic effect will be disregarded only to the extent that they reduce an investor's capital account below the amount he or she is required to restore upon liquidation. To the extent the allocation does not reduce the investor's capital account below this level, it will be considered to have economic effect. Where an allocation is only partially reallocated, however, both the portion that is reallocated and the portion that is considered to have economic effect shall consist of a proportionate share of all items making up the allocation.

---

[15] Regulation Section 1.704-1(b)(2)(ii)(e).

Example 1-5

Recall the facts of example 1-4. A and B form a limited liability company to purchase video arcade equipment. The investors each contribute $1,500 cash to the LLC, which then borrows $12,000 and purchases the equipment for $15,000. A is to be allocated all of the depreciation expense. All other items of partnership income or loss are to be allocated equally. A is not required to restore any deficit in his capital account.

Assume that in the LLC's first year of operations, it reports income before depreciation of $2,000. As in example 1-4, it reports depreciation expense of $3,000. Absent Section 704(b), the investors' capital accounts at the end of the first year would be as follows:

	A	B
Beginning balances	$ 1,500	$ 1,500
Income before depreciation	1,000	1,000
Depreciation expense	(3,000)	—
Ending balances	$ (500)	$ 2,500

Because A is not obligated to restore the deficit in his capital account, the above allocations will not be considered to have economic effect under the general provisions of Section 704(b). If the partnership agreement meets the requirements of the alternate test, however, the allocations to A will be considered to have economic effect to the extent they do not reduce the balance in his capital account below zero (because he is not obligated to restore a deficit balance in his capital account). Thus, under the alternate test only $(500) of the net allocation must be reallocated. Because A's net allocation was $(2,000), 1/4 of each item allocated to A must be reallocated to B. Accordingly, B will be allocated approximately $250 of the income before depreciation that was originally allocated to A, and $750 of the depreciation originally allocated to A. The new allocations will be as follows:

	A	B
Beginning balances	$ 1,500	$ 1,500
Income before depreciation	750	1,250
Depreciation expense	(2,250)	(750)
Ending balances	$ —	$ 2,000

As illustrated, the reallocations will leave A with a zero balance in his capital account. B's capital balance will be $2,000.

KNOWLEDGE CHECK

5. K is a limited partner in a real estate partnership. The balance in her capital account at the beginning of the year was $25,000. She made an additional cash contribution of $5,000 to the partnership during the year. K's percentage shares of the partnership's rental real estate loss and charitable contributions for the year were as follows:

Share of partnership rental real estate loss	(36,000)
Share of partnership charitable contributions	4,000

As a limited partner, K is not obligated to restore deficit balances in her capital account. How much of the rental real estate loss can the partnership allocate to K under Section 704(b)?

a. $36,000.

b. $30,000.

c. $27,000.

d. $25,000.

ADJUSTED CAPITAL ACCOUNTS

The regulations require that in determining whether an allocation will reduce a partner's or member's capital account below the allowed level, adjustments must be made to account for certain reasonably expected future reductions to that account.[16] In applying the alternate test, capital accounts must be adjusted for

- *Reasonably expected* future depletion allowances (because depletion is computed at the partner or member level rather than at the entity level);
- *Reasonably expected* future net distributions (annual distributions of partnership income are disregarded); and
- *Reasonably expected* future allocations under Sections 704(e)(2) (relating to gifted interests in family partnerships), 706(d) (relating to changes in partners' or members' interests), and 1.751-1(b)(2)(ii) (relating to distributions of Section 751 property).

Thus, the regulations require that anticipated future events must be considered in determining the effect of a partnership allocation on the balance in a partner's capital account. Unexpected future events are covered by the required qualified income offset provision.

---

[16] Regulation Section 1.704-1(b)(2)(ii)(d).

Substantiality

OVERVIEW

Once an allocation is determined to have economic effect, it must be determined whether that economic effect is substantial. The substantiality criterion requires that the allocation substantially affect the dollar amounts to be received by the investors upon liquidation, independent of tax consequences. The regulations outline three situations in which an allocation will not satisfy the substantiality criterion.

SHIFTING TAX CONSEQUENCES

Perhaps the most obvious type of allocation that would meet the economic effects test(s) without substantially affecting the investor's non-tax economic interests in the entity is an allocation of capital gain or loss, or non-taxable income, to one investor accompanied by an equivalent allocation of ordinary income or loss to another investor. Here both investors would receive equivalent shares of income or loss, but each would face potentially different tax consequences. The regulations provide that such allocations lack substantiality, even if the requirements for economic effect are met. Specifically, the regulations reject the substantiality of allocations where there is a strong likelihood that

- The net changes in the investors' capital accounts would not differ substantially without the allocation; and
- The total (aggregate) tax liability of the investors will be less than if the allocation were not recognized.[17]

 Example 1-6

A and B are equal partners in the AB partnership. Each is in the 30 percent tax bracket. At the beginning of Y5, the balance in each of their capital accounts was $9,000. For Y5, the partnership reported taxable income consisting of $6,000 of ordinary income from the rental of residential real property and $6,000 of capital gains. The partnership has been in existence since Y1.

The partners agree to allocate all of the rental net income to A and all of the capital gain to B. Assume the allocations have economic effect. If both partners have the same tax attributes outside the partnership (for example, assume that neither has passive losses from any other source, neither has net capital loss carryforwards, and both are in the same tax bracket), then the above allocations may be considered to have substantial economic effect.

---

[17] Regulation Section 1.704-1(b)(2)(iii)(b).

Example 1-6 (continued)

However, if A has passive losses from other sources, so that the allocation of the partnership passive income will not increase his tax liability (and the capital gain would), then the allocations would reduce the combined tax liability of the partners. Alternatively, if B has capital loss carryforwards so that the capital gain allocation does not increase his tax liability (though it would increase A's tax liability), then the allocations would reduce the combined tax liability of the partners. Finally, if B is in a higher tax bracket than A, so that the benefit of the 15 percent tax rate on capital gains would be more beneficial to B than to A, then the allocation will again reduce the aggregate tax liability of the two partners.

In any of the above three situations, the balances in the partners' capital accounts do not differ from those that would result from an equal allocation of each item of partnership income, yet the partners' combined tax liabilities will be reduced by the allocations.

Accordingly, the allocations lack substantiality (although they may have economic effect) and will not be recognized under Section 704(b).

Given that it is less likely that there is a reason to make special allocations of the character, as opposed to the amount, of partnership or LLC income or loss items, allocations of this nature should always draw special scrutiny from practitioners (as they probably will from the IRS). The regulations provide an example where there is a non-tax reason for the allocation of a certain character of income. In that example, 90 percent of a partnership's foreign income was allocated to a non-resident partner.[18] Because the amount of foreign income could not be predicted with any reasonable certainty, the allocation was deemed to be substantial.

TRANSITORY ALLOCATIONS

The Section 704(b) regulations also reject allocations in a taxable year that are likely to be largely offset by other allocations in a subsequent year. The criteria under this test are the same as above. That is, the economic effect of partnership allocations will be deemed insubstantial if there is a strong likelihood that

- The net changes in the investors' capital accounts would not differ substantially without the allocations; and
- The total tax liability of the investors would be less than if the allocations were disregarded.

---

[18] Reg, Section 1.704-1(b)(5), Ex. 10(i).

TRANSITORY ALLOCATIONS VERSUS SHIFTING TAX CONSEQUENCES

The difference between the criteria under the transitory allocation rules and those under the shifting tax consequences guidelines is one of application rather than substance.

The provisions of the transitory allocations test are applied over a five-year period. In contrast, an allocation will be denied under the shifting tax consequences rules only if it violates the above criteria within a single year.

 Example 1-7

E and F form the EF Company, a limited liability company, with equal cash contributions of $10,000. The LLC, which opts to be taxed as a partnership, then uses the money to purchase depreciable five-year equipment.

The LLC elects to depreciate the equipment using the straight-line method. E, who has a sizable net operating loss carryforward that is about to expire, agrees to allocate depreciation expense on the equipment entirely to F for the first two years of such equipment's useful life.

In the 3rd year, E and F will share the depreciation equally, and in years 4 and 5, depreciation will be allocated entirely to E.

If the partnership agreement contains the necessary provisions, the allocations will have economic effect.

However, the economic effect will not be substantial, because the net increases and decreases to the partners' capital accounts over the 5 year period will be the same as they would have been in the absence of the special allocations, and the partners' total tax liability will be reduced by virtue of E's opportunity to use a portion of the expiring NOL carryforward.

Tax Planning Point: An allocation will be disregarded under the transitory allocations rules only if there is a strong likelihood that it will be offset by another allocation within five years.[19] Furthermore, in applying these rules, it is assumed that the fair market value of partnership property is equal to its Section 704(b) book value.[20] Adjustments to book value are presumed to be matched by corresponding changes in fair market value. As a result, there cannot be a strong likelihood that the economic effect of an allocation will be largely offset by a subsequent allocation of gain or loss from the disposition of partnership or LLC property.

---

[19] Regulation Section 1.704-1(b)(2)(c)(2).
[20] Id.

Example 1-8

A and B form the AB partnership for purposes of drilling an oil well. A contributes the leasehold on which the well is to be drilled, and B agrees to drill the well.

The partnership agreement provides that all leasehold depletion will be allocated to A and all intangible drilling costs will be allocated to B. Assume that these allocations will have economic effect.

The partnership agreement also provides that any gain or loss from the subsequent disposition of the property will be allocated in such a way as to balance the partners' capital accounts to the extent possible.

Thus, in the event there is sufficient gain or loss from the disposition of the property to make it possible, the partners will share liquidation proceeds equally. If there is insufficient gain or loss, the partners will share liquidation proceeds in accordance with their capital account balances after allocating gain or loss from disposition in such a way as to bring the capital accounts as close as possible to one another.

The partners fully expect to realize a sizable gain from disposition of the property within two years. However, because the regulations presume that there will be no gain or loss upon disposition of the property, there is not a strong likelihood that the current year allocations of depletion and/or IDC will be largely offset by future allocations of gain or loss.

Accordingly, the economic effect of the current allocations will be substantial.

KNOWLEDGE CHECK

6. G and S form a partnership to drill for oil and gas. G contributes a leasehold with a tax basis and fair market value of $250,000. S contributes $250,000 cash to cover the costs of drilling the well. The partnership agreement allocates 100 percent of the costs of drilling to S. After spending $150,000 on drilling the well, the partners realize that the well is going to be a dry hole. The partners decide to sell the leasehold and liquidate. To that end, they sell the leasehold for $200,000. The partnership agreement provides for balancing allocations of any gain or loss on sale of the leasehold, meaning that the partnership will make liquidating distributions to the partners as close to 50:50 as possible. What is the largest portion of the remaining $300,000 in partnership assets that can be distributed to S if the partnership agreement complies with the requirements of Section 704(b)?

   a. Zero.
   b. $50,000.
   c. $150,000.
   d. $100,000.

OVERALL TAX EFFECTS TEST

The final test which must be met before the economic effect of an allocation will be deemed substantial is much broader than those previously discussed. In an attempt to catch questionable allocations which avoid the limitations of the more specific provisions against transitory allocations and allocations which merely shift the tax consequences of partnership or LLC operations among the investors, the regulations provide an overall tax effects test.

Under this test, the economic effect of an allocation will not be substantial if

- the allocation may, in present value terms, enhance the after-tax economic consequences of at least one partner or LLC member; and
- there is a strong likelihood that no partner or LLC member will suffer substantially diminished after-tax economic consequences, again in present value terms.[21]

Essentially, these provisions provide that allocations that leave some partners or members better off after taxes, while leaving no partners or members worse off after taxes, will not be recognized. As with all the substantiality tests, in applying these rules, the interaction between entity allocations and the investors' individual tax attributes outside the entity will be taken into account.

KNOWLEDGE CHECK

7. Yellowhouse Partners is a general partnership with two equal partners, A and B. In the current year, the partnership has operating income of $18,000 and a net capital loss of ($15,000). A has a large capital gain outside the partnership, whereas B does not, and therefore would be able to deduct only $3,000 of her share of the capital loss. Accordingly, the partners agree to amend the partnership agreement so that ($12,000) of the capital loss (80 percent) is allocated to A. She will be allocated 50 percent of the partnership's net operating income. The partners agree that future capital gain, if any, will be disproportionately allocated to B to rebalance the two partners' capital accounts. Will this allocation have substantial economic effect?

    a. No. The allocation will enhance the after-tax economic consequences to partner A and will not substantially diminish the after-tax economic consequences to partner B.
    b. Yes. The allocation reduces A's economic interest in the partnership by $4,500 ($12,000 reduction for the capital loss allocation, versus $7,500 reduction if the capital loss were allocated 50/50). It increases B's economic interest by the same amount.
    c. No. The agreement to use future capital gains to rebalance the partners' capital accounts violates the requirements of the transitory allocations test.
    d. Yes. Although the allocation reduces A's tax liability outside the partnership, it increases B's tax liability, so the requirements of the overall tax effects test are not violated.

---

[21] Regulation Section 1.704-1(b)(2)(iii)(a).

Denied Allocations: Determining the Partners' or LLC Members' Interests in the Entity

In General

Where allocations are determined not to have substantial economic effect, the affected items must be reallocated in accordance with the partners' or LLC members' interests in the entity. Although not clearly defined, any determination of the investors' interests in the entity should reflect the manner in which the investors have agreed to share the economic benefit or burden of a particular item of income or loss. Where this economic arrangement is not clear, the regulations establish a rebuttable presumption that all investors have an equal interest in each item of entity income or loss.

The determination of the investors' interests in the entity is made on an item-by-item basis. The regulations identify the following four factors which will be considered in the analysis:[22]

1. The investors' relative contributions to the partnership or LLC.
2. The investors' interests in the entity's economic profits and losses.
3. The investors' interests in entity cash flows and other nonliquidating distributions.
4. The investors' liquidation rights.

No Deficit Restoration Requirement

A special rule applies where the reallocation results from the entity's failure to include an unlimited deficit restoration requirement in its agreement. In this situation, if the other two rules of the economic effect test are satisfied, and the substantiality provisions are not violated, the investors' interests will be determined by comparing the manner in which contributions or distributions would be made if all properties of the partnership or LLC were sold at book value and the partnership or LLC were liquidated at the end of the current year to the manner in which such contributions or distributions would have been made upon a similar liquidation at the end of the prior year.[23]

---

[22] Regulation Section 1.704-1(b)(3)(ii).
[23] Regulation Section 1.704-1(b)(3)(iii).

Example 1-9

Q and R form a limited partnership for the purpose of purchasing residential real property to lease. Q, the limited partner, contributes $9,000, and R, the general partner, contributes $1,000.

The partnership purchases a building for $100,000, incurring a recourse mortgage of $90,000. The partners agree to share all items 90 percent to Q and 10 percent to R. Though Q is not required to restore deficits in her capital account, the requirements of the alternate economic effect test are met.

In its first year of operations, the partnership reports a net loss of $(8,000), comprised of depreciation expense of $12,000 and other income of $4,000. The allocation of this loss 90 percent to Q and 10 percent to R has substantial economic effect because it does not create a deficit in Q's capital account.

In the second year, the partnership again reports an $(8,000) loss, comprised of the same items. Allocation of this loss 90 percent to Q and 10 percent to R results in the following capital balances:

	Q	R
Beginning balances	$ 9,000	$ 1,000
Year 1 loss	(7,200)	(800)
[$12,000 x .90] + [.90 x 4000]		
Year 2 loss	(7,200)	(800)
Ending balances	$ (5,400)	$ (600)

Thus, $(5,400) of the year 2 loss allocation does not have economic effect because it reduces Q's capital account below zero.

If the partnership had sold its assets for book value and liquidated at the end of year 1, the $88,000 proceeds from the sale, when added to the $4,000 income retained by the partnership, would enable the partnership to pay off its $90,000 mortgage, leaving $2,000 to be divided among the partners.

Of this $2,000, Q would be entitled to $1,800 ($9,000 beginning capital balance, less $7,200 loss allocation) and R would receive $200. Liquidation at the end of the second year will net the partnership only $76,000 from the sale of its assets to add to its $8,000 in retained earnings.

All $84,000 will be paid to the creditor, leaving the partnership still $6,000 in debt. Because Q is a limited partner, this $6,000 will have to be contributed by R. Comparing these outcomes over the two years in question reveals that R bore $(6,200) of the year 2 loss (loss of his $200 right to receive a distribution in year 1 plus $6,000 required contribution in year 2). Q bore only $(1,800) of the loss (Q would have been entitled to $1,800 at the end of year 1, but gets nothing at the end of year 2). Thus, in addition to the $(800) originally allocated to R in year 2, $(5,400) of the year 2 loss will be reallocated to R from Q.

KNOWLEDGE CHECK

8. Green Egg Partnership had the following book balance sheet just prior to liquidating:

Assets	$2,750,000
Liabilities	$2,000,000
Capital, E	1,000,000
Capital, H	(250,000)
Total Liabilities & Equity	$2,750,000

The partnership sold all its assets for $2,750,000, paid its liabilities, and liquidated. How much will partner E be entitled to receive?

    a. Zero.
    b. $750,000.
    c. $1,000,000.
    d. ($250,000).

9. LG is a limited partnership with one general partner (G), and a group of limited partners (L). The partnership agreement allocates profits and losses 20 percent to G and 80 percent to L. Because the limited partners cannot be compelled to make additional contributions to capital, the partnership agreement contains a qualified income offset. At the beginning of the year, the partners' capital balances were as follows:

Capital, G	$ 10,000
Capital, L	$ 50,000

The partnership lost $100,000 this year. No portion of the loss was attributable to nonrecourse deductions. How much of this loss will be allocable to the general partner G?

    a. $10,000.
    b. $20,000.
    c. $50,000.
    d. $100,000.

Other Issues

DISTRIBUTIONS OF PARTNERSHIP PROPERTY

As previously noted, Section 704(b) requires that investors' capital accounts be reduced by the fair market value of property distributed to them. Where book value differs from fair market value, this requires that a gain or loss be recorded.[24] Such gain or loss must be recorded in the investors' capital accounts in the ratios in which they would share it if the partnership had sold the property in a taxable transaction.

Tax Planning Point: Many partnerships may desire to specially allocate the deemed gain or loss associated with a partnership distribution in order to avoid the creation or expansion of a deficit balance in the retiring partner's capital account. Alternatively, the partnership or LLC could opt to revalue all its property in order to alleviate this problem.

 Example 1-10

A, a 1/3 member in the ABC limited liability company, receives a distribution of property with a Section 704(b) book value of $50,000 and a fair market value of $75,000 in liquidation of his interest.

A's Section 704(b) capital account prior to the distribution is $60,000. Because the distribution must be recorded in the partnership's Section 704(b) records at $75,000, the LLC must first record a gain of $25,000.

This gain would presumably be shared equally by the 3 investors, increasing the balance in each of their capital accounts by $8,333. In this case, however, an $8,333 increase in A's capital account would still leave her with a deficit of $(6,667) after the distribution, which she would be required to restore. If $75,000 is the true value of A's partnership interest, restoration of any deficit would not be consistent with the purpose of the distribution. Thus, the LLC agreement should be amended to provide that $15,000 of the Section 704 (b) book gain from the distribution be allocated to A, with the remaining $10,000 allocated between B and C. This will prevent the distribution from creating a deficit in A's capital account.

SECTION 734(B) ADJUSTMENTS

The distribution of property by a partnership or LLC to a partner or member may allow the entity to adjust the basis of its remaining property under Section 734(b). Where the distribution is in complete liquidation of an investor's interest, these basis adjustments are required to be reflected in the distributee investor's capital account,[25] subject to two restrictions. First, the adjustment can be made to the distributee investor's capital account only to the extent the corresponding basis adjustment can be made

---

[24] Regulation Section 1.704-1(b)(2)(iv).
[25] Regulation Section 1.704-1(b)(2)(iv)(m)(4).

to one or more items of partnership property under Section 755.Second, adjustments must result in an increase or decrease in the amount at which the applicable property is carried on the entity's books.

 Example 1-11

Q, R and S form a general equal partnership, to which each contributes $30,000.

The partnership makes an Internal Revenue Code (IRC) Code Section 754 election. The partnership uses $50,000 of its funds to buy stock of X Corp. After several years the X stock and cash are still the only partnership assets, and the value of the X stock is $80,000.

The partnership then liquidates Q's interest in exchange for $40,000 cash. Assuming Q's basis and capital account are still $30,000, the distribution will cause Q to recognize gain of $10,000. The partnership must increase its basis in the X stock by $10,000 (the amount of gain Q recognizes). Q's capital account must be increased by the $10,000 gain, and must then be reduced by the amount of the distribution, $40,000.

The result is that Q's capital account after the liquidating distribution will be zero. R's and S's capital accounts are not adjusted.

Where a Section 734(b) adjustment arises from a distribution other than in liquidation of a partner's interest, the resulting capital account adjustments are to be reflected in the capital accounts of all the investors, subject to the same restrictions as above. The adjustment is allocated among the investors in the manner in which the unrealized income or loss inherent in the distributed property would have been allocated had the property been sold.

At first glance, the provisions governing the treatment of Section 734(b) adjustments under Section 704(b) may appear to conflict with the general rule of Section 734(b), which says that these special basis adjustments apply to the common basis of all partnership or LLC property to the benefit or detriment of all partners or members therein. It must be noted, however, that the Section 704(b) provisions apply only to the mechanical adjustment of investor capital accounts.

Allocation of the adjustment entirely to the liquidating investor's account is necessary to balance his or her capital account. The adjustment to partnership or LLC basis is still made under the general principle of Section 734(b) to the common basis of partnership or LLC property and thus to the benefit or detriment of all remaining investors.

Example 1-12

Q, R, and S form a general partnership, to which each contributes $30,000. The partnership makes an IRC Code Section 754 election. The partnership uses $50,000 of its funds to buy stock of X Corp.

After several years the X stock and cash are still the only partnership assets, and the value of the X stock is $80,000. The partnership then distributes $40,000 in cash to Q in a nonliquidating distribution.

Assuming Q's basis and capital account are still $30,000, the distribution will cause Q to recognize gain of $10,000. The partnership must increase its basis in the X stock by $10,000 (the amount of gain Q recognizes).

Each partner's capital account must be increased by their share of the $10,000 gain, and Q's capital account must then be reduced by the amount of the distribution, $40,000.

The result is that Q's capital account after the nonliquidating distribution will be $30,000 + $3,333 – $40,000+$6,667 = 0. Q's capital account will be brought to zero because he recognized $10,000 of gain ($3,333 +$6,667). Otherwise Q's capital account would be – $6,667.

A partners' capital account cannot be negative if it is caused by a cash distribution.

TRANSFERS OF PARTNERSHIP INTERESTS

The general rule of Section 704(b) requires that upon the transfer of all or a part of an investor's interest in a partnership or LLC, the capital account of the transferor carries over to the transferee.[26]Adjustments to the tax basis of partnership or LLC property under Section 743(b) are not reflected in the Section 704(b) book capital account of the transferee or any other investor.[27] This rule also applies where the entity does not have a Section 754 election in effect and an investor is allowed a special basis adjustment under Section 732(d). If the transfer causes a partnership or LLC termination under Section 708, capital accounts will carry over to the new partnership that is formed as a result of the technical termination.[28]

Please see chapter 6 for a more detailed discussion of IRC Sections 734(b) and 743(b).

---

[26] Regulation Section 1.704-1(b)(2)(iv)(m)(1).

[27] Regulation Section 1.704-1(b)(2)(iv)(m)(2).

[28] Regulation Section 1.704-1(b)(2)(iv)(1).

Optional Revaluation of Partnership Property

The regulations allow a partnership or LLC to revalue all its property to fair market value, and to make the related necessary adjustments to the partners' or members' capital accounts, in the following four situations:[29]

1. In connection with a contribution of property, including money, to the entity in exchange for an interest therein.
2. In connection with a distribution of property, including money, by the entity in liquidation of all or part of an investor's interest therein.
3. In connection with the grant of an interest in the partnership (after May 5, 2004) in consideration for the provision of services, by either an existing partner or a new partner.
4. In connection with the issuance by the partnership of a noncompensatory option (other than an option for a *de minimis* partnership interest).
5. Under generally accepted industry accounting practices, provided substantially all of the entity's property, excluding money, consists of tradable securities.

Tax Planning Point: Although they may increase accounting costs, asset revaluations will generally be advisable for many partnerships and LLCs. Especially when an investor's interest in an ongoing entity is liquidated, a revaluation may be the best way to avoid the creation of an artificial deficit in the retiring investor's capital account.

The adjustment of the investors' capital accounts in the event of a revaluation must reflect the manner in which the unrealized income, gain, loss, or deduction inherent in partnership or LLC property would be allocated among the investors if there were a taxable disposition of all the entity's property at fair market value at the date of the revaluation. Subsequent computations of book depreciation must be made at the same rate as before the revaluation.

Proposed Regulations: Under Proposed Regulations[30], a revaluation of partnership property is required for a partnership that distributes money or property (other than a *de minimis* amount) to a partner as consideration for an interest in the partnership, and that owns section 751 property immediately after the distribution. In addition, if the partnership (upper-tier partnership) owns another partnership directly or indirectly through one or more partnerships (lower-tier partnership), and the same persons own, directly or indirectly (through one or more entities), more than 50 percent of the capital and profits interests in both the upper-tier partnership and the lower-tier partnership, the lower-tier partnership must also revalue its assets immediately prior to the distribution if the lower-tier partnership owns section 751 property. If the same persons do not own, directly or indirectly, more than 50 percent of the capital and profits interests in both the upper-tier partnership and the lower-tier partnership, the upper-tier partnership must allocate its distributive share of the lower-tier partnership's items among its partners in a manner that reflects the allocations that would have been made had the lower-tier partnership revalued its property.

---

[29] Regulation Section 1.704-1(b)(2)(iv)(f).
[30] Proposed Regulation Section 1.751-1(b)(2)(iv).

Partnership Agreement: Adjustment of Capital Accounts

Following is the provision used by one partnership to assure that capital accounts were properly adjusted:

> Notwithstanding any provision of this Agreement...the General Partnershall revalue Partnership properties, and make corresponding adjustments to the Partners' Capital Accounts, as prescribed by Section 1.704-1(b)(2)(iv)(f) of the Treasury Regulations in connection with any contribution to or distribution by the Partnership of more than a de minimis amount of money or other property in exchange for an interest in the Partnership unless the General Partner reasonably determines that such revaluations and adjustments are not necessary to reflect the economic interests of the Partners in the Partnership. In addition, the book values of Partnership properties shall be increased or decreased, as the case may be, to reflect any adjustments to the adjusted tax bases of such properties pursuant to Section 734(b) or Section 743(b) of the Code to the extent that such basis adjustments are taken into account in determining Capital Account balances pursuant to Treasury Regulations Section 1.704-1(b)(2)(iv)(m) and have not been reflected in adjustments to the book values of such properties...

Note that the above provision addresses the adjustment of capital accounts when contributions or distributions are made to or from the partnership.

DETERMINING FAIR MARKET VALUE

Partnerships and LLCs are given much flexibility in determining the fair market values of their property. The regulations provide that the values assigned to property by a partnership or LLC will generally be presumed accurate as long as such values are reasonably agreed upon by the investors in arm's-length negotiations, and the investors have adverse interests.[31] The penalty for abuse of these provisions is severe, however. Where the IRS determines that partnership or LLC property has been significantly under- or over-valued, the capital account maintenance requirements of Section 704(b) will be considered not to have been met, and all items of partnership or LLC income, gain, loss, and deduction will be subject to reallocation.[32]

---

[31] Regulation Section 1.704-1(b)(2)(iv)(h).
[32] Id.

Allocation of Deductions Attributable to Nonrecourse Debt

OVERVIEW

Nonrecourse debt creates special problems under Section 704(b). For a partnership or LLC loss allocation to have economic effect, those partners or members sharing in the allocation must bear the economic burden of that loss. Generally, this requires that the allocation either reduce the amount to which the recipient investors are entitled at liquidation, or increase the amount they are obligated to contribute in the event of a partnership or LLC liquidation. If the loss being allocated is supported by nonrecourse debt (for example, depreciation), neither of these conditions will be satisfied.

For example, if tax depreciation on a building purchased with nonrecourse debt is matched by actual economic depreciation (as is presumed under Section 704(b)), depreciation in excess of the partners' or members' original contributions (plus any undistributed partnership or LLC income) will not be borne by the partners or LLC members. Because they are not personally liable on a nonrecourse note, only the creditor(s) can bear the economic burden of the depreciation. Thus, the depreciation allocations would not have economic effect under the general provisions of Section 704(b).

Because the outstanding balance of a nonrecourse note is treated as part of the amount realized upon the disposition of the encumbered property (even in foreclosure), however, nonrecourse deductions will affect the tax consequences to the investors if the partnership or LLC disposes of all its assets and liquidates. Because nonrecourse deductions (those deductions supported by nonrecourse debt) will reduce the entity's basis in the encumbered property, they increase the tax gain to be recognized upon disposition of such property. Thus, nonrecourse deductions will increase the eventual tax liability of the partners or members upon liquidation of the entity, and, as a result may be considered to have economic effect if certain requirements are met.

KNOWLEDGE CHECK

10. QL and RR form a limited partnership. QL, the general partner, contributes $50,000. RR, the limited partner, contributes $200,000. The partnership obtains a $750,000 nonrecourse note and purchases depreciable machinery for $1,000,000. The partnership agreement provides that depreciation, computed on a straight-line basis over five years, will be allocated entirely to RR. Everything else will be allocated 80 percent to RR and 20 percent to QL. The partnership agreement meets the requirements of the alternate test for economic effect and does contain a minimum gain chargeback provision. If the partnership breaks even before depreciation, what portion of the first year's depreciation allocation will be reallocated to QL under Section 704(b)? (Assume that year 1 depreciation expense equals $200,000.)

    a. Zero.

    b. $40,000.

    c. $100,000.

    d. $160,000.

NONRECOURSE DEDUCTION DEFINED

A nonrecourse deduction is defined as one that reduces the entity's net assets (on the Section 704(b) balance sheet) to a level below the outstanding principal of its nonrecourse liabilities.[33] Thus, for a nonrecourse deduction to exist, there must be no remaining partner or member capital, or recourse debt, to absorb the partnership loss. At that point, only the nonrecourse creditors will bear economic risk for the loss.

Where a partnership or LLC loss is composed of more than one item, the nonrecourse deduction is composed only of those items specifically attributable to the property encumbered by the nonrecourse debt (typically depreciation expense). Where some partnership or LLC capital exists to support a part of the deduction, but not all of it, only the excess of the deduction over such remaining capital is a nonrecourse deduction.

Example 1-13

A and B form AB, a limited liability company, with contributions of $20,000 each. AB obtained a $110,000 nonrecourse loan and purchased real estate for $150,000. In its first eight years of operations, the LLC had total gross income of $160,000, which was exactly offset by interest and other operating expenses of $160,000. In addition, AB reported total depreciation expense over the eight years of $40,000. The LLC had no nonrecourse deductions in years one through eight. The remaining basis of its real estate was $110,000. It owned no other assets.

Over the next eight years, the LLC's expenses before depreciation again exactly offset its operating income. It again reported depreciation expense of $40,000, giving it a net loss of $(40,000). At the end of this eight-year period, AB's basis in its realty was only $70,000. Assume that it still had no other assets. If the outstanding principal balance of its nonrecourse note were still $110,000, the LLC's nonrecourse deductions would total $40,000. This nonrecourse deduction would be comprised entirely of depreciation expense on the real estate.

KNOWLEDGE CHECK

11. C and D form partnership CD with contributions of $15,000 each. CD then obtains a $270,000 nonrecourse loan and purchases machinery for $300,000. In its first year of operations, the partnership has a gross income of $10,000 which is exactly offset by interest and other operating expenses of $10,000. In addition, CD reports depreciation expense of $60,000. How much of the depreciation expense will constitute a nonrecourse deduction?

    a. Zero.
    b. $30,000.
    c. $60,000.
    d. $10,000.

---

[33] Regulation Section 1.704-2(i)(2).

GENERAL REQUIREMENTS FOR ECONOMIC EFFECT

The regulations under Section 704(b) establish the following four conditions which must be satisfied for an allocation of nonrecourse deductions to have economic effect:[34]

1. The first two requirements of the general test for economic effect (capital account maintenance and distribution of liquidation proceeds) must be satisfied.
2. The allocation of nonrecourse deductions must be reasonably consistent with allocations of some other significant partnership or LLC item(s) attributable to the encumbered property and those other allocations must have substantial economic effect.
3. The partnership or LLC agreement must either require that partners or members are obligated to restore deficit balances in their capital accounts, without limitation, or contain a minimum gain chargeback.
4. All other material entity allocations and capital account adjustments must be recognized under the regulations.

CONSISTENCY WITH OTHER SIGNIFICANT ITEMS

Essentially, the regulations treat the allocation of a nonrecourse deduction as meaningful if it follows other allocations that have substantial economic effect and the partnership or LLC agreement provides protection against the creation of deficits in partner or member capital accounts. The regulations are quite flexible with regard to the determination of whether an allocation is reasonably consistent with the allocation of other items attributable to the property encumbered by the nonrecourse debt. For example, where partnership or LLC income and losses are allocated 90 percent to one partner or member and 10 percent to another until such time as aggregate income equals prior losses, and allocated equally thereafter, the regulations treat any allocation of nonrecourse deductions between 90:10 and 50:50 as reasonably consistent with significant other allocations.[35] The primary question under the regulations is what constitutes a significant other item attributable to the property securing the nonrecourse liability. It seems that depreciation supported by partner or member capital contributions (plus undistributed income) should qualify as a significant other item.

MINIMUM GAIN CHARGEBACK

Partnership or LLC minimum gain is that minimum amount of gain that will result from the disposition of the property securing the nonrecourse debt. Because the forgiveness (by the lender) or assumption (by the buyer) of nonrecourse liabilities is considered an amount realized from the sale of the encumbered property, in no case can the partnership or LLC recognize less gain than the difference between the property's basis and the remaining principal balance of the nonrecourse note upon disposition or abandonment of the property. Thus, minimum gain is computed as the difference between the basis under Section 704(b) of the securing property and the remaining balance of the nonrecourse note.

---

[34] Regulation Section 1.704-2(e).
[35] Regulation Section 1.704-2(f)(7), Example 1.

Each investor's share of partnership or LLC minimum gain is the sum of the nonrecourse deductions previously allocated to such investor (or his or her predecessor in interest), reduced by his or her share of previous decreases in minimum gain.[36] Such minimum gain is added to the investor's deficit restoration obligation to determine the maximum deficit that can be allowed to accumulate in such investor's capital account. Thus, minimum gain increases the amount of losses that can be allocated to a partner or LLC member without creating an improper deficit.

The minimum gain chargeback provision then plays the same role as the qualified income offset provision in the alternate test for economic effect. The minimum gain chargeback provisions are triggered in certain circumstances where there is a decrease in partnership or LLC minimum gain (for example, as when the entity repays a portion of the loan). Minimum gain chargeback is only required in specific situations where minimum gain decreases. Where a partner or member's capital account unexpectedly falls below the permissible deficit, as a result of a decrease in entity minimum gain,[37] the minimum gain chargeback provision requires that such partner or member must be allocated sufficient income (including gross income) to eliminate the excess deficit in his or her capital account.

Partnership Agreement: Allocation of Nonrecourse Deductions

The allocation of nonrecourse deductions is provided for by this representative section of a partnership agreement:

> If the Partnership incurs any borrowings, the Partnership (i) shall allocate any non-recourse deductions, computed and determined in accordance with Sections 1.704-2(b)(1), 1.704-2(c) and 1.704-2(j) of the Treasury Regulations, it may have twenty percent (20 percent) to the General Partner and eighty percent (80 percent) to the Partners in proportion to their Percentages of Contributed Capital, (ii) shall allocate any partner non-recourse deductions, computed and determined in accordance with Sections 1.704-2(i)(1), 1.704-2(i)(2) and 1.704-2(j) of the Treasury Regulations, it may have so as to comply with Section 1.704-2(i) of the Treasury Regulations and (iii) shall make such allocations as are necessary to comply with the minimum gain chargeback provisions of Sections 1.704-2(f), 1.704-2(i) and 1.704-2(j) of the Treasury Regulations, taking into account all exceptions provided by such provisions to the applicability of this clause.

As before, the authors make no representations as to the legality of this provision, but it might provide a basis from which similar nonrecourse deduction provisions in other partnership agreements can be identified.

---

[36] Regulation Section 1.704-2(g)(1).

[37] Decreases in minimum gain generally result from principal payments on a nonrecourse note.

Summary

The Section 704(b) regulations are based on a simple premise. Tax allocations will only be recognized if they mirror the allocations of the economic benefits and detriments of partnership or LLC activities. The economic effects of partnership or LLC activities are best measured over time by reference to the cash flows ultimately attributable to the partners or LLC members. Thus, for a tax allocation to stand, it must ultimately affect the cash receipts to be received by the investor from the entity. It must be properly accounted for in a set of capital accounts that will ultimately be used to determine the distribution of partnership or LLC net assets upon liquidation.

Where deductions are supported by nonrecourse debt, so that only creditor cash flows can be affected, this premise is altered somewhat. Nonrecourse deductions must be allocated in accordance with the manner in which investors will ultimately share the tax gains, and thus the tax liabilities, arising from those nonrecourse deductions. The tax benefits of nonrecourse deductions, rather than following the allocation of associated economic burdens, must be allocated in such a way as to follow the tax burdens that will someday arise from the basis reductions associated with the nonrecourse deductions. Again, these burdens are best reflected in partner or member capital accounts.

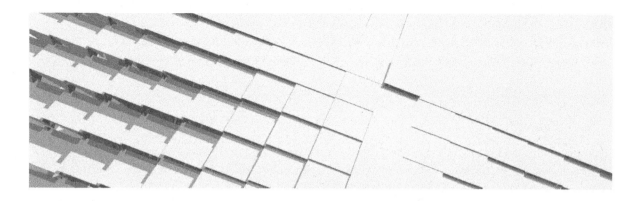

Chapter 2

ALLOCATIONS WITH RESPECT TO CONTRIBUTED PROPERTY: SECTION 704(C)(1)(A)

LEARNING OBJECTIVES

After completing this chapter, you should be able to do the following:

- Distinguish between "book" allocations required under Section 704(b) and "tax" allocations required under Section 704(c).
- Identify the potential tax consequences when a partner or LLC member makes a contribution of appreciated or depreciated property to the entity.
- Distinguish between the various methods prescribed by the regulations to make required special allocations with respect to contributed property.
- Recognize the three methods described in the Section 704(c) regulations to make special allocations with respect to contributed property.
- Determine when a non-contributing partner or LLC member will or will not be protected by required allocations under Section 704(c).

INTRODUCTION

26 CFR Section 704(b), requiring allocations to have substantial economic effect, has as its primary purpose the prevention of tax avoidance by the use of economically meaningless allocations of partnership or LLC income or loss. Partners and LLC members can reduce their tax liabilities by use of

special partnership allocations, but only if those allocations are associated with real economic costs. Section 704(c), on the other hand, requires special allocations that do not cause the partner to suffer nontax economic costs, in order to prevent the use of partnerships and LLCs as tax avoidance vehicles.

 Example 2-1

A contributes land to AB, Ltd., a limited liability company opting to be taxed as a partnership for federal income tax purposes. A and B each own 50 percent of AB. The tax basis of the land at the date of contribution is $100,000 and its fair market value is $250,000. If the land is sold, Section 704(c) will require the first $150,000 of gain to be allocated to A. If not for Section 704(c), the partners would share the gain equally and A would have effectively shifted $75,000 of gain to B.

Section 704(c) applies whenever an investor contributes property to a partnership or LLC with a fair market value that differs from its tax basis. In such a case, tax gains and losses, and depreciation and depletion with respect to the contributed property, differ from the amounts recorded for "book" purposes under Section 704(b). To the extent of these differences, the tax consequences of a partnership or LLC allocation do not reflect the economic cost or benefit associated with that allocation. Accordingly, Section 704(b) cannot, by itself, prevent investors from using partnerships or LLCs to manipulate their tax liabilities when there is a contribution of appreciated or depreciated property.

KNOWLEDGE CHECK

1. Bill contributed non-depreciable property with a tax basis of $15,000 and a fair market value of $32,000 to the BG Partnership in exchange for a 50 percent interest therein. If the property is subsequently sold (two years later) for $40,000, how much of the resulting $25,000 gain must be allocated to Bill?

   a. $12,500.
   b. $25,000.
   c. $17,000.
   d. $21,000.

When it was first enacted, Section 704(c) was an elective provision designed to protect the other investors in a partnership when a partner contributed appreciated property. Thus, where a partner contributed depreciable property with a basis less than its fair market value, the partnership could elect to allocate tax gain from the subsequent disposition of such property to the contributing partner to the extent of the original difference between the value and basis. Similarly, tax depreciation during the period prior to disposition could be allocated away from the contributing partner in a like amount. In this way, the other partners would not be affected by any difference between fair market value (Section 704(b) book value) and tax basis at the date of contribution. Only the contributing partner would receive allocations of tax gain or loss unaccompanied by economic consequence under Section 704(b).

The Tax Reform Act of 1984 changed Section 704(c) from an elective provision to a mandatory one. Special allocations are now required when property is contributed to a partnership or LLC with a tax basis different from its fair market value.

Between 1993 and 1995, the IRS issued new regulations under Section 704(c)(1)(A).[1] The regulations require partnerships and LLCs to take into account built-in gains and losses inherent in contributed properties when making allocations among partners or members. They allow partnerships or LLCs to allocate items of tax depreciation, depletion, gain, or loss with respect to contributed property using any reasonable method, as long as the method is consistently applied. The regulations further identify three reasonable methods: the "traditional" method, the traditional method with curative allocations, and the remedial allocations method. Note that the latter method replaces the deferred sale method originally countenanced by the proposed regulations. Other reasonable methods are presumably allowable, and a partnership or LLC may use different methods with respect to different properties, but once a method has been selected for a given property, it must be consistently applied.

KNOWLEDGE CHECK

2. Ellen contributed land with a tax basis of $23,000 and a fair market value of $35,000 to the Barking Dog Partnership. In return, she received a one-half interest in the partnership. The partnership agreement provides that all items of income, gain, loss, or deduction are to be allocated one-half to Ellen and one-half to her other partner. The partnership subsequently sold the land for $41,000, recognizing a taxable gain of $18,000 ($41,000 sales price less $23,000 tax basis). How much of this gain will be allocated to the other partner?

    a. $0.
    b. $3,000.
    c. $6,000.
    d. $9,000.

3. Clara contributed property with a tax basis of $150,000 and a fair market value of $230,000 to a newly-formed partnership in exchange for a one-fourth interest in partnership capital, profits, and losses. The partnership subsequently sold the property for $310,000, recognizing a $160,000 taxable gain. What portion of the gain will be reported to Clara on her Schedule K-1?

    a. $40,000.
    b. $80,000.
    c. $100,000.
    d. $160,000.

---

[1] Regulations Section 1.704-3, issued 12/ 21/ 93, amended 12/ 27/ 94, 5/ 8/ 97, 8/ 19/ 97, 7/ 15/ 2004, 3/ 21/ 2005, and 5/ 23/ 2005.

The Traditional Method

The traditional method sanctioned by the regulations corresponds with the method outlined in the regulations under Section 704(b). Those regulations require the special allocation of partnership or LLC tax items associated with contributed property on the occurrence of either of two events: (1) disposition by the entity of the contributed asset(s); or (2) depreciation, or other cost recovery, by the partnership or LLC of the tax basis of the contributed property.

ALLOCATIONS OF TAX GAIN OR LOSS

With regard to special allocations of gain or loss on the disposition of contributed property by a partnership or LLC, use of the traditional method is relatively straightforward. Any tax gain or loss recognized by the entity is first allocated to the contributing partner or LLC member to the extent of the remaining built-in gain or loss inherent in the property at the date of the sale. The remainder (equivalent to the Section 704(b) "book" gain on disposition of the property) is then allocated among all the partners or members, including the original contributor, in accordance with the partnership or LLC agreement.

 Example 2-2

J contributed land to JD, Ltd., a limited liability company opting to be taxed as a partnership for federal income tax purposes. The tax basis of the land at the date of contribution was $15,000 and its fair market value was $20,000. D contributed $20,000 cash. The LLC agreement allocates all items of profit and loss equally between the partners. Two years later, the LLC sold the land contributed by J for $25,000, recognizing a tax gain of $10,000. Under Section 704(c), applying the traditional method, the first $5,000 of this gain (the built-in gain of $5,000, measured as the difference between the property's $15,000 tax basis and its $20,000 Section 704(b) "book" value) must be allocated to J. The remaining $5,000 gain is allocated equally between J and D under Section 704(b). Thus, the two investors will receive the following allocations of gain on sale of the property contributed by J:

	J	D	
Section 704(c) gain (in other words, "built-in" gain)	$	$ 5,000	—
Remaining gain (equal to "book" gain)	2,500	2,500	
Total gain reported to each member on K-1	$ 7,500	$ 2,500	
Original basis in JD	15,000	20,000	
Ending basis in JD	$ 22,500	$ 22,500	
Ending capital account (20,000 + 2,500)	$ 22,500	$ 22,500	

As indicated above, the required Section 704(c) allocation will tend to make the tax basis capital account (that is, basis without the effect of partnership liabilities) closer in value to the Section 704(b) "book" capital account.

KNOWLEDGE CHECK

4. Q contributed land to the QL partnership with a tax basis of $350 and a fair market value of $500. L contributed $500 cash. The partnership agreement allocates all items of profit and loss equally between the partners. Two years after formation, the partnership sells the land contributed by Q for $700, recognizing a tax gain of $350. How much of this gain must be allocated to Q?

    a. $150.
    b. $175.
    c. $250.
    d. $350.

COST RECOVERY DEDUCTIONS

The allocation of tax depreciation and/ or other cost recovery deductions using the traditional method is slightly more complex. With regard to these items, the Section 704(c) allocations are determined in two steps. First, to the extent possible, investors other than the contributor (that is, the non-contributing investors) are allocated tax deductions equal to their shares of the book depreciation (or other cost recovery deduction) with respect to the contributed property under Section 704(b). Any remaining tax deduction is then allocated to the contributing investor.

Example 2-3

A, B, and C form the ABC partnership with contributions as follows. A contributes depreciable personal property with a basis of $33 and a fair market value of $45. The property is subject to a $15 debt. B and C each contribute $30 cash. The partnership agreement provides that all items of partnership gain, loss, income, and deduction will be shared equally by the three partners. The property has a remaining depreciable life of 3 years and is depreciated using the straight-line method.

Example 2-3 (continued)

Depreciation expense in the partnership's first year of operations will be $15 for book and $11 for tax. It will be allocated among the partners as follows:

	A		B		C	
	Book	Tax	Book	Tax	Book	Tax
Year 1:						
Book depreciation	$ 5		$ 5		$ 5	
Tax depreciation		$1		$ 5		$ 5
Year 2:						
Book depreciation	$ 5		$ 5		$ 5	
Tax depreciation		$1		$ 5		$ 5
Year 3:						
Book depreciation	$ 5		$ 5		$ 5	
Tax depreciation		$1		$ 5		$ 5
Total allocations	$15	$3	$15	$15	$15	$15

Under Section 704(b), each partner will be allocated $5 of book depreciation. Under Section 704(c), the non-contributing partners (B and C), will be allocated $5 tax depreciation, the same amounts as they are allocated for book purposes. The remaining tax depreciation of $1 will be allocated to A. Thus, A alone bears the tax burden associated with the $12 gain inherent in the property at the date of contribution. Over the remaining 3-year depreciable life of the asset, A will recognize the entire $12 tax gain in the form of reduced deductions for tax depreciation.

KNOWLEDGE CHECK

5. X, Y, and Z form the XYZ partnership with the following contributions. X contributes depreciable personal property with a basis of $90 and a fair market value of $108. The property is subject to a $48 debt. Y and Z each contribute $60 cash. The partnership agreement provides that all items of partnership gain, loss, income, and deduction will be shared equally by the three partners. The property has current tax and book depreciation of $30 and $36, respectively. How much tax depreciation will be allocated to X in the year of formation?

    a. $12.

    b. $10.

    c. $6.

    d. $16.

Tax Planning Point—Relationship between Sections 704(b) and 704(c): As is apparent in the above examples, the application of Section 704(c) is heavily dependent on the allocations prescribed in Section 704(b). Under Section 704(c), the tax allocations to non-contributing partners or members follow the book allocations to those partners or members under Section 704(b). As a result, some observers maintain that partnerships or LLCs that want to avoid the provisions of Section 704(c) can sometimes do so by making special allocations of depreciation or other cost recovery deductions under Section 704(b).

Example 2-4

Assume the same facts as example 2-2. A, B, and C form partnership ABC, with A contributing depreciable property and B and C each contributing cash. In this case, however, assume that the partnership agreement allocates the first two years' depreciation expense entirely to B and C, with the third year's depreciation expense allocable entirely to A. Further assume that these allocations have substantial economic effect.[2] Over the three-year period, the partners would now receive allocations as follows:

	A		B		C	
	Book	Tax	Book	Tax	Book	Tax
Year 1:						
Book depreciation	$—		$7.5		$7.5	
Tax depreciation		$—		$5.5		$5.5
Year 2:						
Book depreciation	$—		$7.5		$7.5	
Tax depreciation		$—		$5.5		$5.5
Year 3:						
Book depreciation	$15		$—		$—	
Tax depreciation		$11		$—		$—
Total allocations	$15	$11	$15	$11	$15	$11

Because B and C are allocated all the book depreciation in years 1 and 2, they receive all the tax depreciation that year also. Moreover, because neither of them is the contributing partner with respect to the depreciable property, no special allocation of tax depreciation is available under Section 704(c) for those years. In year 3, A is allocated all the partnership's depreciation expense for book, and thus will be allocated all $11 tax depreciation in that year as well. As a result, over the three-year period constituting the asset's remaining depreciable life, each partner will be allocated 1/3 of the total tax depreciation taken by the partnership. Even though A was the contributing partner with respect to the depreciable asset, the built-in gain with respect to that asset is not subjected to the provisions of Section 704(c). If this is allowed, the special allocation under Section 704(b) has effectively allowed A to avoid the limitations of Section 704(c).

---

[2] These allocations would seem to be susceptible to disqualification under the transitory allocations provisions of Regulation Section 1.704-1(b)(2)(iii)(c). However, Example 18(ix) of Regulation Section 1.704-1(b)(5) explicitly condones such an arrangement. Thus, so long as the aggregate tax liability of the partners or LLC members is not reduced by this type of "longitudinal" allocation of depreciation deductions, the allocations should withstand scrutiny under Section 704.

6. A, B, and C form the ABC partnership with the following contributions. A contributes depreciable personal property with a basis of $54,000 and a fair market value of $72,000. B and C each contribute $72,000 cash. The partnership agreement provides that all items of partnership gain, loss, income, and deduction will be shared equally by the three partners. The property contributed by A has total current book and tax depreciation of $24,000 and $18,000, respectively. The partnership opts to use the traditional method to make allocations under Section 704(c). How much depreciation expense will be allocated to partner A for tax purposes in the partnership's first year of operations?

    a. $0.

    b. $8,000.

    c. $6,000.

    d. $2,000.

7. Ann contributed five-year depreciable property to the AB partnership with a basis of $54,000 and a fair market value of $162,000. The property, which has been depreciated using the straight-line method, has current tax and book depreciation of $18,000 and $54,000. The partnership agreement allocates all items equally between Ann and the other partner. The partnership uses the traditional method to make tax allocations under Section 704(c). How much tax depreciation will be allocated to Ann in the partnership's first year of operations?

    a. ($9,000) negative share of depreciation.

    b. $0.

    c. $9,000 positive share of depreciation.

    d. $27,000 positive share of depreciation.

DEPRECIATION METHODS

In order to ensure that partnerships or LLCs do not attempt to avoid Section 704(c) by choosing different accounting methods or different useful lives for book and tax, the regulations under Section 704(b) require that book depreciation and other cost recovery deductions be calculated at the same rate used in the tax computations of those items.[3] Thus, where a depreciable asset has three years remaining in its depreciable life for tax purposes, it must be depreciated over three years for book purposes as well. Furthermore, if the percentage rate at which tax depreciation is calculated differs for one or more of the asset's remaining depreciable years, this difference must be reflected in the Section 704(b) depreciation computation as well.

---

[3] Regulation Section 1.704-1(b)(2)(iv)(g)(3).

Example 2-5

A contributes five-year depreciable property to a limited liability partnership in January, year three. The property was purchased in January, year one for $20,000. Its value at the date of contribution is $15,000. Its remaining tax basis is $9,600 ($20,000 original cost – $4,000 depreciation in year one – $6,400 depreciation in year two). The property will be depreciated over another four years for tax purposes (remaining three-year useful life + ½ year depreciation in sixth year). Tax depreciation in the partnership's first taxable year will be $3,840 ($20,000 × 19.20 percent).

Thus, book depreciation under Section 704(b) will be $6,000 ([3,840/9,600] × 15,000). In the partnership's second year, tax depreciation will be $2,304 ($20,000 × 11.52 percent). Section 704(b) book depreciation will be $3,600 ([2,304/9,600] × 15,000).

KNOWLEDGE CHECK

8. Kim contributed five-year depreciable property to a partnership in January, Y3. The property was purchased in January, Y1 for $80,000. Its value at the date of contribution was $60,000. Its remaining tax basis was $38,400 ($80,000 original cost – $16,000 depreciation in year 1 – $25,600 year 2 depreciation). Tax depreciation in year 3 will be $15,360. How much book depreciation will the partnership record under Section 704(b) for Y3, the year of contribution to the partnership?

    a. $15,360.
    b. $20,000.
    c. $24,000.
    d. $32,000.

ANTI-ABUSE PROVISION

The regulations impose an additional barrier to manipulation, adopting an anti-abuse rule under which an allocation method is not reasonable if the contribution of property and the allocation of tax items are made "in a manner that substantially reduces the present value of the partners' aggregate tax liability."[4] The regulations make clear that the traditional method cannot be used if it violates this anti-abuse provision.[5] Thus, it is not clear how much room is available for avoiding one's Section 704(c) gains (or losses) via special allocations of book items under Section 704(b).

---

[4] Regulation Section 1.704-3(a)(10).
[5] Regulation Section 1.704-3(b)(2) example 2.

THE CEILING RULE

The regulations retain the ceiling rule of old Regulations Section 1.704-1(c).[6] Under the ceiling rule, special allocations of tax depreciation, depletion, gain, or loss cannot exceed the actual amounts of those items recognized by the partnership or LLC. The ceiling rule will generally come into play when a contributing partner's percent ownership is less than the percent the contributed property has appreciated. Thus, where a 50 percent partner or LLC member contributes depreciable property to the partnership or LLC with a basis less than half its fair market value, special allocations of depreciation under Section 704(c) will not be sufficient to prevent the shifting of at least some of the pre-contribution gain to the other partners or members. This shifting will occur in the form of reduced depreciation deductions because under the ceiling rule depreciation can be allocated to partners or LLC members only to the extent of the total amount allowed at the partnership or LLC level.

 Example 2-6

A contributes 5-year depreciable property to AB, Ltd., a limited liability company choosing to be taxed as a partnership for federal income tax purposes. The property contributed by A has a tax basis of $9,000 and a fair market value of $27,000. The property, which has been depreciated using the straight-line method, has a remaining depreciable life of 3 years. The LLC agreement allocates all items equally among the members.

For each of the next three years, Section 704(b) book depreciation for the contributed property will be $9,000, of which $4,500 will be allocated to A and $4,500 to B. Tax depreciation each year will total only $3,000, however. Although this is all allocated to B under Section 704(c), it is not enough to match the decrease in his capital account. Thus, A is shifting $1,500 of the built-in gain in the contributed property to B each year. This shift cannot be prevented. Even upon the sale of the asset at the end of its depreciable life, Section 704(c) will provide no further relief to B because the remaining book-tax disparity with respect to the contributed property is zero. (Being fully depreciated, the property has both a book value and tax basis of zero.)

Similarly, tax gain or loss can be specially allocated among the partners only to the extent of the actual amount realized by the partnership. As a result, post-contribution depreciation in the value of a contributed asset will allow the contributor to shift some of the built-in gain at the date of contribution to his partners who will not be allowed to deduct the economic losses they have realized since the date of contribution.

---

[6] Regulation Section 1.704-3(b)(1).

Example 2-7

G contributes land with a tax basis of $50,000, and a fair market value of $90,000, to the GH limited partnership. H contributes $90,000 cash. The partners agree to share all items of partnership gain and loss equally. If the property contributed by G is subsequently sold for $75,000, the partnership realizes a ($15,000) economic (and book) loss, of which ($7,500) is attributable to H. H is not allowed to deduct this loss, however, because for tax purposes, the partnership realizes a $25,000 gain. This gain will be allocated entirely to G under Section 704(c), but this allocation does not prevent G from shifting $7,500 of the pre-contribution built-in gain to H.

KNOWLEDGE CHECK

9. A contributes five-year depreciable property to the AB partnership in exchange for a 50 percent interest therein. The property has a basis of $27,000 and a fair market value of $81,000. The property has current tax and book depreciation of $9,000 and $27,000, respectively. B contributed cash for the remaining 50 percent interest. The partnership agreement allocates all items equally among the partners. The partnership uses the traditional method to make tax allocations under Section 704(c). How much tax depreciation will be allocated to A in the partnership's first year of operations?

    a. $0.
    b. $4,500.
    c. $9,000.
    d. $13,500.

10. M contributes land with a tax basis of $150,000, and a fair market value of $190,000, to the MP partnership. P contributes $190,000 cash. The partners agree to share all items of partnership gain and loss equally. The property contributed by M is subsequently sold for $165,000. How much gain will P be allocated for tax purposes from the sale? Assume the partnership uses the traditional method to make allocations under Section 704(c).

    a. $0.
    b. $7,500.
    c. $15,000.
    d. $40,000.

NONTAXABLE DISPOSITIONS

When a partnership or LLC disposes of Section 704(c) property in a nontaxable exchange (for example, a like-kind exchange under Section 1031, contribution to a corporation under Section 351, and the like), the disposition does not trigger recognition of built-in gain or loss under Section 704(c) using the traditional method. Property received in the exchange, however, becomes Section 704(c) property so that any built-in gain or loss will be subject to Section 704(c) when it is subsequently sold (or otherwise disposed of). Also note that any gain or loss recognized on the exchange itself (that is, upon receipt of boot) is subject to Section 704(c) to the extent of the built-in gain or loss inherent in the property at the date of the exchange.[7]

Example 2-8

A transfers land with a tax basis of $40,000 to the AB limited liability company in exchange for a 50 percent interest therein. At the date of the contribution, the FMV of the land is $75,000. B transfers $75,000 cash. The LLC opts to use the traditional method to allocate gains and losses under Section 704(c). Two years later, AB exchanges the land for like-kind property with a fair market value of $75,000. No boot is received in the exchange and AB recognizes no gain. Thus, A (the contributor-member) will not recognize any gain under Section 704(c) on the exchange. The "new" property, however, retains the Section 704(c) "taint," so that when it is sold in a taxable transaction, the first $35,000 of gain recognized must be allocated entirely to A under Section 704(c).

Example 2-9

Assume the same facts as in example 2-8, except that AB exchanged the property contributed by A for like-kind property worth $55,000, and $20,000 cash. Under Section 1031, AB must recognize a $20,000 gain on the exchange (because it received $20,000 boot), and will take a $40,000 basis in the like-kind property received. This $20,000 gain is allocable entirely to A pursuant to Section 704(c). Moreover, the like-kind property received is again treated as Section 704(c) property, but the built-in gain in such property is reduced to $15,000 (FMV of $55,000 less $40,000 basis). Thus, a subsequent sale of the substitute property for $60,000 would result in a $20,000 gain to AB, of which $17,500 would be allocated to A (first $15,000 plus half of remaining $5,000) and $2,500 to B.

---

[7] Regulation Section 1.704-3(a)(8).

The Traditional Method With Curative Allocations

The second reasonable method sanctioned by the regulations is the traditional method described above, with curative allocations to alleviate distortions caused by the ceiling rule. Curative allocations, first sanctioned in the Committee Reports accompanying the 1984 amendment of Section 704(c), use special allocations of other items of income or loss to make up for any distortions caused by the ceiling rule. Thus, where the ceiling rule limits the allocation of depreciation or depletion from one property to noncontributing partners or members, this limitation can be avoided by specially allocating depreciation or depletion from another property to those non-contributors to the extent of the shortfall. Similarly, where a post-contribution change in the value of contributed property leads to ceiling rule limitations on the allocation of tax gain or loss from the sale of such property, other partnership or LLC gain or loss can be specially allocated to cure the ceiling rule distortion. These curative allocations equalize the book and tax allocations to the noncontributing partners or members, thereby preventing the contributor(s) from shifting built-in gain or loss to non-contributors.

Example 2-10

A and B form the AB partnership with the following contributions.

A contributes 5-year property (P1) valued at $15,000, with a tax basis of $5,000. The property has a two-year remaining depreciable life.

B contributes 5-year property (P2) with a tax basis of $12,000, and a fair market value of $15,000. The property has three years remaining in its depreciable life. Both properties are depreciated using the straight-line method.

The ceiling rule applies here, and will prevent B from being allocated her full share of depreciation with respect to property 1 (contributed by A). Depreciation allocations to the two partners will be as follows:

	A		B	
	Book	Tax	Book	Tax
Depreciation, property 1	$ 3,750	$ —	$ 3,750	$ 2,500
Depreciation, property 2	2,500	2,500	2,500	1,500
Total, w/out curative allocations	$ 6,250	$ 2,500	$ 6,250	$ 4,000

Book depreciation on P1, $7,500, is allocated equally between the two partners under Section 704(b). Using the traditional method to make allocations under Section 704(c), tax depreciation is allocated first to B, the non-contributor, to the extent of her share of book depreciation, or $3,750.

Example 2-10 (continued)

The ceiling rule, however, allows only $2,500 tax depreciation to be allocated to B with respect to P1 (because there is only $2,500 tax depreciation from this property). Thus, using the traditional method, the ceiling rule causes B to recognize, indirectly, $1,250 of the built-in gain inherent in the property contributed by A. If the partnership opts to use curative allocations, this distortion could be cured by re-allocating $1,250 depreciation on P2 away from A and over to B. Thus, total allocations would be as follows:

	A		B	
	Book	Tax	Book	Tax
Depr, P1: book	$ 3,750		$ 3,750	
Depr, P1: tax		$ —		$ 2,500
Depr, P2: book	2,500		2,500	
Depr, P2: tax		2,500		1,500
Curative Allocation:				
Depr, P2	—	(1,250)		1,250
Total depreciation	$ 6,250	$ 1,250	$ 6,250	$ 5,250

Note that the difference between book and tax depreciation for A is $5,000, or one-half the built-in gain inherent in property 1 at the date of contribution. Effectively, the built-in gain in this property is being amortized over the two years remaining in its useful life. Similarly, the difference between book and tax depreciation for partner B is $1,000, or one-third of the built-in gain inherent in property 2, which has three years remaining of its depreciable life.

Of course, for curative allocations to be effective, the partnership must have sufficient amounts of other income or deductions to cure the ceiling rule distortions. The regulations allow ceiling rule limitations on depreciation allocations to be cured with special allocations of items other than depreciation.[8] For example, a ceiling rule limitation of depreciation allocated to a noncontributing partner or member can be cured by allocating additional interest expense to such partner or member (and away from the contributor), or by allocating ordinary income away from the noncontributing partner or member (and to the contributor). Either of the above special allocations will correct the ceiling rule distortion.

The only case in which curative allocations will not be sufficient to cure ceiling rule distortions is when the partnership or LLC has insufficient amounts of other income or deductions of the same character to fully cure the ceiling rule distortion. The regulations clearly prohibit using tax items that would have a different tax effect to the partners to cure ceiling rule distortions. The regulations do provide, however, that shortages in one tax year can be corrected with curative allocations in a subsequent year.[9] The

---

[8] Regulation Section 1.704-3(c)(3)(iii).
[9] Regulation Section 1.704-3(c)(3)(ii).

regulations indicate that the correction should be made within a reasonable time, such as over the economic life of the property.

 Example 2-11

X is a member of the XY limited liability company. In year 1, X's share of book depreciation on a property contributed by Y (the other member of the LLC) exceeded her share of tax depreciation due to the ceiling rule. The LLC had no other depreciable property. Its only other items of taxable income or deduction consisted of a long-term capital gain and a small amount of foreign source income. Because neither of these items have the same tax character as depreciation, X's ceiling rule distortion cannot be cured in year 1. X may, however, be entitled to a special allocation of domestic ordinary income (a negative allocation) or additional depreciation deductions, and the like, in year 2 to cure the ceiling rule distortion caused in year 1.

The Remedial Allocations Method

The third reasonable method of making Section 704(c) allocations that is countenanced by the regulations is the remedial allocations method. The remedial allocations method is designed to allow the partnership or LLC to eliminate ceiling rule distortions by creating remedial accounts, and allocating the amounts in these accounts to the partners or members affected by the ceiling rule. In essence, the entity creates two offsetting remedial accounts—one an expense (or loss) account, and the other an income (or gain) account. Because these two accounts offset one another, they have no effect on the entity's net taxable income or loss, though they do affect the allocation of taxable income or loss among the partners or members.

MECHANICS

The remedial allocations method is really quite simple. Just as under the traditional method, the partnership or LLC computes book depreciation, depletion, gain, or loss with regard to contributed property and allocates these amounts among the partners or members in accordance with the partnership or LLC agreement. Tax depreciation, depletion, gain, or loss with respect to a particular piece of property is then allocated to non-contributors in an amount equal to their book allocations of these items. Any remaining balance, after allocation to the non-contributors, is then allocated to the contributing partner or member.

If there is insufficient amount of tax depreciation, depletion, gain, or loss to support the allocations to the non-contributors, the ceiling rule applies, creating book-tax distortions in the capital balances for these partners or members. Under the remedial allocations method, these distortions are eliminated by creating a remedial account (for example, a remedial depreciation account) in the amount of the deficiency, and allocating the balance in this account to the non-contributors.[10] In effect, the ceiling rule limitation is simply ignored.

To offset the above "remedial" account, a second account is created in a like amount for the contributing partner or member. Where the first remedial account had a debit balance (for example, depreciation expense), the offsetting account must have a credit balance (for example, ordinary income). The balance in this account is allocated entirely to the contributor, thus shifting the entire burden of the pre-contribution built-in gain (or loss) with respect to the contributed property onto the shoulders of the contributor-partner(s) or member(s).

---

[10] Regulation Section 1.704-3(d).

Example 2-12

A contributes depreciable property to the AB limited partnership with a tax basis of $3,000, and a fair market value of $10,000. B contributes $10,000 cash. Assume that book depreciation for the partnership's first year of operations with respect to the property contributed by A is $5,000, and that this depreciation is allocable 50 percent to each partner. Tax depreciation with respect to this property is $1,500. Finally, assume the partnership breaks even before depreciation expense.

Under Section 704(c), the first $2,500 of tax depreciation must be allocated to partner B, with any remainder allocable to A. Applying the ceiling rule, however, B can only be allocated $1,500 of tax depreciation, creating a $1,000 book-tax disparity in B's capital account.

Under the remedial allocations method, this ceiling rule distortion can be eliminated by creating $1,000 in "remedial" depreciation expense, allocable to B, and offsetting this allocation by creating $1,000 "remedial" income to be allocated to A. The effects on the partners' capital accounts would be as follows:

	A		B	
	Book	Tax	Book	Tax
Initial contribution	$ 10,000	$ 3,000	$ 10,000	$ 10,000
Depreciation	(2,500)	—	(2,500)	(1,500)
Remedial depreciation				(1,000)
Remedial income		1,000		
Ending balances	$ 7,500	$ 4,000	$ 7,500	$ 7,500

The only restriction the regulations place on the creation of these remedial accounts is that they be the same in character.[11] Thus, where the first remedial account is depreciation expense, as in the example above, the offsetting account must be ordinary income. Note that the regulations do not require that the partnership or LLC wait to make the offsetting allocation until sufficient income or deductions of the same character occur. For example, the $1,000 of "remedial income" allocated to A in the above example could be negative depreciation. Moreover, if the depreciable property is used in a partnership rental activity, the offsetting allocation to the contributor-partner must be ordinary income from that rental activity. Where the initial remedial account creates loss from the disposition of the contributed property, the offsetting account must be characterized as gain from the sale of that property.

---

[11] Regulation Section 1.704-3(d)(3).

Example 2-13

N and P form a limited liability company, NP. N contributes property with a tax basis of $3,000 and a fair market value of $10,000 in exchange for her one-half interest in the LLC. P contributes $10,000 cash. At the end of NP's first year of operations, it sells the property contributed by N to an unrelated buyer for $2,000. It has zero net taxable income before considering the loss on the sale. The LLC agreement allocates all items of income, deduction, gain, or loss equally between N and P.

Sale of the property triggers an ($8,000) book loss, which is allocated equally between the two investors. The tax loss, however, is only ($1,000) [$3,000 tax basis less $2,000 sales proceeds]. This loss is allocable entirely to P under Section 704(c). If the LLC uses the remedial allocations method, P will also be allocated an additional ($3,000) remedial loss on the sale, offset by a remedial allocation to N of $3,000 gain from the sale:

	N		P		Total	
	Book	**Tax**	**Book**	**Tax**	**Book**	**Tax**
Initial contribution	$ 10,000	$ 3,000	$ 10,000	$ 10,000	$ 20,000	$ 13,000
Loss on sale	(4,000)	—	(4,000)	(1,000)	(8,000)	(1,000)
Remedial loss				(3,000)		(3,000)
Remedial gain		3,000				3,000
Ending balances	$ 6,000	$ 6,000	$ 6,000	$ 6,000	$ 12,000	$ 12,000

KNOWLEDGE CHECK

11. M contributes land with a tax basis of $150,000 and a fair market value of $190,000 to the MP Partnership. P contributes $190,000 cash. The partners agree to share all items of partnership gain and loss equally. The property contributed by M is subsequently sold for $165,000. How much gain or loss will P be allocated for tax purposes from the sale? Assume the partnership uses the remedial allocations method to make allocations under Section 704(c).

    a. $0.

    b. $7,500.

    c. ($12,500) loss.

    d. $15,000.

COMPUTATION OF BOOK ITEMS

The regulations contain a minor departure from the principles of Section 704(b) concerning the computation of book depreciation and depletion with respect to contributed property. Solely for purposes of determining the amounts involved in remedial allocations, the regulations require that book depreciation and depletion be computed as if the contributed property consisted of two assets. To the extent of the tax basis of the property, book depreciation or depletion is computed over the remaining depreciable life of the property (for tax purposes) at the same rates used for tax purposes. Thus, book depreciation will equal tax depreciation for this portion of the asset. Any excess of the book value (fair market value) of the contributed property over its tax basis will be treated as a new asset acquisition for purposes of computing book depreciation or depletion.[12]

 Example 2-14

L and M formed the equal LLC LM, making the following contributions. L contributed depreciable property with a tax basis of $6,000 and a fair market value of $15,000. M contributed $15,000 cash. The property contributed by L has four years remaining in its depreciable life. Under current rules, it is classified as 10-year property. The LLC, like L, opts to use the straight-line method to compute depreciation. For sake of simplicity, the first-year conventions of Section 168 are ignored in the following computations.

Book depreciation of the property contributed by L will be $2,400 for each of the LLC's first four years of operations [($6,000 ÷ 4) + ($9,000 ÷ 10)]. With regard to the first $6,000 book value of this property, book depreciation will equal tax depreciation [straight-line over remaining 4-year useful life]. The remaining $9,000 book value will be recovered using the straight-line method over the 10-year depreciable life of a new asset from this class. Thus, in years one through four, the LLC will make no remedial allocations because tax depreciation will be sufficient to cover M's share of the entity's book depreciation:

	L		M	
	Book	**Tax**	**Book**	**Tax**
Initial contribution	$ 15,000	$ 6,000	$ 15,000	$ 15,000
Depreciation, Y1-Y4	(4,800)	(1,200)	(4,800)	(4,800)
Ending balances	$ 10,200	$ 4,800	$ 10,200	$ 10,200

---

[12] Regulation Section 1.704-3(d)(2).

Example 2-14 (continued)

Beginning in year five, however, remedial allocations of $450 of tax depreciation must be made to M (offset by remedial allocations of $450 ordinary income to L):

	L		M	
	Book	Tax	Book	Tax
Balance, beg. Y5	$ 10,200	$ 4,800	$ 10,200	$ 10,200
Depreciation	(450)	—	(450)	—
Remedial depreciation				(450)
Remedial income		450		
Ending balances	$ 9,750	$ 5,250	$ 9,750	$ 9,750

These remedial allocations will continue over the remaining 6-year life of the property (years 5-10), so that at the end of year 10, the book and tax capital accounts of both members will be equal. In effect the LLC will have amortized L's $9,000 built-in gain over the 10-year useful life of the property she contributed. As is clear from an analysis of the above capital accounts, L recognizes $900 more income (less loss) from the LLC than M in each of the entity's first 10 years of operations.

Special Rules

SECTION 704(B) REVALUATIONS

The regulations require that the principles of Section 704(c) be applied when partnerships or LLCs revalue property under Regulations Section 1.704-1(b)(2)(iv)(f).[13] Under this provision, partnerships and LLCs are allowed to revalue all entity assets at fair market value upon the admission of a new partner or member, the liquidation of all or part of an existing partner's or member's interest, or in connection with the grant of a partnership interest after May 5, 2004, in exchange for services to the partnership.[14] In such cases, all partners or members whose Section 704(b) capital accounts are altered are treated as contributors from that point on,[15] and future tax allocations must reflect the differences between the book and tax values of partnership or LLC assets resulting from the revaluation.

Example 2-15

A and B are equal partners in the AB partnership. On January 1, the partnership had the following balance sheets:

	Book and Tax	
	Basis	FMV
Land	$ 500,000	$ 800,000
Capital, A	$ 250,000	$ 400,000
Capital, B	250,000	400,000
	$ 500,000	$ 800,000

At that date, the partnership admits new partner C as a one-third partner in exchange for a $400,000 cash contribution. To ensure that the partners' book capital accounts reflect the true sharing arrangements between the partners, the partnership elects to "book up" its sole asset (land) to its fair market value of $800,000 at the date of C's admission.

---

[13] Regulation Section 1.704-3(a)(6).

[14] In addition, proposed regulations issued in November 2014 would require the partnership to revalue all its property following a distribution in partial or full liquidation of a partner's interest if the partnership has Section 751 property (ordinary income assets) immediately following the distribution. Prop. Regs. Section 1.704-1(b)(2)(iv)(f). If the partnership owns an interest in a lower-tier partnership, revaluation of the lower-tier partnership's assets may also be required under the proposed regs.

[15] These allocations are known as "reverse" 704(c) allocations.

Example 2-15 (continued)

This revaluation causes A's and B's book capital accounts to be increased to $400,000 each, so that the new partnership balance sheets are as follows:

	Tax Basis	Book Value
Cash	$ 400,000	$ 400,000
Land	500,000	800,000
	$ 900,000	$ 1,200,000
Capital, A	$ 250,000	$ 400,000
Capital, B	250,000	400,000
Capital, C	400,000	400,000
	$ 900,000	$ 1,200,000

For purposes of Section 704(c), the land is now treated as contributed property (contributed by partners A and B to "new" partnership ABC).[16] Accordingly, upon a subsequent sale of the property for $950,000, partners A and B will each be required to recognize their $150,000 shares of the built-in gain inherent in the property before C's admission to the partnership, plus their one-third shares ($50,000) of the post-admission gain.

SMALL DISPARITIES

The regulations allow partnerships and LLCs to ignore Section 704(c) when the disparity between the book and tax values of contributed property is less than 15 percent of the adjusted basis of such property.[17] In order for this exception to apply, the aggregate disparity between book and tax basis for all properties contributed by a contributor-partner or member during the same tax year cannot exceed $20,000. Alternatively, the partnership or LLC can elect to apply Section 704(c), but only upon disposition of the property (that is, it can choose to defer special allocations until it sells or exchanges the contributed property).

---

[16] Additional theories may apply to revaluations. See, for example, "Exploring the Outer Limits of the Section 704 (c) Built-in Gain Rule," by Blake D. Rubin and Andrea R. Macintosh in *The Journal of Taxation* (1998 – part I in vol. 89, no. 3, part 2 in vol. 89, no. 4, and part 3 in vol. 89, no. 5).
[17] Regulation Section 1.704-3(e)(1).

AGGREGATION OF PROPERTIES

An additional simplification provision allows a partnership or LLC to aggregate all properties contributed by an individual partner or member that are included in the same general asset account for depreciation purposes, and treat them as a single asset when making Section 704(c) allocations. This aggregation provision does not apply to real estate.[18]

TIERED PARTNERSHIPS

Finally, the regulations provide that tiered partnerships cannot be used to avoid the requirements of Section 704(c). Where one partnership or LLC contributes Section 704(c) property to a lower tier entity, it must allocate its distributive share of depreciation, gain, loss, and the like, allocated from that entity with respect to that property in such a way as to take into account the original contributor's built-in gain or loss.[19]

---

[18] Regulation Section 1.704-3(e)(2).
[19] Regulation Section 1.704-3(a)(9). See also footnote 14 for application of the revaluation rules in tiered partnership settings.

Summary

The regulations under Section 704(c) provide substantial guidance with respect to special allocations of gains and losses, including cost recovery deductions recognized on items of contributed property. In general, the regulations are quite favorable to taxpayers. Not only do they allow the use of any reasonable method of making such allocations, they also allow the use of different methods by the same partnership or LLC for different properties. The only restriction is that partnerships or LLCs are not allowed to use methods expressly designed to reduce the aggregate tax liabilities of their partners or members.

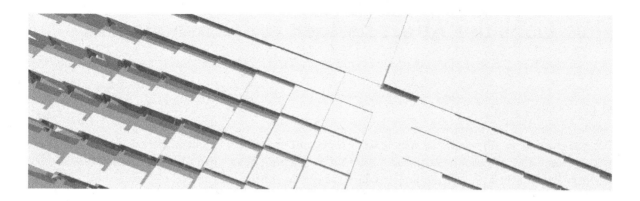

Chapter 3

ALLOCATION OF PARTNERSHIP RECOURSE LIABILITIES UNDER SECTION 752

LEARNING OBJECTIVES

After completing this chapter, you should be able to do the following:

- Recognize how liabilities affect the calculation of a partner's or member's basis and at-risk amount in his or her partnership or LLC interest.
- Calculate the gain that can result from reallocation of liabilities when a partner joins a partnership.
- Distinguish between recourse and nonrecourse liabilities of a partnership or LLC.
- Calculate a partner's or member's share of recourse liabilities of a partnership or LLC.

How Liabilities Affect Partner Tax Consequences

BASIC CONCEPTS

Because partners are (in theory) ultimately liable for partnership debts, liabilities increase the partners' potential losses in the event of partnership dissolution. Accordingly, they must be included in the partners' bases in their partnership interests, and changes in either the total level of partnership indebtedness or in the way in which partners share in that indebtedness must be accounted for on an ongoing basis.

The partnership is essentially disregarded from a tax standpoint when accounting for partnership debts. The partners' shares of partnership indebtedness flow through to the partners who are then treated as if they had made cash payments to the partnership in a like amount. Of course, since the statute treats partnership debts as indirect cash payments made by the partners, any reduction in partnership indebtedness must also be treated as a cash payment, albeit to the partners, rather than from them. Thus, accounting for partnership liabilities is important for tax purposes, not only in that a partner's share of partnership debt increases the amount of losses he or she can deduct (since deductions are limited to basis) but also because in certain cases, a reduction in partnership indebtedness can trigger unexpected gain recognition for one or more partners. It is also important to understand that because Section 752 treats the assumption by a partner of partnership debt as a cash payment by the partner to the partnership, liabilities attached to properties received as a distribution from the partnership increase the partner's basis in the partnership interest, rather than in the encumbered property.

TRANSACTIONS THAT CHANGE PARTNERS' SHARES OF PARTNERSHIP LIABILITIES

The mechanical application of Section 752 is relatively straightforward. Section 752(a) provides that increases in a partner's share of partnership debt, or the assumption by a partner of a partnership debt, are treated as contributions of money by the partner to the partnership, thus increasing the partner's basis in his or her partnership interest. Section 752(b) provides that decreases in a partner's share of partnership debt, or assumptions by the partnership of a partner's debt, are treated as distributions of money by the partnership to the partner. Deemed distributions under Section 752(b) decrease the partner's basis in his or her partnership interest and, as noted above, may trigger the recognition of gain to the partner under Section 731.

Thus, whenever a partnership obtains additional financing or pays down existing loans, the increased or decreased debt levels will have a flow-through effect on the partners just as if they had made or received cash payments to or from the partnership. Other, less obvious, transactions, however, will also impact the partners' shares of partnership indebtedness. For example, the admission of a new partner, the contribution of additional capital to the partnership by an existing partner, the distribution of encumbered property to an existing partner, and the reduction or termination of an existing partner's interest in the partnership will all have potential consequences for partners that might initially appear to be uninvolved in the transaction. Even if uninvolved in the transaction, partners can be treated as receiving cash distributions or making cash contributions, as the case may be. One final caveat – even if the partnership has not been involved in any of the above transactions during the year, and has neither paid down existing debt nor incurred additional financing, if it makes special allocations of gain, loss, income or deductions among the partners, the partners' shares of debt will generally change. Thus, it is important that the proper allocation of partnership liabilities be recalculated every year.

Contribution of Encumbered Property

The application of Section 752(b) can trigger gain under Section 731(a) when a partner contributes property encumbered by a liability in excess of its basis. Such a gain is not precluded by Section 721 because it arises, not from the contribution of property in exchange for a partnership interest, but rather from a deemed distribution under Section 752(b) resulting from the partner's entry into the partnership.

It should be noted, however, that in computing any such gain under Section 731 (a) upon a partner's entrance into the partnership, the provisions of Section 752(a) and Section 752(b) are applied simultaneously.[1] Thus, gain will be triggered under Section 731(a) only to the extent that the amount of liability shifted from the contributing partner to the other partners exceeds the sum of the basis of property contributed and the increase in the contributor's share of partnership debts.

Example 3-1

A and B form the AB partnership with the following contributions of property and cash. A contributes land with a basis of $15,000, and a fair market value of $30,000, but encumbered by a debt of $20,000. B contributes $10,000 cash. A and B are equal partners. Assume that they share liability for the new partnership debt 50:50. Under Section 752(b), A will be treated as if she received a distribution of $20,000 cash when the partnership assumes the $20,000 debt encumbering the land. A will recognize no gain under Section 731(a), however, because she is also treated, under Section 752(a), as if she had contributed $10,000 cash (representing her 50 percent share of the partnership debt) in addition to the land. Thus A will have sufficient basis in her partnership interest to absorb the deemed distribution under Section 752(b). After fully accounting for the debt transfer, A's basis in her partnership interest is reduced to $5,000 [$15,000 Basis of Land - $20,000 Liability Relief + $10,000 (Share of Liabilities)]. B has a $20,000 basis in her partnership interest. ($10,000 cash contributed directly plus $10,000 deemed contribution under Section 752(a)).

---

[1] Regulations Section 1.752-1(f). See also Revenue Ruling 87-120, 87-2 CB 161. The provisions of Section Section 752(a) and (b) are applied simultaneously whenever both are triggered by the same transaction, whether the transaction involves a contribution to the partnership or a distribution from the partnership. See also Private Letter Rulings 199943005, 199943006 and 199943007 (July 16, 1999), in which the Service ruled that the contribution of encumbered properties to a partnership and the refinancing of such properties by the partnership constituted simultaneous transactions. Note, however, that where Sections 752(a) and (b) are triggered in two separate, though related transactions, the Service has ruled that they are not to be applied simultaneously. See Revenue Ruling 81-242, 1981-2 CB 147, involving the involuntary conversion of mortgaged property and its subsequent replacement under Section 1033.

KNOWLEDGE CHECK

1. R and Q form RQ partnership with the following contributions of property and cash. R contributes land with a basis of $500 and a fair market value of $1,000, but encumbered by a debt of $800. Q contributes $200 cash. R and Q are equal partners. Assume that they share liability for the new partnership debt 50:50. What will be R's basis in his partnership interest?

   a. $0.
   b. $100.
   c. $200.
   d. $500.

Example 3-2

J and D form the JD Partnership. J contributes property with a tax basis of $10,000, and subject to a recourse mortgage of $24,000.

The FMV of the property is $30,000. D contributes $12,000 cash.

Assume the partners share the partnership debt in accordance with their capital interests – one-third to J and two-thirds to D.

Under Section 752(a), J will be deemed to have contributed property with a basis of $10,000 and $8,000 cash (one-third of the liability) to the partnership. She will simultaneously be treated under Section 752(b) as if she received a distribution of $24,000 cash upon the partnership's assumption of the mortgage encumbering her property.

Since her basis in the partnership interest cannot be less than zero, she must recognize a $6,000 gain under Section 731(a). Her basis in her partnership interest will be zero after taking the gain into account. D will recognize no gain on the contribution of cash to the partnership and will have a tax basis in her partnership interest of $28,000 ($12,000 cash contributed plus $16,000 share of the mortgage).

Note that while J cannot have a negative basis in her partnership interest, she can and does have a negative balance in her capital account on the partnership's tax basis balance sheet (unless a Section 754 election is in effect). (She has a positive $30,000 - $24,000 = $6,000 capital balance on the partnership's Section 704(b) balance sheet.) A deficit in a partner's capital balance on the books of the partnership is okay. It means that in the event of partnership liquidation, the partner would owe additional monies to the partnership.

In contrast, a partner can never individually have a negative tax basis in the partnership interest – any event that would cause the partner's basis to fall below zero will trigger recognition of gain by the partner in an amount necessary to restore basis to zero.

Caveat: Note that the above results would not apply if the mortgage on the property contributed by J had been a nonrecourse, rather than recourse, debt. In such a case, the nonrecourse mortgage would have been allocated first to J to the extent of the minimum amount of gain that would be allocated to her under Section 704(c) in the event that the lender were to foreclose upon the property in satisfaction of the nonrecourse mortgage.

In this case, the minimum gain would be $14,000 under the facts above. This concept, "Section 704(c) minimum gain," is based on the tax treatment of forgiven indebtedness under Section 1001, and is discussed in more detail in chapter 4. However, the 704(c) gain does not override the 704(b) gain.

---

2. A and B form the equal AB partnership with the following contributions. A contributes property with a basis of $200,000 and a fair market value of $600,000, but subject to a recourse debt of $400,000, incurred several years ago to finance the original acquisition of the property. B contributes property with a basis of $200,000 and a fair market value of $300,000. It is subject to a debt of $100,000, also incurred several years ago when the property was originally acquired. A and B share all items of partnership income, gain, loss, and deduction equally. They share partnership liabilities in the same ratio. What will be A's basis in her partnership interest immediately after formation?

    a. $0.

    b. $200,000.

    c. $50,000.

    d. None of the above.

If a continuing partner contributes encumbered property to a partnership, that partner will only recognize gain if the net debt relief exceeds the basis of the property contributed and the partner's pre-contribution basis in the property. Note that where more than one encumbered property is contributed to the partnership, the partners each account for their shares of aggregate partnership debt in determining whether they must report any gain on formation.

Example 3-3

Q and R form an equal partnership with the following contributions:

	Q				R		
	Basis	**FMV**	**Liability**		**Basis**	**FMV**	**Liability**
Prop 1	$ 160	$ 480	$ 300				
Prop 2					$ 150	$ 450	$ 360

Q receives a two-thirds interest in the partnership and R receives a one-third interest. Assume they share partnership liabilities in these same ratios. Under Section 752(a), Q will be deemed to have contributed money to the partnership in the amount of $440 (two-thirds of the partnership's aggregate indebtedness of $660). Her deemed distribution under Section 752(b) is $300. Thus, she recognizes no gain under Section 731, and her basis in her partnership interest is $300 ($160 basis in property 1, plus $440 share of partnership debt, less $300 deemed distribution under Section 752(b)).

In addition to property 2, R will be treated as having contributed money of $220 to the partnership, and will have a deemed distribution of $360. Thus, he will recognize no gain under Section 731 and will have a $10 basis in his partnership interest ($150 plus $220, less $360).

Section 752(b) poses a potentially dangerous trap for the unwary. As noted above, distributions in excess of a partner's basis in her partnership interest trigger taxable gain under Section 731 (a). This gain is taxed as a gain from the sale of the partnership interest. Since Section 752(b) treats a decrease in a partner's share of partnership debts as a distribution of cash, an unexpected gain under Section 731(a) may be triggered as a result of a partnership's payment of its debts, or on the admission of a new partner

 Example 3-4

A and B form the equal AB partnership with the following contributions. A contributes property with a basis of $100 and a fair market value of $600, but subject to a recourse debt of $300. B contributes property with a basis of $200 and a fair market value of $400. It is subject to a debt of $100. Six months later, C is admitted as a 25 percent partner in exchange for $200 cash. Following C's entry, A's and B's interests in partnership capital fall from 50 percent to 37.5 percent. Assume they share partnership liabilities in the same ratios.

Neither partner A or B recognizes income or loss as a result of his original contribution to the partnership. A's basis in his partnership interest is zero ($100 property contributed + $200 increase in his share of partnership debt – $300 debt transferred to the partnership). B takes a basis of $300 in his partnership interest ($200 property contributed + $200 increase in his share of partnership debt – $100 debt transferred to the partnership).

C's subsequent entry, however, changes the partners' debt sharing ratios. C now shares 25 percent of the partnership debt, reducing A's and B's shares by 12.5 percent, or $50, each. This reduction is treated as a cash distribution under Section 752(b) of $50 each to A and B. This deemed distribution reduces B's basis in his partnership interest to $250. A's deemed $50 distribution triggers a $50 gain under Section 731(a).[2] His basis remains zero.

Caveat: Regulations Section 1.704-1(b)(2)(iv)(f) allows partnerships to revalue their properties following the admission of a new partner. Revaluation of the partnership's assets, and thus the partners' capital accounts, is generally advisable in these situations. If the partnership in this example had opted to revalue its assets following C's admission, the resulting tax consequences would depend on the nature of the partnership's debt. If the debt were recourse, as in the original example, the same results would apply—A would recognize a $50 gain under Section 731(a) following C's entry to the partnership. However, if the debt were nonrecourse, revaluation of the partnership's assets would create Section 704(c) minimum gain, allocable to A, "protecting" his share of partnership liabilities, and preventing them from being shifted away from him to C (see chapter 4).

---

[2] Note that the Service has taken the position that a taxpayer who owns both a limited and a general interest in a partnership must pool his basis in the limited and general partnership interests to determine whether an "excess" distribution has occurred. Revenue Ruling 84-53, 1984-1 CB 159. See also Letter Ruling 8350006, August 22, 1983 (may not be used or cited as precedent).

KNOWLEDGE CHECK

3. Assume the same facts as in the previous question. Assume further that the partnership admits a third partner, C, six months later in exchange for a cash contribution of $200,000. C will receive a one-third interest in partnership capital, profits, and losses. Assume further that she is allocated one-third of the partnership's liabilities under Section 752. A and B's shares of partnership liabilities under that statute decline to one-third each. Assuming no change in other facts, how much gain will A be required to recognize upon the admission of C?

    a. $0.
    b. $33,333.
    c. $83,333.
    d. None of the above.

Distributions in Partial Liquidation of a Partner's Interest

Receipt of a non-liquidating distribution by a partner is generally nontaxable unless the partner receives cash in excess of basis.[3] In some cases, however, a seemingly nontaxable distribution can trigger gain under Section 731(a) if the distribution alters the partner's share of partnership liabilities. Recall that Section 752(b) treats a reduction in the partner's share of partnership debt as a distribution of money by the partnership to the partner. This deemed distribution, when coupled with an actual cash distribution, can trigger unexpected gain to the partner.

Example 3-5

Until December, Z was a one-third partner in Alphabet Partners, an insurance partnership. Her tax basis in her partnership interest was $10,000, consisting of her deficit capital balance of ($20,000) and her one-third share of the partnership's $90,000 in outstanding liabilities.

On December 18, Z received an $8,000 cash distribution from the partnership. Assume that the distribution reduces Z's interest in the partnership from one-third to one-fifth, and reduces her share of partnership liabilities to 20 percent as well.

The reduction in her share of partnership liabilities from $30,000 (one-third) to $18,000 (one-fifth) is treated under Section 752(b) as a cash distribution in the amount of $12,000. When coupled with the actual cash distribution of $8,000, Z's total "cash" distribution is $20,000, which exceeds her basis in the partnership interest by $10,000. Accordingly, she must recognize a $10,000 gain under Section 731(a).[4]

---

[3] A number of exceptions to this general rule have been legislated over the years. See Sections 751(b) [relating to disproportionate distributions], 704(c)(1)(B) [relating to distributions of contributed property], 737 [relating to distributions received by partners previously contributing appreciated property to the partnership] and 707 [relating to disguised sales] for exceptions.

[4] This example assumes that Sections 751(b), 707 and 737 do not apply to this distribution.

Note that the deemed cash contribution under Section 752(b) is accounted for before accounting for any distribution of property (other than money) associated with the redemption of some or all of the partner's interest in the partnership.[5] Thus, unless the partner's net debt relief as a result of the distribution exceeds his or her basis in the partnership interest (for example, the partner has a negative tax basis capital account before the distribution), a property distribution never triggers gain under Section 731(a), even if it reduces the partner's allocable share of partnership liabilities.

 Example 3-6

S received a distribution of property valued at $500 from the TSX Partnership (tax basis of the property was $325). The distribution reduced S's interest in the partnership from one-third to one-fifth. It also reduced her share of partnership liabilities from one-third to one-fifth. Immediately prior to the distribution, S's basis in her partnership interest was $250 and her share of partnership liabilities was $200 (one-third of the partnership's $600 in outstanding debt).

Under Section 752(b), S will be treated as having received a cash distribution of $80 (the difference between one-third and one-fifth of the partnership's outstanding indebtedness) in addition to the property actually distributed.

The deemed cash distribution is accounted for first, reducing her tax basis in the partnership interest from $250 to $170. She will then take a $170 basis in the property received from the partnership under Section 732. Her remaining basis in her partnership interest will be zero.

Distributions of Encumbered Property

When a partner receives a distribution of property encumbered by liabilities, the consequences are slightly more complicated. Under Section 752(a), the assumption by the partner of partnership liabilities is treated as a contribution of cash by the partner to the partnership. This deemed contribution must be taken into account for purposes of applying the basis determination rules of Sections 732 and 733.

The tax treatment in these situations is further complicated by Section 752(b), which treats a decrease in a partner's share of partnership liabilities as a cash distribution by the partnership to the partner. Since a distribution of encumbered property will generally decrease the partnership's outstanding liabilities, it will decrease every partner's share of partnership debt. The actual distribution of encumbered property to a single partner will thus be accompanied by a deemed cash distribution to all partners. The distributee-partner must account for both the deemed cash contribution and the deemed cash distribution in addition to the actual distribution of property received from the partnership. Note that the deemed cash contribution will, in most cases, result in an increase in the partner's basis in the partnership interest rather than in the encumbered property.

---

[5] Section 733. See also Revenue Ruling 79-205, 1979-2 CB 255.

Example 3-7

ABC Partnership had the following balance sheet as of December 31:

	Basis	FMV		Basis	FMV
Cash	$ 45,000	$ 45,000	Mtg, P1	$ 15,000	$ 15,000
Prop 1	30,000	95,000	Mtg, P2	30,000	30,000
Prop 2	15,000	55,000	Capital, A	15,000	50,000
			Capital, B	15,000	50,000
			Capital, C	15,000	50,000
	$ 90,000	$ 195,000		$ 90,000	$ 195,000

On that date, the partnership distributed property 2 to C, reducing her interest in the partnership from one-third to one-fifth. Assume that C's share of partnership liabilities was also reduced from one-third to one-fifth. C took property 2 subject to the related mortgage.

Under Section 731(a), C recognizes no gain on the distribution of property 2, since she did not receive cash in excess of her basis in her partnership interest. Prior to the distribution, C's basis in her interest was $30,000 (her $15,000 tax basis capital account plus her one-third share of the partnership's liabilities). The distribution reduces her interest in the partnership from one-third to one-fifth. It also reduces the partnership's outstanding liabilities from $45,000 to $15,000. Thus, her share of partnership debt falls from $15,000 (one-third of $45,000) to $3,000 (one-fifth of $15,000), and she is treated under Section 752(b) as having received a distribution of $12,000 cash from the partnership.

At the same time, her assumption of the partnership's $30,000 mortgage on property 2 is treated as a cash contribution to the partnership. Thus, although property 2 is encumbered by a $30,000 liability, her basis in it is only $15,000 (carryover basis). Meanwhile, her basis in her partnership interest actually increases by $3,000, to $33,000 (original $30,000 basis, plus $30,000 deemed cash contribution, less $12,000 deemed cash distribution, less $15,000 basis in property 2 received from the partnership).

The transfer of liabilities from the partnership to C also has tax consequences for the other two partners. Although their interests in the partnership increase from 33 percent to 40 percent, after accounting for the transfer to C, their shares of partnership liabilities fall by $9,000 (from one-third of $45,000 to 40 percent of $15,000). Thus, although they were not directly involved in the transaction, each of their bases in their partnership interests fall from $30,000 to $21,000.

4. ABC Partnership had the following balance sheets as of December 31:

	Basis	FMV		Basis	FMV
Cash	$ 45,000	$ 45,000	Mtg, P1	$ 45,000	$ 45,000
Prop 1	30,000	80,000	Mtg, P2	30,000	30,000
Prop 2	15,000	70,000	Capital, A	5,000	40,000
			Capital, B	5,000	40,000
			Capital, C	5,000	40,000
	$ 90,000	$ 195,000		$ 90,000	$ 195,000

On that date, the partnership distributed property 2 to C in complete liquidation of her interest in the partnership. C took property 2 subject to its mortgage. How much gain will C recognize in connection with the distribution?

   a. $0.
   b. $55,000.
   c. $65,000.
   d. $35,000.

EFFECT OF LIABILITIES ON PARTNERS' AND LLC MEMBERS' AMOUNTS AT RISK

Under Section 465, a partner or LLC member's deduction for flow-through losses allocated to him or her from the partnership or LLC is limited to the amount he or she has "at risk" as a result of his or her investment in the entity. The partner's or member's amount at risk is computed in a manner similar to the computation of basis, except that it does not include the partner's or member's share of entity -level nonqualified nonrecourse financing or seller-financing. Thus, in measuring the amount at risk under Section 465, the investor must distinguish among his/ her share of different types of entity liabilities.

Nonrecourse financing is generally not considered to increase the partners' or members' amounts at risk unless it is "qualified" nonrecourse financing. Generally, speaking, qualified nonrecourse financing is financing that is obtained from a qualified, unrelated lender and that is secured by real estate. A qualified lender is broadly defined as a lender whose regular business includes lending money or a lender whose loans are backed by the U.S. government or an agency thereof.

Most nonrecourse financing obtained by real estate partnerships or LLCs is obtained from a qualified lender and can be included in the at-risk amounts of the partners or members. One problem for LLCs is that the members are legally protected from personal liability from creditors of the entity (subject to many restrictions as described in the beginning course). As a result, many of the LLC's debts will be classified as nonrecourse liabilities because no member has personal responsibility for repayment in the event of default by the LLC. These liabilities cannot be included in the at-risk amounts of the LLC's members unless they are secured by real estate (and were obtained from a qualified lender).

In many cases, however, certain debts of the LLC will be guaranteed by one or more members. In such cases, as discussed in chapter 4, the debt will be classified as a recourse liability, because the guarantor, at least, has personal risk of loss in the event of LLC default. If the guarantor would not have recourse against other members of the LLC in the event the entity defaulted and the guarantor had to make the payment, the liability would be allocated to the guarantor-member. In such cases, the debt should be treated as a recourse liability and included in the amount at risk for the guarantor member.[6]

KNOWLEDGE CHECK

5. Under what circumstances will debt allocated to a partner or an LLC member increase both the tax basis of the partnership interest and the partner's or member's amount at risk?

    a. When the debt is nonrecourse.
    b. When the debt is encumbered by real estate.
    c. When the partner is a general partner.
    d. When the debt is recourse debt or qualified nonrecourse debt.

---

[6] See FSA 200025018 (March 17, 2000).

Allocation of Liabilities Among the Partners: In General

Prior to 1989, the allocation of partnership liabilities was a relatively simple process. Recourse liabilities were allocated among general partners in accordance with their loss-sharing ratios. This allocation scheme was intended to reflect the way in which the true risks of these liabilities were actually shared by partners. Since recourse lenders have no access to the personal assets of limited partners, limited partners were not allocated any share of recourse liabilities. Moreover, the rules were based on the conceptual foundation that these debts would only be paid by general partners if the partnership lost a sufficiently substantial portion of its assets so that it could no longer pay them on its own. Thus, general partners would become liable for recourse debts of the partnership only in the event it lost money. They were therefore deemed to share in these debts in the same ratios in which they shared in partnership losses.

Nonrecourse liabilities were subject to a different allocation scheme. By definition, no partner would be personally liable for a partnership nonrecourse debt. Thus, the partners would bear the burden of repayment of these debts only in the form of a reduced share of partnership operating profits. Accordingly, these debts were allocable among all partners and were to be shared in accordance with the partners' profit-sharing ratios. Agreements between partners to shift the risk of certain liabilities were generally ignored.

Indeed, in *Raphan*,[7] the court held that a general partner's guarantee of a partnership nonrecourse loan did not affect the character of that loan under Section 752. The limited partners were allowed to increase their basis by their proportionate shares of the loan. In response to the *Raphan* decision, Congress instructed the IRS to revise the regulations under Section 752 so that the allocation of partnership liabilities more closely resembled the economic reality of the partners' true risks.[8] The Service issued the first set of temporary regulations under Section 752 on January 30, 1989. A second set of slightly modified regulations was issued on July 29, 1991.

Caution: The allocation of debt to a partner under Section 752, while increasing the partner's basis in his or her partnership interest, does not necessarily increase the partner's amount at risk under Section 465. As discussed above, the partner's at-risk amount is only increased by allocations of recourse and qualified nonrecourse debt.

The regulations now provide a more substantive framework for analysis of the partners' economic risk with respect to debts incurred by the partnership. This framework is consistent with that established in the Section 704(b) regulations issued during the same time period. Together, these two sets of regulations provide a comprehensive approach to evaluating the underlying economic impact of partnership operations on the partners and require that the tax consequences of the allocation of partnership liabilities more closely reflect economic reality.

---

[7] 55 AFTR 2d 85-1154 (1985).
[8] Committee Reports on P.L. 98-369.

RECOURSE VERSUS NONRECOURSE LIABILITIES

The regulations retain much of the conceptual framework of the old rules. Recourse liabilities can only be allocated to partners who would actually have to pay those liabilities in the event of partnership default, while nonrecourse liabilities can be allocated among all partners. This means that recourse liabilities generally cannot be allocated to limited partners.

The allocation of recourse liabilities among the partners is based on an analysis of the partners' individual responsibilities in the event of partnership default. Since partnership default occurs only if the partnership loses money, the focus remains on how the partners share the risks associated with nonprofitable operations. However, this analysis is much more thorough than merely looking to the partner's shares of partnership or LLC loss. The regulations require an analysis of the partners' liability - sharing responsibilities in a hypothetical, worst-case scenario known as a "constructive liquidation."

The regulations also impose a comprehensive approach to allocating nonrecourse liabilities. These provisions are discussed in detail in chapter 4.

RECOURSE LIABILITY DEFINED

A Partner is responsible for a recourse liability to the extent that the partner, or related person, bears the economic risk of loss for that liability in the event of a partnership default (under § 1.752-2). For example, unless the debt contract states explicitly that the lender's only recourse in the event of partnership default is against the property serving as collateral for that debt, the lender can pursue payment from the general partners. Such a debt will be classified as a recourse liability with respect to the general partners.[9]

In many cases, the debt contract may say on its face that the lender has recourse only against property serving as collateral for the loan. Such a loan would ordinarily be characterized as a nonrecourse liability. In some cases, however, other circumstances may apply that result in a debt which is nonrecourse on its face being classified as a recourse liability. For example, if the lender is a partner in the partnership (or is related to a partner in the partnership), the lender or partner will suffer economic loss in the event of a partnership default. In that case, the debt is reclassified as recourse and will be allocable solely to the lender or partner.

Similarly, if a partner guarantees part or all of a note, or interest payments on the note, the note will be wholly or partly reclassified as recourse debt with respect to the guarantor. The same result will apply if a partner pledges property as collateral for an otherwise nonrecourse note. Because partnership default would cause the partner to lose the property serving as collateral, the note will be reclassified as recourse to the extent of the value of the property (and will be allocable solely to the partner pledging collateral).

---

[9] Regulation Section 1.752-1(a)(1) and (2).

Under Proposed Regulations issued in January 2014,[10] the IRS identifies five commercial requirements all of which must be satisfied for a liability to be classified as a recourse liability. The requirements are as follows:

- Borrower is required to maintain a commercially reasonable net worth or is subject to commercially reasonable restrictions on asset transfers for inadequate consideration.
- Borrower required to provide documentation of its financial condition periodically.
- Payment obligation does not end before term of liability.
- Borrower not required to maintain liquidity in excess of reasonable needs.
- Borrower received arm's length consideration for assuming the payment obligation.

As proposed regulations, these rules will not be effective until published in the Federal Register as final regulations. They dramatically change the definition of recourse liabilities, and have drawn criticism from the profession.[11] At this point, therefore, it is difficult to estimate the likelihood that these new requirements will ultimately be formally adopted by the Treasury Department.

---

[10] Prop. Regs. Section 1.752-2(b)(3)(ii), issued January 30, 2014. Note: these proposed regulations were issued in addition to proposed regulations issued under Section 752 on January 6, 2014.

[11] For example, see the letter from the American Bar Association (ABA) to the Commissioner of Internal Revenue dated August 8, 2014, in which the ABA strongly criticizes the requirements of the proposed regulations (available at: www.americanbar.org/ content/ dam/ aba/ administrative/ taxation/ policy/ 081114comments.authcheckdam.pdf).

Allocation of Recourse Liabilities

GENERAL RULES: "CONSTRUCTIVE LIQUIDATION"

Partnership recourse liabilities are allocated among general partners in accordance with the way those partners bear the economic risk of loss for those liabilities. Partners bear the economic risk of loss for a liability to the extent they would be required to make a net contribution to the lender, or to the partnership, in the event of a partnership constructive liquidation. In this hypothetical constructive liquidation scenario all the partnership's assets (including money) are sold for no consideration, and the partnership is liquidated without paying any of its outstanding liabilities. The losses recognized in the deemed sale are then allocated to the partners in accordance with their loss-sharing ratios and their capital accounts are analyzed to determine each partner's potential personal liability.

This hypothetical liquidation determines each partner's economic risk for partnership liabilities in a manner quite similar to the determination of his or her economic interest in partnership items of income and loss under Section 704(b). In fact, it follows the rationale under Section 704(b) – the hypothetical book losses are allocated to the partners as provided in the partnership agreement, and recorded in their capital accounts. Those partners with deficits in their capital accounts following this hypothetical transaction would be obligated to restore those deficits under Section 704(b). Restoration of deficit capital accounts would be required in order for the partnership to pay its creditors. Thus, their shares of the partnership's recourse liabilities are equal to the deficit balances they would be required to repay in the hypothetical worst-case scenario reflected in the constructive liquidation.

Example 3-8

A and B form a general partnership with cash contributions of $50,000 each. The partners agree to share all items of income and loss equally. The partnership borrows $90,000 on a recourse note and purchases a shopping center for $190,000. A constructive liquidation of the partnership, in which all partnership assets are assumed to become worthless, and all liabilities payable in full, would yield the following partner capital accounts:

	A	B
Beginning Capital	$ 50,000	$ 50,000
Loss on Shopping Center	(95,000)	(95,000)
Hypothetical capital balance	$ (45,000)	$ (45,000)

Since A and B would each be required by law to make a net contribution of $45,000 to the partnership, they share risk of loss for the partnership recourse debt equally.

KNOWLEDGE CHECK

6. Which of the following definitions of a constructive liquidation is the most accurate?

    a. A constructive liquidation is a hypothetical scenario in which all the partnership's assets (including money) are sold for no consideration and it is liquidated without paying any of its outstanding liabilities.

    b. A constructive liquidation is a hypothetical scenario in which the all of the partnership's liabilities are deemed to come due and are payable by the partners in accordance with the ratio established in the partnership agreement.

    c. A constructive liquidation is a hypothetical scenario in which all the partnership's assets are sold for their book values and the partnership is liquidated.

    d. A constructive liquidation is a hypothetical scenario in which all the partnership's assets are sold for their tax bases and the partnership is liquidated.

7. Which capital accounts do the regulations look to in determining the partners' shares of partnership recourse debts in a hypothetical constructive liquidation?

    a. The Section 704(b) book capital accounts.

    b. The capital accounts under GAAP.

    c. The tax capital accounts.

    d. The hypothetical capital accounts.

LIMITED PARTNERS

Because limited partners typically cannot be obligated to make payments to the partnership or to the partnership's creditors beyond their initial contributions, the regulations generally prevent them from sharing in partnership recourse debts. However, where a limited partner is required to restore a deficit in his or her capital account, this obligation will entitle him or her to a share of partnership recourse debts. Similarly, where a limited partner obtains his or her partnership interest in exchange for cash and a promissory note obligating him or her to make additional contributions in the future, he or she will be entitled to share in partnership recourse debts to the extent of the outstanding balance of the promissory note.

KNOWLEDGE CHECK

8. Q and L form a limited partnership to invest in residential rental property. Q, the general partner, invests $50,000 for a 10 percent interest in partnership capital, profits, and losses. L, a group of limited partners, invests $450,000 in exchange for the remaining 90 percent interest in capital, profit, and loss. The partnership borrows $1,500,000 to construct the rental property. The initial financing takes the form of a recourse bridge loan, guaranteed by Q. Upon completion of construction, the project is to be refinanced with a nonrecourse loan. What is partner Q's share of the recourse bridge loan?

    a. $0.
    b. $1,500,000.
    c. $750,000.
    d. $150,000.

BOOK VERSUS TAX CAPITAL ACCOUNTS

The regulations under Section 752 are corollaries of the earlier regulations issued under Section 704(b). The Section 704(b) regulations, governing partnership accounting generally, form the foundation on which the liability sharing regulations are based. Thus, it is important to recognize that the hypothetical capital account calculations required in the constructive liquidation process are based on the partners' book capital accounts under Section 704(b).

Example 3-9

Q and L form a partnership with the following contributions of property and/or cash. Q contributes real estate with a fair market value of $750,000 and a tax basis of $450,000. The real estate is unencumbered by liabilities of any kind. L contributes cash of $750,000. The partnership then borrows $500,000 against the real estate contributed by Q to construct an office building. The loan is a recourse loan for which Q and L, as general partners, each assume joint and several liabilities. Q and L agree to share in partnership capital, profits and losses equally. A constructive liquidation immediately after the partnership incurs the liability would yield the following results:

	Q	L
Beginning capital balances	$ 750,000	$ 750,000
Hypothetical loss	(1,000,000)	(1,000,000)
Hypothetical capital balance	$ (250,000)	$ (250,000)

Example 3-9 (continued)

Note that the hypothetical loss allocated between the two partners is the amount of the book loss that would result if the partnership disposed of all its assets for no consideration. Where the partnership has only recourse liabilities outstanding, the hypothetical loss will be equal to the aggregate book value of the partnership's assets. In this case, the partnership would lose $2 million. Allocating this loss equally among the two partners leaves each with a $250,000 deficit balance in their hypothetical capital accounts. These reflect the amounts each partner would be required to pay the partnership in order to allow the partnership to pay its creditors. Since each partner would owe $250,000, they share the $500,000 partnership recourse liability equally.

EFFECT OF PARTNER GUARANTEES

Where one or more partners or LLC members guarantee partnership or LLC liabilities, the guarantee may or may not affect the allocation of the guaranteed debt. The consequences of a guarantee depend on the nature of the debt being guaranteed (in other words, recourse versus nonrecourse) and the nature of the guarantor's claims against the partnership or one or more individual partners should he or she have to make good on the guarantee.

Guarantees of Recourse Debt

Partner guarantees of partnership recourse debts may be relevant in determining who bears economic risk. However, the regulations provide that where the guarantor has recourse against another partner, such as a general partner (as is usually the case under state law), or where the guarantee is enforceable only after the creditor exhausts his or her remedies against the partnership, the guarantee is disregarded. In such cases, the guarantor is not obligated to make a net payment to the partnership, or its creditors, in excess of that amountwhich would be required without the guarantee, and so the partners' d ebt sharing ratios are not affected.[12]

 Example 3-10

E and F form a limited partnership with cash contributions of $20,000 each. E, the general partner, and F, the limited partner, agree to share all profits and losses equally.

The partnership purchases real property for $40,000 cash and a recourse note for $60,000. F guarantees the recourse note. In the event of a partnership default, F would be obligated to pay the outstanding balance of the note, but would be subrogated to the seller's rights against the partnership. F has no other obligations to make additional payments to the partnership. Because F is subrogated to the seller's rights against the partnership, he would be entitled to recover from the partnership any amount paid under the guarantee upon partnership default. Thus, F would not be obligated to make a net payment with respect to the liability in a constructive liquidation.

---

[12] Regulations Section 1.752-2(b)(5) and (6).

Example 3-10 (continued)

E, the sole general partner, would, however, be required under state law to make a $60,000 payment to the partnership in a constructive liquidation. Thus, F's guarantee is disregarded and E is considered to bear the economic risk of loss for the entire $60,000 partnership liability.

Guarantees of Nonrecourse Debt

Different results apply when a partner or LLC member guarantees a nonrecourse debt of the partnership or LLC. In this case, the lender has no claim against any partners in the partnership other than the guarantor. Thus, even if the guarantor has the right of subrogation, he or she would have no claim against the partnership or any other partner for reimbursement after satisfying his or her guarantee. Thus, in these cases, the nonrecourse note is reclassified as recourse debt and is allocated wholly to the guarantor.

KNOWLEDGE CHECK

9. S is a 10 percent partner in ST Partners. T, a group of limited partners, owns the remaining 90 percent interest in the partnership. All items of partnership income and loss are shared proportionately by each of the partners. The partnership borrowed $1,000,000 on a nonrecourse loan to construct an apartment complex on land purchased earlier by the partnership. S guaranteed this loan. How much of the loan will be allocated to S under Section 752?

    a. 0 percent.
    b. 10 percent.
    c. 100 percent.
    d. The portion that exceeds the aggregate capital balances of the limited partners.

Note that an interesting aspect of these provisions is that the allocation of the partnership's liabilities and the allocation of partnership losses will generally match. For recourse liabilities, the allocation of the liabilities is expressly tied to the measurement of how the partners would truly share in a catastrophic loss of the partnership. Where one or more partners have guaranteed a nominally nonrecourse debt of the partnership, in contrast, the partnership will essentially be required to allocate its losses to the partners to whom the (now recourse) liability has been allocated. This requirement follows the prohibition in the Section 704(b) regulations against creating or increasing deficits in the partners' capital accounts in excess of the amounts they are required to restore (either through recognition of "minimum gain" or by making an additional contribution to capital) upon liquidation of the partnership. Thus, Section 752 and 704(b) fit together seamlessly.

Example 3-11

B and Z form a limited partnership to construct and manage residential rental property. B, the general partner, contributes $50,000 cash in exchange for a 10 percent general partnership interest. Z, a group of limited partners, contributes $450,000 in exchange for an aggregate, limited, interest in the partnership of 90 percent. The partnership borrows $1,500,000 on a nonrecourse loan to acquire real estate and construct an apartment complex. In order to secure agreeable terms, B guarantees the loan. Since the loan is now a recourse loan, it must be allocated using the constructive liquidation process. Immediately after the loan is obtained, a constructive liquidation would yield the following results:

	B	Z
Beginning capital balances	$ 50,000	$ 450,000
Hypothetical loss (10:90)	(200,000)	(1,800,000)
Hypothetical balances	(150,000)	(1,350,000)
Reallocation to avoid deficit in Z's capital account	(1,350,000)	1,350,000
Adjusted hypothetical balances	$ (1,500,000)	$ —

Although the partnership agreement allocates 90 percent of the partnership's losses to Z, this allocation will not be recognized under Section 704(b). Allocations to the partners can create a deficit balance in their capital accounts only to the extent of their obligations to restore those deficits at liquidation, or their shares of partnership minimum gain. Since the partnership liability is properly classified as a recourse liability (due to B's guarantee), there is no partnership minimum gain. Thus, loss allocations can create a deficit balance in B's capital account, since she is a general partner, but not in Z's.

Accordingly, the bulk of the partnership's actual and potential future losses must be allocated to B, as must the recourse liability.

Arrangements Tantamount to a Guarantee

The regulations provide that certain contractual arrangements which have the effect of insulating the lender from risk will be treated as guarantees. If a partner or related person enters into a contractual obligation with the lender, which has the effect of insulating "substantially all the risk to the lender that the partnership will not satisfy its obligations under the loan," and a principal purpose of the contractual arrangement is to allow other partners to be allocated shares of the loan, then the partner or related person will be treated as having guaranteed the loan.[13] The regulations suggest that a lease agreement between a partner or related person and the partnership in which the partnership receives above-market lease payments is an example of this type of "indirect" guarantee.

Loans by a Partner or Related Person

Similar rules apply to loans obtained from partners or related parties. If the loans are recourse, so that the lender has a claim against the partnership, and thus against all the general partners, the loan is allocated

---

[13] Regulations Section 1.752-2(j)(2).

among the general partners following the hypothetical constructive liquidation scenario. If, in contrast, the loan from a partner or related party is structured as a nonrecourse loan, so that the lender has no claim against the partnership or any partner, in the event of default, it will be classified as a recourse loan, allocable to the partner who either made the loan, or is related to the lender. Where more than one partner is related to the lender, the loan is allocated to that partner with the most significant relationship. If multiple partners are equally related to the lender, the loan is allocated equally among these partners.

SPECIAL ALLOCATIONS OF PARTNERSHIP INCOME AND LOSS

The allocation of recourse debts generally follows the allocation of partnership capital, profits, and losses unless partnership losses are not allocated in accordance with capital ratios. Where the partnership agreement provides for special allocations of partnership profits or losses, the allocation of partnership recourse liabilities can differ dramatically from both the partners' loss-sharing ratios and capital ratios.

KNOWLEDGE CHECK

10. Q and L form a general partnership with the following contributions of property and cash. Q contributes real estate with a fair market value of $750,000 and a tax basis of $450,000. The real estate is encumbered by a recourse liability of $500,000, incurred to finance the original acquisition of the property. L contributes cash of $250,000. The partnership agreement allocates profits equally between Q and L. Losses, however, are allocated 80 percent to Q and 20 percent to L. How much of the $500,000 recourse liability will be allocated to partner L under Section 752?

    a. $0.

    b. $100,000.

    c. $250,000.

    d. None of the above.

 Example 3-12

J and D form a general partnership with cash contributions of $150,000 each. The partnership subsequently borrows $300,000 on a recourse note and purchases a shopping center for $600,000. The partners agree that profits are to be shared equally, but losses will be allocated 75 percent to J and 25 percent to D. At inception of the partnership, a constructive liquidation would yield the following capital accounts:

	J	D
Beginning capital balances	$ 150,000	$ 150,000
Hypothetical loss on Shopping Center	(450,000)	(150,000)
Ending Balance	$ (300,000)	$ —

Example 3-12 (continued)

Thus, J would be required to make a net contribution of $300,000 to the partnership which would be used by the partnership to retire its debt. Accordingly, J bears the economic risk of loss for the entire $300,000 of partnership recourse debt. Although she is only allocated 75 percent of the partnership's losses, she will be allocated 100 percent of the debt.

Note that special allocations of partnership profits can also affect the allocation of recourse debts under the constructive liquidation process.

Example 3-13

M, N, and S form a general partnership, each contributing $50,000 for a one-third interest in partnership capital. The partnership agreement allocates profits 50 percent to M and 25 percent each to N and S. The three partners share losses equally.

Shortly after formation, the partnership borrows $350,000 on a recourse loan and purchases depreciable real estate for $500,000. Over its first few years of operations, it reports net profits of $200,000, of which $100,000 are allocated to M and $50,000 each to N and S. Assume it has the following balance sheet at the end of this period:

Cash and equivalents	$ 225,000
Land and improvements	500,000
Accumulated depreciation	(50,000)
Total assets	$ 675,000
Mortgage, real estate	$ 325,000
Capital, M	150,000
Capital, N	100,000
Capital, S	100,000
Total liabilities and capital	$ 675,000

A constructive liquidation at this point would yield the following hypothetical results:

	M	N	S
Beginning capital balance	$ 150,000	$ 100,000	$ 100,000
Hypothetical loss	(225,000)	(225,000)	(225,000)
Constructive capital balance	$ (75,000)	$ (125,000)	$ (125,000)

Thus, the partnership allocates the recourse liability $75,000 to M, $125,000 to N and $125,000 to S, even though their loss ratios are one-third each.

As the above examples illustrate, the constructive liquidation computations should be recalculated every time the partnership is required to report to the partners their shares of partnership indebtedness. For example, the computations should be recalculated every year when the partnership files its tax returns and the accompanying Schedules K-1. Fresh computations are also necessary whenever a partner sells all or part of his or her interest in the partnership, whenever a new partner is admitted to the partnership and whenever partnership property is distributed to a partner, whether in partial or total redemption of his or her interest in the partnership.

KNOWLEDGE CHECK

11. D and E form a general partnership with cash contributions of $150,000 each. The partners agree to share income equally. Losses are to be allocated 60 percent to D and 40 percent to E. The partnership borrows $700,000 on a recourse note and purchases a shopping center for $1,000,000. How much of the debt will be allocated to D under Section 752 in the partnership's first year of operations?

    a. $0.
    b. $350,000.
    c. $450,000.
    d. $700,000.

12. A and B formed a general partnership with cash contributions of $100,000 each. The partnership subsequently borrowed $400,000 on a recourse note and purchased a shopping center for $600,000. The partners agreed that profits were to be shared equally, but losses would be allocated 75 percent to A and 25 percent to B. How much of the recourse liability will be allocated to B under Section 752?

    a. $0.
    b. $150,000.
    c. $300,000.
    d. $50,000.

Chapter 4

Allocation of Partnership Nonrecourse Liabilities and Related Deductions Under Sections 752 and 704(b)

Learning Objectives

After completing this chapter, you should be able to do the following:

- Distinguish between recourse and nonrecourse liabilities of a partnership or LLC.
- Calculate a partner's or member's share of nonrecourse liabilities of a partnership or LLC.
- Analyze the impact of a partner or LLC member's guarantee of a recourse or nonrecourse liability of the entity.
- Calculate a partner or LLC member's share of nonrecourse deductions of a partnership or LLC.
- Recognize when to treat a liability as a recognized versus contingent liability and understand how to account for partnership or LLC contingent liabilities.

Distinguishing Between Recourse and Nonrecourse Liabilities

A recourse liability is one for which any partner or related person bears personal risk of loss in the event of a partnership default.[1] For this purpose, a partner bears a personal risk of loss if he or she would be obligated to make a payment, either to a creditor or to the partnership, in the event the partnership's assets (including cash) became completely worthless, and it was unable to satisfy its obligations. If no partner would be obligated to make any additional payments with respect to a partnership debt in this hypothetical scenario (known as a *constructive liquidation*), the liability is classified as a nonrecourse liability.

OBLIGATION TO MAKE PAYMENT

In determining whether a partner would be obligated to make a payment in the event of partnership default, the regulations consider contractual obligations outside the partnership (for example, guarantees, indemnifications, and so on), obligations imposed by the partnership agreement (for example, deficit restoration requirements, additional capital contributions, and so on), and obligations imposed by state law.[2] Contingent obligations, however, are generally disregarded.[3] Thus, if a partner would be obligated to make a payment only in the event that, say, another partner defaulted on his or her obligation, this obligation would be disregarded.

PARTNER GUARANTEE OF INTEREST ON NONRECOURSE LOAN

As noted in chapter 3, the regulations expressly require that a partner's guarantee of an otherwise nonrecourse loan will cause such loan to be recharacterized as a recourse debt. The regulations also require recharacterization of a portion of a nonrecourse loan where a partner (or partners) has guaranteed more than 25 percent[4] of the interest which accrues on the loan. In such a case, the loan is recharacterized as a recourse debt to the extent of the present value (discounted at the interest rate charged on the loan) of the remaining interest payments which the guarantor(s) would be obligated to pay if the partnership should default.[5] Any excess of the loan amount over the present value of the guaranteed interest payments is treated as a nonrecourse loan. This recharacterization rule does not apply if the interest guarantee covers a period of no more than five years or one-third of the term of the loan, whichever is less.[6]

---

[1] Regulations Section 1.752-1(a)(1).

[2] Regulations Section 1.752-2(b)(3).

[3] Regulations Section 1.752-2(b)(4).

[4] Regulations Section 1.752-2(e).

[5] If interest is imputed under either Sections 483 or 1274, the present value of the guaranteed interest must be computed using the applicable federal rate, compounded semi-annually. See Regulations Section 1.752-2(e)(2).

[6] Regulations Section 1.752-2(e)(3).

Example 4-1

C and D form a general partnership to purchase an apartment complex. The partnership obtains a $1,500,000 nonrecourse loan and purchases an apartment building for $2,000,000. The terms of the loan call for annual payments of interest only over 10 years, with the principal payable in a lump sum at the end of the ten-year loan term. C guarantees the payment of all interest on the loan. Interest accrues at a 14 percent annual rate.

At the time the partnership obtains the loan, the present value of the remaining interest payments guaranteed by C is $1,095,384.[7] Accordingly, only $404,616 of the $1,500,000 loan is a nonrecourse obligation under Section 752. If the partnership makes the first annual interest payment, the amount of its nonrecourse obligations in year 2 will increase to $461,262 ($1,500,000 less $1,038,738, the present value of the remaining 9 years interest payments). C's basis in the partnership would in general decrease with the decrease in recourse debt from the interest assumed by C, even though it is partially offset by the increase in nonrecourse debt, because D would also share in the nonrecourse debt (qualified nonrecourse financing).

KNOWLEDGE CHECK

1. C and D form a general partnership to purchase an apartment complex. The partnership obtains a $1,500,000 nonrecourse loan, bearing interest at 8 percent per year, and purchases an apartment building for $2,000,000. The terms of the loan call for annual payments of interest only over 10 years, with the principal payable in a lump sum at the end of each period. C guarantees the payment of all interest on the loan. How much of the loan will be recharacterized as a recourse loan, allocable to C?

    a. None of it.
    b. All of it.
    c. 80 percent of it.
    d. An amount equal to the present value of the guaranteed interest.

PARTNER PROVIDING COLLATERAL FOR A PARTNERSHIP NONRECOURSE LOAN

The regulations also reclassify otherwise nonrecourse loans where such loans are collateralized by property owned by a partner, rather than the partnership. In such cases, the partner who owns the collateral bears the ultimate economic risk in the event the partnership defaults on the loan and the loan will be recast as a recourse debt to the extent of the fair market value of the property serving as collateral, as of the date such property was pledged against the loan.[8] A promissory note contributed to the

---

[7] Present value of a $210,000 annuity (14 percent of $1,500,000) for 10 years at a 14 percent discount rate.
[8] Regulations Section 1.752-2(h)(1) and (3).

partnership by a partner does not count as property unless it is readily tradable on an established securities market.[9]

The regulations treat certain property contributions as indirect pledges against partnership loans. Specifically, where a partner contributes property to a partnership which is used by the partnership as security for a nonrecourse loan, and substantially all of the items of income, gain, loss or deduction attributable to such property are allocated to the contributor, the contributor will be treated as having collateralized the nonrecourse loan. As a result, the loan will be recharacterized as a recourse loan to the extent of the fair market value of the property serving as collateral.[10]

KNOWLEDGE CHECK

2. E and F form a general partnership to purchase an apartment complex. The partnership obtains a $1,000,000 nonrecourse loan and purchases an apartment building for $1,500,000. E owns real estate outside the partnership that she pledges as collateral for the loan. How much of the loan will be recharacterized as a recourse loan, allocable to E?

    a. None of the loan will be recharacterized as a recourse loan unless the bank seizes the collateral pledged by E. At that point, a portion of the loan equal to the value of the collateral will be recharacterized as a recourse loan.

    b. An amount equal to the present value of the property pledged as collateral, measured as of the date of the loan.

    c. An amount equal to the present value of the property pledged as collateral, measured as of the end of each partnership taxable year as long as the loan remains outstanding.

    d. An amount equal to the excess of the loan balance over the value of the apartment building purchased with the proceeds of the loan.

NONRECOURSE LOANS BY PARTNERS

Similarly, where a nonrecourse loan is obtained from a partner or from a lender related to a partner, such partner will be considered to bear the economic risk of loss for the loan, and the loan will be treated as a recourse debt.[11] Related lenders are defined by reference to Sections 267 and 707, except that siblings and less than 80 percent owned corporations are not treated as related parties.[12]

---

[9] Regulations Section 1.752-2(h)(3).
[10] Regulations Section 1.752-2(h)(2).
[11] Regulations Section 1.752-2(c).
[12] Regulations Section 1.752-4(b).

Example 4-2

A and B form a general partnership with cash contributions of $50,000 each. The partnership then purchases an office building for its $100,000 cash and a nonrecourse note in the amount of $300,000 that is secured by the building. The nonrecourse financing is obtained from a bank owned 100 percent by B. Because B owns the bank, she bears the ultimate economic risk of loss in the event of partnership default. Accordingly, the loan will be treated as a recourse obligation. Note that if B owned less than 80 percent of the outstanding stock of the bank, and the remainder was owned by an unrelated party (to B), the loan would be treated as a nonrecourse loan for purposes of Section 752.

"WRAPPED" DEBT

Where the nonrecourse loan provided by a partner or related lender wraps around another nonrecourse loan provided by an unrelated lender, only the excess of the wrap-around note over the original loan will be treated as a recourse debt.[13]

 Example 4-3

Assume similar facts as in example 4-2. A and B form a partnership with cash contributions of $50,000 each. The partnership then purchases a building for $400,000. It pays $100,000 cash and borrows the remainder obtaining a nonrecourse mortgage in the amount of $300,000 from a bank owned 100 percent by partner B. The nonrecourse loan obtained from B's bank wraps around a $250,000 underlying nonrecourse note issued by the seller to an unrelated lender in connection with her original acquisition of the building. In this case, if the partnership defaults on the loan, B will be at risk for only $50,000 – the remaining risk on the mortgage will be borne by the other lender. Accordingly, of the $300,000 note obtained from B's bank, only $50,000 will be reclassified as a recourse obligation of the partnership.

DE MINIMIS EXCEPTIONS

A qualified nonrecourse loan obtained from a partner or related person is not recharacterized as recourse debt if the partner who makes the loan, or to whom the lender is related, has an interest in "each item of partnership income, gain, loss, deduction or credit" of 10 percent or less for every taxable year that the partner is a member of the partnership.[14] Similarly, a partner's guarantee of an otherwise qualified nonrecourse liability, or the interest thereon, does not cause the loan, or any portion thereof, to be

---

[13] Regulations Section 1.752-2(c)(2).
[14] Regulations Section 1.752-2(d)(1).

recharacterized as recourse if the partner's interest in partnership income, gain, loss, deduction or credit does not exceed 10 percent in every taxable year in which the partner is a member of the partnership. [15]

Whether a nonrecourse loan is qualified for purposes of the *de minimis* exception is determined under Section 465(b)(6), disregarding the type of activity financed by the loan. Thus, a qualified nonrecourse loan for this purpose is a nonconvertible loan for which no person is personally liable for repayment and which is obtained from a qualified lender. Qualified lenders include any Federal, State, or local government or instrumentality thereof, and any lender whose loans are guaranteed by a Federal, State, or local government or instrumentality thereof. In addition, any other lender who is "actively and regularly engaged in the business of lending money" is a qualified lender unless such lender is the person from whom the borrower acquired the property financed by the nonrecourse debt (or a person related to the seller), or a person receiving a fee with respect to the borrower's investment in such property.

KNOWLEDGE CHECK

3. Under the *de minimis* exception in the Treasury Regulations, a qualified nonrecourse loan received by the partnership from a lender who has an interest in the partnership will not be recharacterized as recourse if

    a. The lender is a limited partner, rather than a general partner in the partnership.
    b. The lender does not own a direct interest in the partnership, but is merely related through one or more partners.
    c. The lender has a 10 percent or lesser interest in each item of partnership capital and profits (including credits) in all tax years of the partnership.
    d. The lender agrees not to pursue any individual partner for repayment in event of a partnership default.

---

[15] Regulations Section 1.752-2(d)(2). See Regulations Section 1.752-2(e)(4) for application of the *de minimis* exception to guaranteed interest on an otherwise qualified nonrecourse loan. Note that the *de minimis* exceptions appear to apply if the lender or guarantor-partner has a greater than 10 percent interest in partnership *capital*, so long as his or her interest in profits, losses and credits does not exceed 10 percent.

Allocation of Nonrecourse Debts

CONCEPTUAL DIFFICULTIES IN ALLOCATING NONRECOURSE LIABILITIES

As discussed, nonrecourse liabilities are those liabilities for which no partner or LLC member (or related person) bears personal risk of loss. In the event of default by the entity, the lender can foreclose upon any property serving as collateral for the loan, but has no further recourse against either the partnership or LLC or any partner therein. If the lender is itself a partner or LLC member, or a related party to a partner or member, then at least one partner bears personal risk of loss and the liability, although structured as a nonrecourse loan, will be treated as a recourse loan for purposes of Section 752 (subject to the *de minimis* exceptions discussed previously). Similarly, if the loan is guaranteed by one or more partners, then it will not be treated as a nonrecourse loan under Section 752.

Nonrecourse liabilities create interesting problems from a tax policy standpoint. Although none of the partners has any personal obligation to repay them, the lender would not make a loan that it did not expect to be repaid, so the indebtedness is real. It therefore is included in each partner's tax basis. The question then becomes how to allocate the debt (and the related tax basis) among the partners. An evaluation of the partners' economic risks is irrelevant to the question—none of them have any economic risk. Thus, the question becomes how the partners will share in the repayment of the loan. Historically, Section 752 has looked to the partners' interests in partnership profits to answer this question.

NONRECOURSE LIABILITIES ALLOCATED BY REFERENCE TO PARTNERS' PROFITS INTERESTS

If they are to be repaid at all, partnership nonrecourse liabilities will essentially be paid from partnership profits. If the partnership is not profitable, it will be more likely to default on the loan. Thus, the regulations provide that nonrecourse liabilities are to be allocated in accordance with the partners' profit-sharing ratios. The regulations do, however, give priority to certain kinds of partnership profits over others. In particular, because partnership minimum gain is used in the Section 704(b) regulations as a mechanism for restoring deficit capital balances, the Section 752 regulations look first to minimum gain to guide the allocation of partnership liabilities.

MINIMUM GAIN

Partnership minimum gain is that gain which will be recognized by the partnership upon a disposition of property encumbered by a nonrecourse debt, even if the property becomes worthless. Because the satisfaction of nonrecourse debt in exchange for the encumbered property (for example, as in foreclosure) is treated as a sale or exchange, the minimum sales price that can be realized from the disposition of any property is the amount of the outstanding nonrecourse debt encumbering that property. Thus, where the book value (in other words, Section 704(b) value) of the property falls below the outstanding principal balance of the nonrecourse mortgage, the minimum amount of gain that would be recognized upon disposition of such property is the difference between the basis of the property and the remaining principal. More gain could be recognized, but never less.

 Example 4-4

Partnership GH owns real estate acquired several years ago with a remaining tax basis of $500,000. The property is encumbered by a $750,000 nonrecourse mortgage incurred to finance acquisition of the property. The lender has no recourse against the partnership. Should the partnership default on its loan payments, the lender has the right to foreclose upon the property, taking it in complete satisfaction of the outstanding debt balance. In effect, in the event that the partnership becomes unwilling or unable to make payments on its loan, it will transfer the property to the lender in satisfaction of the loan.

Thus, for tax purposes, foreclosure will be treated by the partnership as a taxable sale of the property; even if the property becomes completely worthless, the partnership will merely transfer it to the lender in satisfaction of the remaining unpaid balance of the nonrecourse loan.

This feature of the loan agreement effectively creates a minimum selling price for the partnership. Regardless of economic circumstances, it can sell its property to the lender for this minimum sales price. Sale at this price would generate a gain, in this case, of $250,000.[16] This gain, the minimum amount that can be triggered for tax purposes, is known as the *minimum gain*.

Knowledge Check

4. J Dean Properties is a partnership that owns real property with a tax basis and book value of $800,000. The property is encumbered by an $850,000 nonrecourse mortgage. The fair market value of the property is $1,000,000. What is the minimum gain associated with the property?

   a. $150,000.
   b. $50,000.
   c. $0.
   d. $200,000.

Under the Section 704(b) regulations, the existence of partnership minimum gain allows partners' capital accounts to fall below zero even in the absence of any requirement on their parts to make additional capital contributions to restore these deficit balances. As long as the deficits do not exceed the partners' shares of partnership minimum gain, any deficit in their capital accounts can be made up – restored – with an allocation of minimum gain. This allocation has tax consequences in that it increases the partner's taxable income. These consequences give the underlying loss allocations economic effect under the Section 704(b) regulations. Following the same rationale, the regulations under Section 752 look to the allocation of minimum gain to support the allocation of the underlying nonrecourse debt associated with that minimum gain.

---

[16] See Regulations Section 1.1001-2(c), examples (7) and (8).

Example 4-5

A and B form a limited partnership to acquire a shopping center. A, the general partner, contributes $20,000, and B, the limited partner, contributes $180,000 to the partnership. The partnership borrows $1,800,000 on a nonrecourse loan and purchases the shopping center for $2,000,000. The partners agree to share losses 10 percent to A and 90 percent to B. Partnership income is to be shared equally. The partnership agreement complies with the requirements of Section 704(b). Minimum gain is to be shared 10/90 in order to substantiate the loss-sharing arrangement. In each of its first three years, the partnership's revenues just offset its operating expenses giving it net income of $0 before depreciation. Its annual depreciation deduction of $90,000 results in a ($90,000) annual tax loss, yielding the following partner capital accounts:

	A	B
Beginning Capital	$ 20,000	$ 180,000
Loss in years 1 and 2	(18,000)	(162,000)
Capital, end of year 2	$ 2,000	$ 18,000
Year 3 loss	(9,000)	(81,000)
Capital, end of year 3	$ (7,000)	$ (63,000)

At the end of years 1 and 2, there is no partnership minimum gain so the nonrecourse liability is allocated equally between the partners in accordance with their general profit-sharing ratios. At the end of year 3, however, partnership minimum gain is $70,000 (basis = 2,000,000 – 270,000 = 1,730,000; principal amount of loan = $1,800,000). Thus, the first $70,000 of the nonrecourse loan is allocated 10 percent to A and 90 percent to B in accordance with the partners' interests in partnership minimum gain. The remaining nonrecourse liability of $1,730,000 (1,800,000 – 70,000) is allocated equally. Thus, at the end of year 3, A's share of partnership nonrecourse debt is $872,000 ($7,000 share of partnership minimum gain plus $865,000 share of the excess) and B's share is $928,000 ($63,000 + $865,000).

TAX VERSUS BOOK MINIMUM GAIN

Profit allocations under Section 704(c) also take priority over other profits in some cases. Where partnership property is encumbered by a nonrecourse debt, and the exchange of such property in full satisfaction of the note would generate a gain that would be allocated to one or more partners under Section 704(c), the nonrecourse liability attached to the property will also be allocated in this way. That is, where minimum gain would be allocated under Section 704(c) to one or more partners, the allocation of the nonrecourse liability follows the allocations of the minimum gain, to the extent of the minimum gain.

Example 4-6

J and K form a general partnership to provide residential property to renters. J contributes $100,000 to the partnership that it uses to acquire residential property. K contributes an apartment building valued at $175,000. The basis of the contributed building is $50,000 and it is subject to a nonrecourse debt of $75,000. The partners share all profits and losses equally. The $75,000 nonrecourse loan, however, is not shared equally by the partners. The first $25,000 of such loan is allocated to K because K would be allocated $25,000 of partnership gain under Section 704(c) if the partnership disposed of the apartment building in full satisfaction of the nonrecourse liability.[17] The remainder of the nonrecourse liability is allocated between the partners in proportion to their equal interests in partnership profits. Thus, J's share of the $75,000 nonrecourse liability is $25,000 (1/2 of 50,000) and K's share is $50,000 ($25,000 + 1/2 of (50,000)).

KNOWLEDGE CHECK

5. Q Lynn Properties is a partnership that owns real property with a tax basis of $750,000 and a book value of $800,000. The property is encumbered by a $900,000 nonrecourse mortgage. The fair market value of the property is $1,000,000. What is the tax and book minimum gain associated with the property?

    a. Tax minimum gain $50,000; book minimum gain $100,000.
    b. Tax minimum gain $50,000; book minimum gain $200,000.
    c. Tax minimum gain zero; book minimum gain $150,000.
    d. Tax minimum gain $150,000; book minimum gain $100,000.

OTHER PARTNERSHIP PROFITS

In summary, each partner's share of partnership nonrecourse debts will be equal to the sum of

1. the partner's share of partnership minimum gain under Section 704(b);
2. the amount of any partnership Section 704(c) minimum gain which would be allocated to such partner; and
3. the partner's proportionate share of any remaining nonrecourse liabilities determined by reference to her interest in general partnership profits.[18]

---

[17] Note that there is no Section 704(b) gain in this problem.

[18] In lieu of step 3, the regulations provide that a partnership may choose to allocate excess nonrecourse liabilities first to the contributing partner up to the amount of built-in gain allocable to that partner under Section 704(c) which exceeds the amount of Section 704(c) minimum gain as determined under step 2. See Regulations Section 1.752-3(a)(3).

If the property serving as collateral for the loan is not Section 704(c) property (in other words, property contributed to the partnership by a partner), there will be no Section 704(c) minimum gain – all minimum gain in such cases will be Section 704(b) minimum gain. Nonrecourse liabilities are generally allocated on a liability-by-liability basis, so that an accurate measurement of book and tax minimum gain, and the partners' interests therein, can be determined.[19] The separately computed amounts are then added together to determine each partner's aggregate share of partnership nonrecourse liabilities.

KNOWLEDGE CHECK

6. Which of the following is not considered in determining a partner's share of partnership nonrecourse debts?

    a. The partner's share of partnership book minimum gain under Section 704(b).
    b. The partner's share of partnership losses.
    c. The partner's share of partnership profits.
    d. The partner's share of partnership tax minimum gain.

Example 4-7

Bedlam Partners was formed several years ago by three partners, B, F, and W. B contributed depreciable property with a tax basis of $450,000 and a fair market value of $600,000. The property was encumbered by a $400,000 nonrecourse debt. F contributed $200,000 cash and W contributed $400,000 cash. The partnership agreement allocates partnership profits 25 percent to B, 25 percent to F and 50 percent to W. Depreciation is allocated equally among the partners.

Shortly after formation, Bedlam borrowed $900,000 on a nonrecourse mortgage and began development of a large real estate project at a total cost of $1,500,000. At the end of its first year, the partnership had properties with an aggregate tax basis of $1,950,000 and an aggregate book value of $2,100,000. Its total nonrecourse debt was $1,300,000. Because the partnership has no minimum gain for book or tax, it would allocate its liabilities based on the partners' general profit shares. Thus, the liabilities would be allocated among the partners 25 percent to B, 25 percent to F and 50 percent to W.

Assume that at the end of the current year, after several years of operation, the remaining tax basis of the property contributed by B was $200,000 and its remaining book value was $266,667. The tax basis and book value of the property acquired just after formation was $1,200,000. The principal balances of the two nonrecourse liabilities remained $400,000 and $900,000 respectively. The partnership had no other properties. The nonrecourse liabilities would be allocated as follows:

---

[19] Regulations Section 1.704-2(d)(1).

Example 4-7 (continued)

	B	F	W
Mtg on property contr. by B:			
Book minimum gain[1]	$ 44,444	$ 44,444	$ 44,444
Tax minimum gain[2]	66,667	—	—
General profits	50,000	50,000	100,000
Mtg. on acquired property:			
Book minimum gain[3]	—	—	—
Tax minimum gain	—	—	—
General profits	225,000	225,000	450,000
Totals	$ 386,111	$ 319,444	$ 594,444

Notes:

[1] Book minimum gain on property contributed by B is $133,333 (400,000 – 266,667 book value). This gain is allocated equally among the partners (because they share depreciation deductions equally).

[2] Tax minimum gain on property contributed by B is $66,667 ($266,667 book value less $200,000 tax basis). This gain is allocated entirely to B under Section 704(c). Total minimum gain on this property is thus $200,000.

[3] There is no book or tax minimum gain on the acquired property because the book and tax basis of this property exceed the outstanding debt balance.

KNOWLEDGE CHECK

7. J and D form a limited partnership to acquire a shopping center. J, the general partner, contributes $100,000, and D, the limited partner, contributes $500,000 to the partnership. The partnership borrowed $3,400,000 on a nonrecourse loan and purchased the shopping center for $4,000,000. The partners agree to share losses 20 percent to J and 80 percent to D. Partnership income is to be shared equally. The partnership agreement complies with the requirements of Section 704(b). Minimum gain is to be shared 20/ 80 in order to substantiate the loss-sharing arrangement. How much of the nonrecourse liability will be allocated to J in the partnership's first year of operations?

    a. $100,000.

    b. $680,000.

    c. $850,000.

    d. $1,700,000.

8. Assume the same facts as in the previous question. Assume further that in year 7, accumulated depreciation on the shopping center is $720,000. How much of the nonrecourse liability will be allocated to J in year 7?

    a. $120,000.

    b. $1,640,000.

    c. $1,700,000.

    d. $1,664,000.

9. El Dorado LLC has property with a tax basis and book value of $850,000 that is encumbered by a $910,000 nonrecourse mortgage. The fair market value of the property is $1,250,000. Walter is a member in the LLC. His share of partnership minimum gain is 25 percent. His share of other partnership income is 10 percent. What will be his share of the partnership's nonrecourse mortgage? (Assume the partnership has no other properties or liabilities.)

    a. $85,000.

    b. $91,000.

    c. $100,000.

    d. $227,500.

Alternative Approach to Allocation of Portion of Nonrecourse Liabilities in Excess of Minimum Gain

The current regulations offer an alternative to the third layer of allocation, under which partnerships may allocate excess nonrecourse liabilities (in other words, amounts in excess of those allocated to reflect minimum gain and Section 704(c) minimum gain) in accordance with:

i. the way in which other "significant items" of partnership income or gain are allocated, or

ii. the way in which partners are reasonably expected to share in the future deductions attributable to those nonrecourse liabilities.[20]

Similar to the significant item method, future deductions attributable to nonrecourse liabilities, labelled 'nonrecourse deductions" in the Sec. 704(b) regulations,[21] can be specially allocated to the partners so long as the allocation of nonrecourse deductions is "reasonably consistent with allocations that have substantial economic effect of some other significant partnership item attributable to the property securing the nonrecourse liabilities."[22] Although the regulations do not provide much insight regarding the interpretation of this clause, it is reasonable (and consistent with common practice) to assume that the allocation of depreciation deductions other than nonrecourse depreciation deductions and the allocation of unrecaptured Sec. 1250 gain are significant partnership items that are attributable to the property securing the nonrecourse liabilities.[23]

---

[20] Regulations Section 1.752-3(a)(3).

[21] Regulations Section 1.704-2(b).

[22] Regulations Section 1.704-2(e)(2).

[23] A partner's share of depreciation deductions attributable to the period before the point at which the basis of the depreciable property falls below the balance of the nonrecourse liability would be a depreciation deduction other than a nonrecourse depreciation deduction.

Example 4-8

Assume the same facts as example 4-7, except that the partnership agreement allocates depreciation expense on the property contributed by B entirely to B. Further, the partners agree to allocate excess nonrecourse liabilities in accordance with the manner in which the deductions attributable to those nonrecourse liabilities will be allocated. If the agreement to allocate 100 percent of the depreciation deductions to partner is valid under Section 704(b), the partnership can allocate the excess $200,000 of nonrecourse debt on the property contributed by B entirely to B. This nonrecourse liability would thus be allocated in the following manner:

	B	F	W
Mtg on property contr. by B:			
Book minimum gain	$ 44,444	$ 44,444	$ 44,444
Tax minimum gain	66,667	—	—
Remainder	200,000	—	—
Total share of this NR debt	$ 311,111	$ 44,444	$ 44,444

KNOWLEDGE CHECK

10. To be recognized for tax purposes, the allocation of a nonrecourse deduction must be "reasonably consistent" with the allocation of other significant partnership items attributable to the encumbered property (among other requirements). Which of the following is not considered an "other significant partnership item?"

    a. Interest expense.
    b. Gain on sale of property.
    c. Cancellation of debt income.
    d. The allocation of partnership recourse debt.

11. C and D form partnership CD with contributions of $25,000 each. CD then obtains a $450,000 nonrecourse loan and purchases machinery for $500,000. In its first year of operations, the partnership has a gross income of $45,000, which is exactly offset by interest and other operating expenses of $45,000. In addition, CD reports depreciation expense of $100,000. It makes no principle payments on the nonrecourse note. How much of the depreciation expense will constitute a nonrecourse deduction?

    a. $0.
    b. $50,000.
    c. $90,000.
    d. $100,000.

The premise behind the allocation of nonrecourse liabilities is that such liabilities, if paid at all, will be paid out of partnership profits, and thus should be shared among partners by reference to how their shares of such profits will be diminished by the repayment of the nonrecourse debt. Expressing concern that the allocation of excess liabilities under the "significant item" method may not accurately reflect the partners' shares of partnership profits, new Proposed Regulations (issued injanuary 2014) replace the "significant item" approach with a new approach based on the partners' "liquidation value percentages."[24] The liquidation value percentage measures the portion of the partnership's net equity that each partner would be entitled to receive if the partnership sold all of its assets for their fair market values, paid off all of its debts, and liquidated.[25] It is not clear how significant this change will be, once implemented in final regulations. The primary concern for limited partners is that they can be allocated sufficient nonrecourse debt to offset any deficit in their capital accounts triggered by the special allocation of depreciation with respect to property encumbered by such nonrecourse debt. This allocation is determined by the manner in which partners share in partnership minimum gain (steps 1 and 2 of the allocation process) and therefore will not be affected by the share of debt allocated to them in step 3. Of course, to the extent that the new approach would reallocate partnership nonrecourse debt following a revaluation of partnership assets, it may pose a trap for the unwary. At any rate, the changes implemented by the proposed regulations do not take effect until issued in the form of final regulations in the *Federal Register*.

---

[24] REG-119305-11, Federal Register, Vol. 79, No. 20. (1/ 30/ 2014).

[25] This concept is similar to the constructive liquidation framework imposed for the allocation of recourse deductions, except that the partnership is deemed to sell its assets for their fair market values, rather than for no consideration as is required in a hypothetical constructive liquidation.

Treatment of Contingent Liabilities

GENERAL

Regulations issued in May 2005 govern the tax treatment of so-called "Section 1.752-7 liabilities."[26] Although poorly defined in the regulations, a Section 1.752-7 liability is essentially a contingent liability which, due to the uncertainty of either the amount of the debt or the likelihood of repayment, is not treated as a liability for purposes of Section 752(a) or (b).

The purpose of the regulations is to prevent partners or LLC members from transferring the tax deductions associated with certain contingent liabilities to the other partners or members of an LLC or partnership. They are also intended to prevent a partner or LLC member from accelerating his or her loss by disposing of his or her interest in the partnership or LLC before property subject to a contingent liability is actually disposed of. Accordingly, the new rules require that the principles of Section 704(c) (relating to built-in gains or losses inherent in contributed property) apply to contingent debt transferred between a partner or LLC member and a partnership or LLC.

MECHANICS

Under the regulations, the assumption of a partner's or member's contingent liability by a partnership or LLC in connection with the transfer of property to the partnership or LLC is treated as a built-in loss under Section 704(c). Accordingly, when the partnership or LLC satisfies all or part of a contingent liability, any resulting tax deduction or loss must be allocated to the contributing partner or member to the extent of the built-in loss at the date of contribution.[27]

---

[26] Regulations Section 1.752-7, effective June 24, 2003. [T.D. 9203] These regulations replace Proposed Regulations Section 1.752-7, issued to deny tax benefits in "son-of-BOSS" tax shelters in which a partner would sell Treasury notes or other securities short, transferring the proceeds, along with the open short sale obligation, to a partnership in exchange for a partnership interest. Because the exact amount of the partnership's obligation to close the short sale by purchasing and delivering securities was not fixed at the date of the transfer, the partnership treated it as a contingent liability not recognized under Section 752. Accordingly, the partner's basis in the partnership interest would be increased by the transfer of the proceeds from short sale of the securities, but would not be decreased by the partnership's assumption of the contingent liability. Although the regulations are purportedly designed to prohibit this treatment, they are not restricted to such obviously abusive transactions and thus may pose a significant trap for the unwary.

[27] Regulations Section 1.752-7(c)(1).

Example 4-9

A, B, and C form Waste Solutions, LLC to develop and operate a landfill. The LLC elects to be treated as a partnership for federal tax purposes. A contributes vacant land with a fair market value and tax basis of $400,000. The land is subject to potential environmental liabilities in the amount of $100,000. In exchange, A receives a 25 percent interest in the LLC. B contributes $300,000 cash in exchange for a 25 percent interest in the LLC, and C contributes $600,000 cash in exchange for a 50 percent interest. The LLC subsequently pays $250,000 to satisfy the environmental liability on the property contributed by A. Assume that the $250,000 payment is deductible by the LLC. The first $100,000 of this deduction must be allocated to A. The remainder will be allocated in accordance with the members' loss-sharing ratios (presumably 25:25:50, although a different sharing ratio will be acceptable as long as the requirements of Section 704(b) are satisfied).

Note: The regulations imply that Section 1.752-7 liabilities are treated as liabilities for book (in other words, Section 704(b)) purposes, but not for tax purposes (if a liability is recognized for purposes of Section 752(a) or (b), it is by definition not a Section 1.752-7 liability). Thus, a partner's or member's Section 704(b) capital account must be reduced by the value of the contingent liability, while his or her capital account on the entity's tax balance sheet will not be affected. See Regulations Section 1.752-7(c)(2) example.

Caution: The regulations do not provide a meaningful description of the valuation of a Section 1.752-7 liability. The term is defined as "the amount of cash that a willing assignor would pay to a willing assignee to assume the Section 1.752-7 liability in an arm's-length transaction."[28] Thus, at this point, practitioners are on their own for purposes of attempting to measure such liabilities.

SALE OR TRANSFER OF INTEREST IN PARTNERSHIP OR LLC

When a partner or LLC member sells his or her interest in the partnership or LLC before the Section 1.752-7 liability has been satisfied by the partnership or LLC, the regulations require that the basis of the partnership or LLC interest be reduced by the remaining Section 1.752-7 liability amount.[29] The basis reduction is deemed to occur immediately before the sale, exchange, or other disposition of the interest. The effect of this provision is to increase the selling partner's or member's gain (or reduce the recognized loss). If and when the partnership or LLC subsequently satisfies the Section 1.752-7 liability, it is not allowed a deduction or capital expense to the extent of the remaining built-in loss associated with the liability. Moreover, no adjustment is required to be made to the capital accounts of the remaining partners or LLC members. If the partnership or LLC notifies the original contributing partner that the Section 1.752 liability has been satisfied, such partner will be allowed a loss or deduction to the extent of the lesser of the built-in loss (the reduction in basis) or the amount paid to satisfy the liability.

---

[28] Regulations Section 1.752-7(b)(3)(ii).
[29] Regulations Section 1.752-7(e)(1).

Example 4-10

Assume the same facts as example 4-9. A contributes raw land with a tax basis and fair market value of $400,000 to Waste Solutions, LLC, in exchange for a 25 percent interest therein. A's tax basis in her Waste Solutions interest will be $400,000. However, due to a contingent environmental liability of $100,000, her interest is worth only $300,000. Assume that A later sells her LLC interest to F for $300,000. Under Section 1.752-7(e)(1), A must reduce her tax basis in the LLC interest by the $100,000 potential environment liability. Thus, she will recognize no gain or loss on the sale to F. If the LLC subsequently satisfies the obligation for $250,000, it will be entitled to a $150,000 deduction (the amount paid to satisfy the obligation over the estimated amount of the liability at the date of A's contribution to the LLC). If the LLC contacts A, she will be entitled to a $100,000 deduction for the built-in loss inherent in the property attributable to the environmental liability.

Warning: Nothing in the regulations obligates the partnership or LLC to notify the former partner or LLC member that the Section 1.752-7 liability has been satisfied. Departing partners or LLC members would be wise to obtain a commitment from the entity to provide notification in the event that the Section 1.752-7 liability is subsequently paid in a future year. The Section 1.752-7 partner must attach a copy of the notification received from the partnership or LLC to his or her tax return in the year the deduction is claimed. The notification must include[30]

- the amount paid in satisfaction of the liability;
- whether the amount(s) paid was in partial or complete satisfaction of such liability;
- the name and address of the person satisfying the liability;
- the date of payment of such liability; and
- the character of the loss triggered by payment of the liability.

KNOWLEDGE CHECK

12. G sold U.S. Treasury Bonds short, receiving $5 million in proceeds. She contributed these proceeds, along with the obligation to close the short position, to a real estate partnership in which she owned a 20 percent interest. Prior to making the contribution to the partnership, her tax basis in her partnership interest was $1 million. What will be her tax basis in the partnership interest immediately following the contribution?

    a. $1 million.
    b. $6 million.
    c. $2 million.
    d. $5 million.

---

[30] Regulations Section 1.752-7(h).

13. Assume the same facts as in the previous question. If G sells her interest in the partnership for $6,000,000 before the partnership has closed the short sale, how much gain will be recognized on the sale?

    a. $4,000,000.

    b. $5,000,000.

    c. $0.

    d. $6,000,000.

LIQUIDATING DISTRIBUTION TO A SECTION 1.752-7 PARTNER OR DISTRIBUTION OF PROPERTY SECURED BY A SECTION 1.752-7 LIABILITY TO ANOTHER PARTNER

Two other types of transactions trigger the application of the basis adjustment rules described previously:

1. Receipt of a liquidating distribution by a Section 1.752-7 partner or member from the partnership or LLC;[31]

or

2. Assumption of the Section 1.752-7 liability by another partner or member of the partnership or LLC[32] (for example, as when the property encumbered by the Section 1.752-7 liability is distributed to another partner).

In such cases, the Section 1.752-7 partner or member (in other words, the partner or member who contributed the property subject to the contingent liability) is required to reduce his or her basis in the partnership interest by the remaining built-in loss associated with the Section 1.752-7 liability. To the extent of the built-in loss at the date of distribution or assumption, neither the partnership or LLC nor the assuming partner or member are allowed a deduction should the liability subsequently be satisfied.[33] If the partnership or LLC notifies the Section 1.752 partner that the liability has been discharged (fully or partially), the partner will be entitled to a deduction in an amount equal to the lesser of the built-in loss associated with the liability or the amount paid in satisfaction thereof.

Special rules apply where another partner or member assumes the contributor's responsibility for the Section 1.752-7 liability. First, immediately following the assumption of the Section 1.752-7 liability from the partnership or LLC by a partner or member other than the Section 1.752-7 liability partner or member, the partnership or LLC must reduce its basis in its assets by the remaining built-in loss associated with the liability. The basis adjustment is allocated among the entity's assets as if it were an adjustment under Section 734(b).

---

[31] Regulations Section 1.752-7(f)(1).

[32] Regulations Section 1.752-7(g)(1).

[33] A deduction is allowed in the event that the liability is satisfied in exchange for a payment that exceeds the built-in loss inherent in the liability at the date of the distribution or assumption of such liability by another partner/ member. See Regulations Section 1.752-7(f)(2) and Section 1.752-7(g)(4).

The assuming partner or member, on the other hand, is not allowed to account for the Section 1.752-7 liability until such time as the liability is satisfied. At that time, the assuming partner or member adjusts his or her basis in the partnership interest, any assets distributed by the partnership or LLC to such partner, or gain or loss on disposition of the partnership or LLC interest as if a recognized liability had been assumed. The amount of the adjustment is equal to the lesser of the amount paid in satisfaction of the debt or the remaining built-in loss associated with the debt. Any amounts paid in excess of such amount are deductible or treated as a capital expenditure by the assuming partner.[34]

 Example 4-11

J, D, and R form the JDR Partnership. J contributes property 1 with a tax basis and fair market value of $5,000,000. The property is subject to a contingent liability valued at $2,000,000. In return, she receives a 25 percent interest in the partnership. D contributes $3,000,000 in cash in exchange for a 25 percent interest, and R contributes $6,000,000 cash in exchange for a 50 percent interest. The partnership uses the cash provided by D and R to purchase additional property.

Two years later, the partnership distributes property 1 to R in partial liquidation of R's interest in the partnership. R took the property subject to the $2,000,000 Section 1.752-7 liability. Upon the distribution of property 1 to R, J is required to reduce her basis in her partnership interest by $2,000,000 (to $3,000,000). Similarly, the JDR Partnership is required to reduce its tax basis in its other properties by $2,000,000. R takes a $5,000,000 carryover basis in property 1, equal to its tax basis in the hands of the partnership. Assuming that R's tax basis in the partnership interest remained $6,000,000 prior to receipt of the distribution, her remaining tax basis in the interest will be reduced to $1,000,000.

Assume that R subsequently pays $1,500,000 to satisfy the Section 1.752-7 liability. R will not be entitled to a tax deduction for the payment. Instead, R will increase the tax basis of the encumbered property (property 1) by the $1,500,000 payment. If R notifies J that the debt has been satisfied, J will be entitled to a $1,500,000 ordinary loss for the amount paid by R in satisfaction of the debt, and a $500,000 capital loss deduction for the excess of the built-in loss over the amount paid in satisfaction of the Section 1.752-7 liability.

---

[34] Similar rules apply when the encumbered property is contributed by the partnership to another partnership or corporation. See Regulations Section 1.752-7(i).

EXCEPTIONS

The provisions of Regulations Section 1.752-7 do not apply to contingent liabilities transferred in either of the following situations:

- The partnership or LLC assumes the liability in connection with a contribution by the partner or LLC member of the trade or business with which such liability is associated and the entity continues to carry on that trade or business after the contribution.
- Just prior to the contribution, the remaining built-in loss associated with the Section 1.752-7 liability(ies) is less than the lesser of 10 percent of the gross value of all partnership assets or $1,000,000.
- The Section 1.752-7 partner transfers his or her interest in the partnership or LLC (in whole or in part) in a nonrecognition transaction (for example, under Sections 351 or 721).

Chapter 5

ADVANCED DISTRIBUTION RULES

LEARNING OBJECTIVES

After completing this chapter, you should be able to do the following:

- Calculate the basis of each property received by a partner or member receiving multiple properties in a non-liquidating distribution from a partnership or LLC.
- Calculate the basis of each property received by a partner receiving multiple properties in a liquidating distribution from a partnership or LLC.
- Recognize which properties will receive a step-up or step-down in basis when multiple properties are received from a partnership or LLC.
- Assess basis increases or decreases among multiple properties for federal income tax purposes.

Non-Liquidating Distributions Generally

Non-Cash Distributions

The Code lays out a relatively straightforward framework for analyzing the tax consequences of proportionate non-liquidating distributions. This framework begins with the general rule of Section 731(a)(1), which states that neither the partner nor the partnership recognizes gain on receipt of property other than cash in a non-liquidating distribution.[1]Partners must realize that relief of liabilities is treated as a distribution of cash, but aside from this caveat, it is relatively easy to structure a distribution to ensure tax-free treatment to both the partner and the partnership.

Any gain realized by the partner on the receipt of a non-cash, non-liquidating distribution is deferred until the partner disposes of the property received. Under Section 732(a)(1), partners generally take a carryover basis in property received from the partnership in a non-liquidating distribution (in other words, any distribution which does not completely terminate the partner's interest in the partnership). That is, the partnership's basis in the property becomes the partner's basis. The partner's basis in his or her partnership interest (in other words, the partner's outside basis) is then reduced, pursuant to Section 733, by an amount equal to the basis assigned to the property received from the partnership.

 Example 5-1

John Smith has a tax basis of $20,000 in his interest in the PH Partnership. In December, John receives a tract of land, valued at $25,000, and having a tax basis to the partnership of $17,000. Neither Smith nor PH Partnership recognizes any gain on the distribution under Section 731(a)(1). Smith takes a $17,000 basis in the land, and reduces his basis in his partnership interest from $20,000 to $3,000.

There is one exception to the carryover basis rule. Where the partnership's tax basis in distributed property exceeds the partner's tax basis in his or her partnership interest, Section 732(a)(2) provides that the partner's basis in the distributed property is limited to her outside basis in the partnership interest. This is a corollary to the requirement that the partner reduce his or her tax basis in the partnership interest by the basis taken in the distributed property. Since the basis in the partnership interest cannot be less than zero, the basis in the distributed property cannot exceed the distributee's pre-distribution basis in the partnership interest.

---

[1] There are exceptions, of course, for certain distributions of contributed property (Secs. 704(c)(1) and 737), disguised sales (Section 707), disproportionate distributions of "hot" assets (Section 751(b)), and liquidating distributions to retiring partners (Section 736).

KNOWLEDGE CHECK

1. Jamie is a partner in Lion Partners. Her basis in her partnership interest is $50,000. In a non-liquidating distribution, Jamie received a distribution of property 1 which had a tax basis of $54,000 and a fair market value of $62,000. The distribution was not a disproportionate distribution, and the provisions of Sections 704(c) and 707 do not apply. How much gain must Jamie recognize on receipt of the non-liquidating distribution?

    a. $0.
    b. $62,000.
    c. $12,000.
    d. $4,000.

 Example 5-2

Assume the same facts as in example 5-1. John Smith has a tax basis of $20,000 in his interest in the PH Partnership. In December, John receives a non-liquidating distribution consisting of a tract of land valued at $25,000. Assume, however, that the partnership's tax basis in the land was $27,000 rather than $17,000. As before, neither Smith nor PH Partnership recognizes any gain on the distribution under Section 731(a)(1). Smith takes a $20,000 basis in the land, and reduces his basis in his partnership interest (outside basis) from $20,000 to zero.

KNOWLEDGE CHECK

2. Lynn is a partner in QLL Partners. Her basis in her partnership interest is $23,000 and her share of the fair market value of the partnership's assets is $124,000. In a non-liquidating distribution, Lynn received a distribution of property 1 which had a tax basis of $30,000 and a fair market value of $62,000. The distribution was not a disproportionate distribution, and the provisions of Sections 704(c) and 707 do not apply. What will be Lynn's tax basis in property 1 received from the partnership?

    a. $23,000.
    b. $30,000.
    c. $62,000.
    d. $39,000.

CASH DISTRIBUTIONS

Most cash distributions received by a partner from a partnership are also nontaxable to the partner. Where a partner receives a distribution of cash from the partnership, the partner will recognize gain only to the extent the amount of cash received exceeds his or her tax basis in the partnership interest. This is a corollary to the general rule that basis in the partnership interest is reduced by the basis allocated by the distributee partner to the property received in the distribution. As with a non-cash distribution, the basis of the partnership interest cannot be reduced below zero. Unlike a property distribution, however, the tax basis of cash received cannot be reduced below its face value. Thus, the partner must recognize income if cash is received in excess of the basis of the partnership interest.

 Example 5-3

Sharon's tax basis in her 25 percent interest in Deep Eilum Partners is $15,000. Assume that she receives a non-liquidating distribution from Deep Ellum of $20,000 cash. The first $15,000 of this distribution will be nontaxable, and will reduce her tax basis in her partnership interest to zero. Because her basis cannot be reduced below zero, however, the remaining $5,000 received as part of the distribution will be taxable to her as a capital gain.

Note that a reduction in a partner's share of partnership liabilities is treated as a cash distribution from the partnership to the partner. This can present a trap for the unwary, turning an otherwise nontaxable distribution into a taxable one. For example, where a cash distribution reduces a partner's interest in the partnership and thus in partnership liabilities, the total amount of the distribution will include both the cash received and the reduction in the partner's share of partnership debt. If the sum of these two figures exceeds the partner's basis in his or her partnership interest, then gain must be recognized to the extent of the excess.

 Example 5-4

Assume the same facts as in example 5-3. Sharon's tax basis in her interest in Deep Ellum Partners is $15,000. She receives a $20,000 cash distribution from the partnership. Assume that this distribution reduces her interest in partnership capital, profits, losses, and liabilities from 25 percent to 15 percent. Further assume that the partnership has total liabilities of $100,000. Thus, the distribution reduces her share of partnership liabilities from $25,000 (25 percent) to $15,000 (15 percent). Since this reduction in her share of partnership debt is treated as a distribution of cash to her from the partnership, her total cash distribution is now $30,000, rather than $20,000. Accordingly, she must now recognize a capital gain of $15,000 (rather than $5,000 as in the previous example). Her tax basis in her partnership interest is reduced to zero.

RECEIPT OF CASH AND PROPERTY

Where a partner receives a distribution consisting of both cash and other property, he or she accounts for the cash portion of the distribution first, and then the property portion. The result of this ordering rule is that the basis of the partnership interest is first reduced by the cash received. If insufficient basis is left to absorb the property distribution, the partner takes a stepped down basis in the property as described previously.

Example 5-5

Ed is a 20 percent partner in Horton Partners. His tax basis in his partnership interest is $28,000. He received a non-liquidating distribution consisting of $8,000 cash and property with a fair value of $45,000 and a tax basis of $25,000. Ed will recognize no gain on receipt of the distribution. The cash reduces his tax basis in the partnership interest to $20,000 ($28,000 pre-distribution basis less $8,000 cash distribution). He then accounts for the property distribution. His remaining basis in the partnership interest is less than the partnership's basis in the distributed property. Thus, he takes a $20,000 tax basis in the property received, and his basis in his partnership interest is reduced to zero.

Note that if the partnership had distributed the property to Ed first, and then distributed the cash in a separate transaction, he would have taken a $25,000 tax basis in the property, reducing his tax basis in the partnership interest to $3,000. He would then have recognized $5,000 on receipt of the subsequent distribution of the cash ($8,000 cash received less $3,000 tax basis in the partnership interest). It is important for both the partner and the partnership to recognize the importance of planning partnership distributions.

KNOWLEDGE CHECK

3. Perry is a partner in PLT Partners. His basis in his partnership interest is $23,000. In a non-liquidating distribution, Perry received a distribution of $15,000 cash and property 1 (tax basis of $30,000 and of $62,000). The distribution was not a disproportionate distribution, and the provisions of Sections 704(c) and 707 do not apply. What will be Perry's tax basis in property 1 received from the partnership?

    a. $23,000.
    b. $30,000.
    c. $62,000.
    d. $8,000.

Finally, recall that a reduction in a partner's share of partnership liabilities is treated as a cash distribution under Section 752(b). Thus, where a partnership property distribution reduces the partner's interest in partnership liabilities, determining the tax consequences of the distribution requires the partner to account for the reduction in liabilities in addition to the receipt of property from the partnership. As in example 5-4, the deemed cash distribution arising from the reduction in the partner's share of debt is accounted for before accounting for the property distribution.

Example 5-6

Norma was a 25 percent partner in Peoria Partners until December when she received a property distribution in partial redemption of her interest in the partnership. Prior to receipt of the distribution, Norma's tax basis in her partnership interest was $50,000, consisting of her $20,000 capital investment in the partnership and her $30,000 share (25 percent) of partnership debt. (Assume the partnership's outstanding liabilities total $120,000.)

She received a distribution of property with a tax basis of $36,000 and a fair market value of $75,000. The property was not encumbered by debt. Assume that in connection with the distribution, Norma's interest in partnership capital, profits, and liabilities was reduced to 10 percent. Thus, in addition to the property, Norma must account for the reduction in her share of partnership liabilities from $30,000 (25 percent of $120,000) to $12,000 (10 percent of $120,000). As discussed previously, this reduction is treated as a cash distribution from the partnership to Norma, and must be accounted for before determining Norma's basis in the property.

The deemed cash distribution of $18,000 ($30,000 − $12,000) will reduce Norma's tax basis in her partnership interest to $32,000 ($50,000 original tax basis less $18,000 deemed cash distribution). Rather than taking a carryover basis in the property received from the partnership (which would be $36,000), her basis in the property will be limited to her remaining basis in the partnership interest ($32,000). Her basis in her partnership interest will be reduced to zero.

KNOWLEDGE CHECK

4. Until last month, Carlos was a partner in CLR Partners. His basis in his partnership interest was $23,000—consisting of the $15,000 balance in his capital account and his $8,000 share of partnership liabilities. In a liquidating distribution, Carlos received a distribution of property 1 (tax basis of $30,000 and fair market value of $62,000). The distribution was not a disproportionate distribution, and the provisions of Sections 704(c) and 707 do not apply. What will be Carlos' tax basis in property 1 received from the partnership?

    a. $15,000.
    b. $23,000.
    c. $62,000.
    d. $30,000.

Thus, to recap the basic distribution rules, partners generally do not recognize gain or loss on receipt of a distribution from a partnership or LLC. Instead, any gain realized on the distribution is deferred and built into the tax basis of the property(ies) received in the distribution. As a result, understanding the rules determining the partner's tax basis in distributed property is very important. Although these rules are relatively straightforward, they become more complex when multiple properties are included in a single distribution.

Distribution of Multiple Properties

Allocation of basis among multiple assets follows a basic set of ordering rules. Basis is first allocated to cash, then to ordinary income assets, and then to other assets. This hierarchy of ordering rules ensures that capital gain realized on the distribution is not converted to ordinary income when distributed properties are subsequently sold. For example, if a partner receives a distribution consisting of both ordinary income property and capital gain property, he or she is allocated a carryover basis in the ordinary income property (equal to the partnership's basis in such property) before basis is allocated to the capital gain property. As a result, any increase or decrease to the basis of any of the properties received in the distribution is allocated to the capital gain assets first. If the partner still needs to reduce basis in distributed property to avoid recognition of income, the basis of ordinary income property received in the distribution will be reduced only after the basis of capital gain property (or Section 1231 property) has been reduced to zero.

 Example 5-7

Jill is a partner in Oak Motte Partners. Her tax basis in her partnership interest is $24,000. She received a non-liquidating distribution consisting of $5,000 cash, inventory with a tax basis of $10,000 and a fair market value of $20,000, and capital gain property with a tax basis of $13,000 and a fair market value of $36,000. She recognizes no gain on the sale and determines her tax basis in the cash and properties received as follows:

Pre-distribution tax basis in partnership interest	$ 24,000
Less: cash received	(5,000)
Less: carryover basis in inventory received	(10,000)
Remaining basis in partnership interest	$ 9,000

Jill's tax basis in the capital gain property will be equal to the lesser of her $9,000 remaining basis in the partnership interest or the carryover basis of the property ($13,000). Thus, her tax basis in the capital gain property will be limited to $9,000. Note that the result of these ordering rules is that the entire step-down in the basis of the distributed assets in Jill's hands is allocated to the capital gain property.

A different problem arises when the distributee-partner receives multiple assets in the same class, and the aggregate basis of these assets must be increased or decreased under Section 732. The question then becomes how to allocate the basis adjustment among the assets received.

Example 5-8

J is a one-third partner in the JDR Partnership. Her basis in her partnership interest is $20,000. In December, J received a distribution from the partnership consisting of the following assets:

	Tax Basis	FMV
Cash	$ 5,000	$ 5,000
Inventory	8,000	12,000
Capital asset 1	12,000	22,000
Capital asset 2	10,000	11,000
	$ 35,000	$ 50,000

J cannot take a carryover basis in all these assets because her outside basis in her partnership interest, $20,000, is less than the aggregate carryover basis of the assets received, $35,000. Thus, the question becomes how to allocate the $20,000 aggregate basis she will take in these assets to the individual assets received. Under Section 732, J must first reduce her basis in the partnership by the $5,000 cash portion of the distribution. She will then allocate $8,000 to the inventory. The remaining $7,000 must be allocated between capital assets 1 and 2.

In situations like the one illustrated in example 5-8, the process by which a reduction in basis is allocated among multiple assets is a function of both the tax basis (to the partnership) and the fair market value of the affected properties. A series of steps must be followed in allocating a basis reduction among multiple assets received in a non-liquidating distribution.

DECREASE IN BASIS OF UNREALIZED RECEIVABLES AND/ OR INVENTORY

Under the ordering rules, outside basis is first allocated to cash distributed. Outside basis is then allocated to unrealized receivables and inventory to the extent of the partnership's basis in these assets.[2] If there is insufficient outside basis to cover the unrealized receivables and inventory, the shortage is allocated first to assets having unrealized depreciation, resulting in a decreased basis for these assets. If the reduction in basis is smaller than the total amount of unrealized depreciation inherent in the distributed assets, the available reduction is allocated to the properties in proportion to their respective amounts of unrealized depreciation.

---

[2] Note that the term "unrealized receivables" includes not only zero basis accounts receivable, but also the portion of any gain inherent in partnership depreciable property that would be classified as ordinary income if such property were sold for fair market value. Thus, potential depreciation recapture on depreciable equipment, furniture & fixtures, and other depreciable assets other than realty is an unrealized receivable. Potential depreciation recapture on partnership real estate, which would be classified as 25 percent capital gain, is *not* an unrealized receivable.

Example 5-9

Q is a one-third partner in the QLR Partnership. Her outside basis in her partnership interest is $20,000. Q receives a distribution consisting of cash, unrealized receivables and inventory as follows. Assume that the distribution does not change Q's interest in partnership ordinary income assets.

	Tax Basis	FMV	Difference
Cash	$ 2,000	$ 2,000	$ —
Accounts Receivable	12,000	10,000	(2,000)
Inventory	10,000	4,000	(6,000)
	$ 24,000	$ 16,000	$ (8,000)

Q cannot take a carryover basis in the assets received from the partnership, because the aggregate basis of these assets ($24,000) exceeds her basis in her partnership interest ($20,000). Her aggregate basis in the distributed assets is limited to $20,000.

Again, she first reduces her outside basis by the $2,000 cash portion of the distribution.

She then allocates the remaining $18,000 basis between the receivables and inventory. Since these assets had an aggregate basis to the partnership of $22,000, the task is to divide the remaining ($4,000) reduction in basis between them. This amount is allocated in accordance with the relative amounts of excess of basis over fair market value inherent in the two assets.

Thus, 2/8 of the excess (1,000) will be allocated to the receivables and 6/8 (3,000) to the inventory. Q will thus take an $11,000 basis ($12,000 - $1,000) in the receivables, and a $7,000 basis ($10,000 - $3,000) in the inventory.

When the reduction in basis exceeds the aggregate unrealized depreciation inherent in the distributed properties, the reduction is first allocated to those properties with unrealized depreciation, until their basis equals their respective fair market value. The remainder is then allocated among all remaining properties in proportion to their remaining basis (as adjusted in the preceding sentence). If there are no properties with unrealized depreciation, the basis reductions will be allocated based on the properties' separate basis.

Example 5-10

R is a one-half partner in the RW Partnership. His basis in his partnership interest is $14,000. He receives a distribution of cash, unrealized receivables and inventory as follows. The distribution does not alter his interest in partnership "hot" assets.

	Tax Basis	FMV	Difference
Cash	$ 2,000	$ 2,000	$ —
Accounts Receivable	10,000	8,000	(2,000)
Inventory	10,000	5,000	(5,000)
	$ 22,000	$ 15,000	$ (7,000)

R's basis in the distributed property, in the aggregate, is limited to his outside basis in his partnership interest of $14,000. This basis is first reduced by the $2,000 cash distribution received. The remaining $12,000 is allocated to the unrealized receivables and inventory, requiring a total reduction in basis of $8,000. This $8,000 reduction, in turn, is first allocated between the two assets in accordance with the unrealized depreciation inherent in each: $2,000 to the receivables and $5,000 to the inventory. The remaining $1,000 reduction in basis is then allocated between the two assets in proportion to their remaining basis. Thus, 8/13 of this reduction ($615) is allocated to the receivables, and 5/13 ($385) is allocated to the inventory. R's total basis in the receivables will be $7,385 ($10,000 – $2,000 – $615). His total basis in the inventory will be $4,615 ($10,000 – $5,000 – $385).

DECREASE IN BASIS OF OTHER ASSETS

Where the partner's outside basis in the partnership interest exceeds the amount of cash and the basis of inventory and receivables received, but is insufficient to cover the aggregate tax basis of all assets received, the necessary reduction is allocated to capital assets. If multiple capital assets are received, the allocation process follows the same process described previously. First, the reduction is allocated to those properties which have unrealized depreciation, to the extent thereof. If the reduction is less than the total unrealized depreciation, it is allocated among those properties with unrealized depreciation in proportion to the relative amounts thereof. If the reduction exceeds the aggregate amount of unrealized depreciation inherent in the distributed properties, the remainder is allocated in proportion to the properties' remaining basis.

It is important to note, however, that the ordering provisions described previously continue to apply. That is, basis is first allocated to cash, then to unrealized receivables and inventory to the extent of their basis to the partnership, and finally, to other assets. If the partner's outside basis exceeds the amount of cash and the basis of ordinary income assets received, any reduction in basis required under Section 732(a)(2) will be applied solely to the remaining other assets, even if the ordinary assets contain unrealized depreciation. This requirement is necessary to preserve the character of the partner's share of partnership unrealized loss inherent in the distributed ordinary income assets.

Example 5-11

Elise is a partner in KidSmart Partners. Her basis in her partnership interest is $35,000. She receives a distribution of cash, inventory, and capital assets as follows. The distribution does not alter her interest in partnership "hot" assets.

	Tax Basis	FMV	Difference
Cash	$ 2,000	$ 2,000	$ —
Inventory	20,000	12,000	(8,000)
Capital asset 1	15,000	20,000	5,000
Capital asset 2	10,000	5,000	(5,000)
	$ 47,000	$ 39,000	$ (8,000)

Although the aggregate basis of the cash and property received by Elise is $47,000, her basis in those assets is limited to $35,000 under Section 732(a)(2). Thus, in the aggregate, a reduction in basis of ($12,000) must be allocated to the assets received. Under Section 732, her $35,000 outside basis must first be reduced by the $2,000 cash portion of the distribution. Next, she allocates $20,000 of her remaining basis to the inventory, notwithstanding the fact that it has declined in value to $12,000. Her remaining basis of $13,000 must then be allocated between capital assets 1 and 2, requiring a total basis reduction in these assets of ($12,000). The first ($5,000) of this basis reduction is applied to capital asset 2, reflecting the unrealized depreciation inherent in that asset. No reduction is applied to capital asset 1 at this point because it has no unrealized depreciation. The remaining ($7,000) of the required reduction, however, is allocated between both assets, in proportion to their remaining basis. (The total basis of the two assets is now $15,000 + $5,000 = $20,000). Thus, 15/20 of this ($7,000) reduction ($5,250) will be applied to capital asset 1. The remaining 5/20 ($1,750) will be applied to capital asset 2. Elise's final basis in the assets received would be as follows:

Cash	$ 2,000
Inventory	20,000
Capital asset 1 ($15,000 - $5,250)	9,750
Capital asset 2 ($10,000 - $5,000 - $1,750)	3,250
	$ 35,000

5. Amy is a partner in Xiowa Partners. Her basis in her partnership interest is $69,000. In a non-liquidating distribution, Amy received three properties. Property 1 was worth $40,000 and had a tax basis of $30,000. Property 2, valued at $15,000, had a tax basis of $23,000. Property 3 was worth $35,000 and had a tax basis of $22,000. The distribution was not a disproportionate distribution and the provisions of Sections 704(c) and 707 do not apply. How much gain must Amy recognize on receipt of the non-liquidating distribution?

   a. $0.
   b. $70,000.
   c. $31,000.
   d. $21,000.

6. In the previous question, what would be Amy's aggregate basis in the three properties received from Xiowa Partners?

   a. $69,000.
   b. $75,000.
   c. $90,000.
   d. $88,000.

7. In the previous question, what will be Amy's tax basis in property 2 received from Xiowa Partners?

   a. $15,000.
   b. $17,000.
   c. $23,000.
   d. $22,000.

8. Keith is a partner in Cellar Dweller Partners. His tax basis in his partnership interest is $42,000. He receives two tracts of land in a non-liquidating distribution from the partnership. The first tract has a tax basis of $30,000 and a fair value of $50,000. The second tract is worth $30,000, with a tax basis of $20,000. The distribution is not disproportionate and does not trigger the provisions of either Section 704(c) or Section 707. What portion of the resulting $8,000 step-down in basis will be allocated to the second tract?

   a. $4,000.
   b. $3,200.
   c. $3,000.
   d. $0.

LIQUIDATING DISTRIBUTIONS

Different rules apply when a partner receives property other than cash in a liquidating distribution. In this case, assuming no gain or loss is recognized on the liquidation, the partner's basis in properties received, in the aggregate, is equal to his or her outside basis in the partnership interest, regardless of the partnership's basis in the distributed properties.[3] Thus, in contrast to a non-liquidating distribution, in which any necessary adjustment to the basis of properties received from the partnership will only be negative,[4] the basis of properties received in a liquidating distribution may be either increased or decreased.

 Example 5-12

Rebecca's outside basis in her partnership interest is $25,000. In complete liquidation of that interest, she receives property with an aggregate fair market value of $50,000, and an aggregate basis to the partnership of $17,000. Under Section 732(b), Rebecca's aggregate basis in the assets received will be $25,000, notwithstanding the fact that the aggregate basis of these properties to the partnership was only $17,000. (Had the partnership's basis in the distributed properties been $37,000, Rebecca would still take an aggregate basis of $25,000.)

The rationale for the substitute basis requirement of Section 732(b) is that the partner's remaining outside basis in the partnership interest must be zero after the distribution, since the partnership interest no longer exists. Thus, the entire pre-distribution outside basis must be assigned to the property or properties received in the liquidating distribution.

The procedure for allocating any necessary increase or decrease in basis among the assets received in a liquidating distribution is similar to that described previously. Indeed, where the application of Section 732(b) requires a reduction in the basis of assets received in the liquidating distribution, the process is identical to that described previously. See examples 5-10, 5-11, and 5-12. Where an increase, rather than a decrease, in basis is required, the process mirrors that described previously.

---

[3] IRC Section 732(b).

[4] This is because the partner's basis in such assets is equal to the *lesser of* the basis of such assets to the partnership or the partner's outside basis in the partnership interest.

9. R is a one-third partner in the RW Partnership. His basis in his partnership interest is $14,000. He receives a liquidating distribution consisting of cash, inventory, and capital assets as follows. The distribution does not alter his interest in partnership "hot" assets and does not trigger the provisions of Sections 704(c) or 707.

	Tax Basis	FMV
Cash	$ 2,000	$ 2,000
Inventory	10,000	25,000
Capital asset	10,000	13,000
	$ 22,000	$ 40,000

What basis will R take in the capital asset?

a. $0.
b. $2,000.
c. $10,000.
d. $13,000.

10. Z is a 20 percent partner in the EZ Partnership. His basis in his partnership interest is $30,000. He receives a liquidating distribution consisting of cash and capital assets as indicated in the following table. The distribution does not alter his interest in partnership "hot" assets and does not trigger the provisions of Sections 704(c) or 707.

	Tax Basis	FMV
Cash	$ 2,000	$ 2,000
Capital asset	18,000	13,000
	$ 20,000	$ 15,000

What is Z's deductible loss on receipt of the liquidating distribution?

a. ($15,000).
b. ($5,000).
c. $0.
d. ($10,000).

11. Jamie was a partner in New Deal Partnership until December 31, when she received a liquidating distribution of cash, unrealized receivables, and inventory as indicated in the following table. The distribution did not alter her interest in partnership "hot" assets.

	Tax Basis	FMV
Cash	$ 5,000	$ 5,000
Receivables	20,000	25,000
Inventory	18,000	20,000

Jamie's basis in her partnership interest prior to the distribution was $45,000. What basis will Jamie take in the accounts receivable?

    a. $0.
    b. $20,000.
    c. $25,000.
    d. $22,000.

ALLOCATING AN INCREASE IN BASIS AMONG MULTIPLE PROPERTIES: ORDINARY VERSUS "OTHER" ASSETS

Again, in a case where the basis of distributed property must be increased, the ordering rules require that outside basis first be reduced by the cash portion of the distribution.[5] Any remainder is then applied to unrealized receivables or inventory to the extent of the partnership's basis in those assets, with any remainder beyond that being allocated to other assets. Under Section 732(c), the partner cannot take a basis in unrealized receivables or inventory greater than the partnership's basis in those assets. If the partner receives no assets other than cash, unrealized receivables and/ or inventory, any excess of his or her outside basis in the partnership interest over the partnership's basis in these assets is charged as a loss.

---

[5] If the partner receives nothing other than cash, any difference between the amount of cash received and the outside basis in the partnership interest triggers recognition of gain or loss. No adjustment to the basis of property in the partner's hands is necessary.

Example 5-13

Lynn was a partner in Pheasant Ridge Partnership until December 31, when she received a liquidating distribution of cash, unrealized receivables and inventory as indicated in the following table. The distribution did not alter her interest in partnership "hot" assets.

	Tax Basis	FMV
Cash	$ 2,000	$ 2,000
Receivables	10,000	18,000
Inventory	15,000	20,000
	$ 27,000	$ 40,000

Prior to the liquidation, Lynn's basis in her partnership interest was $30,000. Under the general rule of Section 732(b), Lynn would take a substitute basis of $30,000 in the distributed properties. However, pursuant to Section 732(c), she cannot take a basis in the receivables or inventory greater than the partnership's basis in those assets. Thus, under Section 731(a)(2), she is required to recognize a loss (capital in nature) of ($3,000), the amount by which her basis in her partnership interest exceeds the amount of cash and basis of the receivables and inventory which constituted the sole assets received in the liquidating distribution.

Note that if the partner receives any property other than cash, receivables or inventory, he or she cannot recognize a loss under Section 731(a)(2). Instead, pursuant to Section 732(b), the basis of such other property is increased to reflect the partner's remaining outside basis in the partnership interest after the allocation to cash and ordinary income assets. Thus, in example 5-13, had Lynn received any other asset(s), she would have taken a $3,000 basis in that asset(s) and no loss would have been recognized. Essentially, this prevents the avoidance of the recognition of ordinary income on a later sale by increasing the basis of distributed ordinary income assets.

ALLOCATING AN INCREASE IN BASIS AMONG MULTIPLE "OTHER" ASSETS

As noted previously, any basis increase required under Section 732(b) is allocated solely to capital assets. Allocation of this increase among multiple assets requires consideration of both the basis and fair market value of the affected assets.

The rules governing the allocation of basis increases among multiple capital assets mirror those governing the allocation of basis decreases. First, the basis increase is allocated to those assets which have unrealized appreciation to the extent of such unrealized appreciation. If the basis increase is less than the aggregate amount of unrealized appreciation inherent in the distributed assets, the increase is allocated among all appreciated assets in proportion to the amount of appreciation inherent therein

Example 5-14

Jordan was a partner in the CB partnership until his interest was liquidated. In liquidation of his entire interest, Jordan received a distribution of cash, unrealized receivables, and capital and Section 1231 assets as follows. The distribution did not alter his interest in partnership "hot" assets. Moreover, assume that capital is a material income-producing factor in the partnership.

	Tax Basis	FMV	Difference
Cash	$ 2,000	$ 2,000	$ —
Section 179 property (original cost $18,000; fully expensed under Section 179)	—	18,000	18,000
Capital asset 1	9,000	11,000	2,000
Capital asset 2	16,000	19,000	3,000
	$ 27,000	$ 50,000	$ 23,000

Jordan's basis in his partnership interest prior to the liquidating distribution was $30,000. Under Section 732(b), this becomes his aggregate basis in the assets received from the partnership. First, his outside basis is reduced by the $2,000 in cash received. Next, he allocates 0 basis to the Section 179 property, since that is the basis of such property to the partnership. Thus, the remaining $28,000 of basis must be allocated to capital assets 1 and 2. This amount exceeds by $3,000 the basis of these assets to the partnership. This excess must be allocated between the two capital assets.

Under the allocation rules, the first $5,000 of basis increases will be allocated in accordance with the unrealized appreciation inherent in each asset ($2,000 in capital asset 1 and $3,000 in capital asset 2). Since the total increase to be allocated is less than the total amount of unrealized appreciation inherent in the assets, the increase must be allocated pro rata in accordance with the relative amounts of unrealized appreciation inherent in each asset. Thus, 2/5 of the ($3,000) increase ($1,200) is allocated to capital asset 1 and 3/5 ($1,800) to capital asset 2. Jordan's basis in capital asset 1 will be thus $10,200 ($9,000 + $1,200). His basis in capital asset 2 will be $17,800 ($16,000 + $1,800).

Where the basis increase to be allocated to capital assets exceeds the aggregate unrealized appreciation inherent in those assets, the increase is first allocated to those assets with unrealized appreciation to the extent thereof. Remaining basis is then allocated among all capital assets received in proportion to their respective fair market values (which now equal their basis). This rule is the mirror image of that applied to allocate a basis reduction that exceeds the aggregate amount of unrealized depreciation inherent in affected assets.

Example 5-15

Myra received a liquidating distribution from her partnership consisting of cash, inventory and Section 1231 and capital assets as follows. Capital is a material income-producing factor for the partnership. The distribution did not alter her interest in partnership "hot" assets.

	Tax Basis	FMV	Difference
Cash	$ 2,000	$ 2,000	$ —
Inventory	10,000	20,000	10,000
Capital asset 1	15,000	19,000	4,000
Capital asset 2	10,000	16,000	6,000
	$ 37,000	$ 57,000	$ 20,000

Myra's outside basis in her partnership interest prior to the liquidation was $50,000. This will be her aggregate basis in the assets received pursuant to Section 732(b). The first $2,000 of this basis is allocated to the cash received. The next $10,000 is applied to inventory. The remaining $38,000 is applied to capital assets 1 and 2, requiring an increase in their basis of $13,000.

The first $10,000 of this $13,000 increase is applied to eliminate the unrealized appreciation inherent in these two assets: $4,000 of the increase is applied to capital asset 1 and $6,000 to capital asset 2. These adjustments increase the basis of these assets to $19,000 and $16,000, respectively. The remaining $3,000 increase in basis is then apportioned between the two assets in accordance with their relative fair market values. Thus, 19/35 of this amount ($1,629) is allocated to capital asset 1, and 16/35 ($1,371) to capital asset 2. Myra's total basis in these assets ($20,629 and $17,371, respectively) thus exceeds their values, even though Myra also received inventory as part of the distribution, which still contains unrealized (built-in) appreciation.

KNOWLEDGE CHECK

12. Vicki is a 20 percent partner in the Arnold-Sutton Partnership. In September, when her basis in her partnership interest was $60,000, she received a liquidating distribution consisting of the following assets:

	Tax Basis	FMV
Cash	$ 3,000	$ 3,000
Capital asset 1	$ 24,000	$ 24,000
Capital asset 2	$ 24,000	$ 48,000
Totals	$ 51,000	$ 75,000

What basis will Vicki take in capital asset 1 received from the partnership?

    a. $33,000.

    b. $28,500.

    c. $24,000.

    d. $27,000.

13. In the previous question, what basis will Vicki take in capital asset 2?

    a. $24,000.

    b. $33,000.

    c. $48,000.

    d. $28,500.

Summary

When a partner receives a distribution of property, his or her basis in the asset(s) received depends on the nature of the distribution. For nonliquidating distributions, the partner generally takes a carryover basis in the asset(s) received, limited to his or her basis in the partnership interest. As a result of this limitation, partners often take a lower basis in distributed partnership property than the partnership had in that property. In such cases, allocation of the basis decrease is computed by reference to both the basis and fair market values of the properties involved. Thus, these rules place significant importance on accurate appraisal of the values of distributed assets, and may therefore inject additional uncertainty into the measurement of subsequent gains and losses (or depreciation deductions) in some situations.

In contrast, where a partner receives a distribution of property from the partnership in liquidation of his or her interest therein, the aggregate basis of the distributed properties will be equal to the basis of the partnership interest just prior to receipt of the distribution. In such cases, the partner may take an increased or decreased basis in the distributed property. Again, allocation of the increase or decrease in basis among multiple properties is a function of both the basis and the fair market values of the properties received. Thus, practitioners should carefully consider potential partnership distributions for planning opportunities.

Chapter 6

ADJUSTMENTS TO THE BASIS OF PARTNERSHIP OR LLC ASSETS

LEARNING OBJECTIVES

After completing this chapter, you should be able to do the following:

- Determine when an Internal Revenue code (IRC) Section 754 election will allow a partnership or LLC to adjust its basis in its assets.
- Assess when a partnership or LLC should make a Section 754 election in order to allow it to adjust the basis of its assets.
- Recognize when a Section 754 election will require a partnership or LLC to decrease its basis in its assets.
- Assess required basis adjustments among partnership or LLC assets.

INTRODUCTION

Partnerships offer more flexibility in tax planning than any other form of business. One area that exemplifies this flexibility is the ability of the partnership to adjust the basis of partnership assets to reflect the economic reality of certain transactions between the partnership and one or more of its partners, and even between two or more partners outside the partnership.

These basis adjustments are made under Section 754, in tandem with either Section 734 or Section 743. Mechanically, Section 754 governs only the method for making the required election to adjust basis in the case of certain distributions[1] or upon certain transfers of partnership interests.[2] A Section 754 election, once made by the partnership, applies to all subsequent distributions and transfers. This chapter will first describe situations in which a basis adjustment is permissible and the reasons for making a Section 754 election. It will then describe the mechanics of adjusting the basis of partnership property and discuss making the election itself. Finally, this chapter will address a special situation for which relief may be available if the election is not made.

---

[1] IRC Section 734(b).
[2] IRC Section 743(b).

Section 743: Adjustments Following the Transfer of a Partnership Interest

The transfer of a partnership interest almost always creates a difference between inside and outside basis. This is so because the transfer price (the outside basis) is to a large extent based on the fair market value (FMV) of the underlying partnership assets, but this value seldom has any relationship to the tax basis of those assets. No adjustment to basis is permissible as a result of a transfer of a partnership interest by sale or exchange or on the death of a partner unless the election provided by Section 754 is in effect.[3] Absent a Section 754 election, transfers of partnership interests may result in recognition of essentially the same income by both the transferor and transferee partners, and may affect the nature of the income to be recognized.

 Example 6-1

D acquires A's interest in the ABC Partnership for a cash payment of $30,000. A's basis in his partnership interest is $10,000. A's share of partnership assets immediately before the transfer is as follows:

	Basis	FMV
Trade Receivables	$ —	$ 10,000
Land	10,000	20,000
	$ 10,000	$ 30,000

A will recognize $20,000 gain on the sale as follows:

Ordinary Income (unrealized receivables) – Section 751(a)	$ 10,000
Capital Gain – Section 741	10,000
	$ 20,000

Because D purchased A's interest in the partnership, rather than A's share of partnership assets, the acquisition does not affect the partnership's basis in its assets unless the partnership has a Section 754 election in effect. Assume that the partnership does not have such an election in effect, and chooses not to make one. Assume further that shortly after D's purchase of A's interest, the partnership collects the receivables. D will be allocated $10,000 in ordinary income from the transaction, and will increase the basis in his partnership interest to $40,000. In effect, A and D have both recognized the same income attributable to the unrealized receivable. Note that collection of the receivable did not change the value of D's interest in the partnership. Thus, if D subsequently sells the interest for its $30,000 value, he will recognize a capital loss of $(10,000), offsetting, to a certain extent, the income allocated to him from the collection of the receivables. Note however that any loss recognized by D on sale of the partnership interest will be characterized as a capital loss, while his income was ordinary. And, of course, no loss at all can be recognized until he sells the partnership interest, which may be far into the future.

---

[3] IRC Section 743(a).

If a Section 754 election is in effect, the difference between the transferee partner's basis in the partnership and the proportionate share of the partnership's basis in its underlying assets is treated as an adjustment to the basis of partnership assets. This adjustment is made solely for the benefit of the transferee partner. The adjustment can result in either an increase or a decrease in the transferee-partner's share of the partnership's basis in its assets. The allocation of the adjustment among partnership assets is made in accordance with rules established in Section 755. The following example demonstrates the effect of such a basis adjustment.

 Example 6-2

Assume the same facts as example 6-1, except that the partnership has a Section 754 election in effect at the time that D acquires his interest from A. The partnership will be entitled to increase its basis in its assets under Section 743(b) to reflect the gain recognized by A. This $20,000 basis adjustment will be allocated between the partnership's two assets as follows:

	Old Basis	743(b) Adjust	New Basis
Trade Receivables	$ —	$ 10,000	$ 10,000
Land	10,000	10,000	20,000
	$ 10,000	$ 20,000	$ 30,000

Note that the preceding adjustments are made to D's share of the basis of partnership assets only. Basis adjustments under Section 743(b) are made solely for the benefit of the transferee partner. The other partners' shares of the partnership's basis in its assets are unaffected. Now when the receivable is collected, D will have $10,000 basis to offset against his share of the proceeds. He therefore will recognize no taxable income and will not adjust his outside basis in his partnership interest.

KNOWLEDGE CHECK

1. Pygmalion LLC had the following balance sheets at December 31:

	Basis	FMV
Cash	30,000	30,000
Property 1	145,000	225,000
Property 2	80,000	140,000
Property 3	105,000	145,000
Total Assets	360,000	540,000
Capital, Ernie	180,000	270,000
Capital, Carl	90,000	135,000
Capital, Angie	90,000	135,000
Total Liabilities & Capital	360,000	540,000

    On that date, Angie, who was a 25 percent partner in the partnership, sold her interest to Gary for $135,000 cash. None of the LLC's assets constitute inventory or unrealized receivables. Assuming that the LLC does not have a Section 754 election in effect and chooses not to make one, what will be Gary's share of the inside basis of the LLC's assets?

    a. $90,000.
    b. $135,000.
    c. $360,000.
    d. $540,000.

2. Assume the same facts as in the previous question, except that the LLC makes a Section 754 election for the year of the sale. Whatwill be the amount of the LLC's required basis adjustment under Section 743(b)?

    a. $0.
    b. $45,000.
    c. $90,000.
    d. $135,000.

3. In the previous question, what will be the LLC's basis in Property 1 after making the required basis adjustment under Section 743(b)?

    a. $145,000.
    b. $165,000.
    c. $225,000.
    d. $190,000.

Distributions of Partnership Property

Under the general distribution rules of Sections 731 and 732, a difference between inside and outside basis may result from a distribution of partnership property. This difference may arise as a result of the recognition of gain or loss by the distributee-partner under Section 731, or as a result of the peculiarities of the provisions of Section 732, which governs the distributee-partner's basis in distributed property. If the partnership has a Section 754 election in effect (or chooses to make one for the year of the distribution), Section 734(b) requires the partnership to adjust its basis in its remaining assets in order to eliminate the resulting difference between outside and inside basis. The purpose of Section 734(b) is to prevent the double recognition of income or loss by both the distributee-partner and the remaining partners in the partnership. Thus, unlike Section 743(b) adjustments which are made solely for the benefit of the new partner, adjustments under Section 734(b) are made for the benefit of all remaining partners in the partnership. There are essentially four situations in which an effective Section 754 election permits an adjustment to the partnership's basis in its assets under Section 734(b).

GAIN RECOGNIZED BY DISTRIBUTEE PARTNER

When a distributee partner recognizes gain (whether or not the distribution is in complete liquidation of his or her partnership interest) and there is a Section 754 election in effect, the basis of undistributed partnership property is increased by the amount of the gain recognized.[4] Gain is recognized only when the amount of cash received in the distribution exceeds the distributee partner's basis in his or her partnership interest. Because cash always has a basis equal to its fair market value, recognition of gain by the distributee partner means that the basis of the remaining assets is less than the remaining partners' basis in their partnership interests. Failure to increase the basis of undistributed partnership assets results in taxation of the same gain to the distributee partner at the time of the distribution and also to the remaining partners at the time of any subsequent sale of the partnership's remaining assets. This double taxation would eventually be offset, but not until the liquidation of the partnership when a loss or reduced gain would be recognized by the distributee partner.

---

[4] IRC Section 734(b)(1)(A).

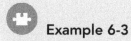 **Example 6-3**

The ABC Partnership has the following balance sheet at December 31:

	Basis	FMV
Cash	$ 30,000	$ 30,000
Property A	20,000	20,000
Property B	10,000	40,000
	$ 60,000	$ 90,000
Capital, A	$ 20,000	$ 30,000
Capital, B	20,000	30,000
Capital, C	20,000	30,000
	$ 60,000	$ 90,000

On that date, the partnership distributed $30,000 cash to A in complete liquidation of her partnership interest. Prior to the distribution, A's basis in her partnership interest was $20,000, as indicated in the previous balance sheet.

A must recognize a $10,000 capital gain on the distribution under Section 731(a) ($30,000 cash received less $20,000 basis in her partnership interest). If the partnership does not have a Section 754 election in effect, the partnership's balance sheet after the distribution will be as follows:

	Basis	FMV
Property A	$ 20,000	$ 20,000
Property B	10,000	40,000
	$ 30,000	$ 60,000
Capital, B	$ 20,000	$ 30,000
Capital, C	20,000	30,000
	$ 40,000	$ 60,000

Note that the gain recognized by A equals her one-third share of the unrealized gain inherent in the partnership's remaining assets. When these assets are sold, this share will be recognized again by the partnership, and allocated to partners B and C. That is, the partnership will recognize a $30,000 gain when these assets are sold, and B and C will each be allocated $15,000 of this gain, rather than $10,000 as would have been the case had A remained in the partnership. Thus, A's share of the gain is recognized twice – once when she retires from the partnership and again when the partnership sells its remaining assets.[5]

---

[5] Note that the extra gain recognized by partners B and C will increase their basis in their partnership interests. Thus, upon sale or liquidation of their partnership interests, each would recognize a capital loss (or a lesser capital gain) in the same amount. This benefit will not be realized, however, until the remaining partners dispose of their partnership interests.

Example 6-3 (continued)

If the partnership has a Section 754 election in effect, Section 734(b) requires that it increase its basis in its remaining assets by the $10,000 gain recognized by A on the cash distribution. This adjustment will prevent partners B and C from having to recognize this gain again. It will also allow the partnership's tax balance sheet to balance without adjusting the capital accounts of the remaining partners, thus preserving the integrity of the partnership's tax balance sheet as well as the K-1s issued to the remaining partners.

KNOWLEDGE CHECK

4. The DEF Partnership has the following balance sheet at December 31:

	Basis	FMV
Cash	$ 50,000	$ 50,000
Property 1	30,000	30,000
Property 2	10,000	55,000
	$ 90,000	$ 135,000
Capital, D	$ 30,000	$ 45,000
Capital, E	30,000	45,000
Capital, F	30,000	45,000
	$ 90,000	$ 135,000

On that date, the partnership distributed $45,000 cash to D in complete liquidation of her partnership interest. Prior to the distribution, D's basis in her partnership interest was $30,000 as indicated in the previous balance sheet. Assume that the partnership has a Section 754 election in effect. What will be the amount of its basis adjustment required under Section 734(b)?

a. $45,000.
b. $30,000.
c. $15,000.
d. $0.

LOSS RECOGNIZED BY DISTRIBUTEE PARTNER UPON DISTRIBUTION OF PARTNERSHIP PROPERTY

Under Section 731(a)(2), it is possible for a partner to recognize a loss upon receipt of a distribution in liquidation of his or her partnership interest. A loss may be recognized only if

- the distribution is in complete liquidation of the distributee partner's interest in the partnership;
- the cash and basis of ordinary income assets (so-called "hot" assets such as inventory and unrealized receivables) distributed are less than the distributee partner's basis in the partnership interest; and
- no other assets are distributed to the partner.

In this situation, the distributee partner recognizes loss equal to the excess of his or her basis in his or her partnership interest over the sum of the cash received plus the basis (to the partnership) of the ordinary income assets received. This represents the exact reverse of the gain situation illustrated in example 6-3 in which cash is distributed in excess of the partner's basis in the partnership interest.

When a loss is recognized on a distribution, the basis of assets remaining in the partnership will generally exceed the aggregate basis of the remaining partners in their partnership interests. A subsequent sale of those assets by the partnership, when combined with the loss recognized by the withdrawing partner, results in more total loss (or less gain) being recognized than would be the case had the retiring partner remained in the partnership. As previous, the double deduction will be offset eventually when the remaining partners dispose of their interests in the partnership (or when the partnership liquidates). If a Section 754 election is in effect at the time of the distribution, however, a negative adjustment to the basis of the remaining partnership assets is required and the double deduction will never take place.[6] The negative adjustment amount is generally equal to the loss recognized by the withdrawing partner.

 Example 6-4

The ABC Partnership has the following balance sheet:

	Basis	FMV
Cash	$ 30,000	$ 30,000
Property A	40,000	20,000
Property B	20,000	10,000
	$ 90,000	$ 60,000
Capital, A	$ 30,000	$ 20,000
Capital, B	30,000	20,000
Capital, C	30,000	20,000
	$ 90,000	$ 60,000

---

[6] IRC Section 734(b)(2)(A).

Example 6-4 (continued)

The partnership distributes $20,000 cash to partner A in complete liquidation of her partnership interest. Assuming A's basis in her partnership interest is $30,000, she will recognize a $(10,000) capital loss on receipt of the distribution.

The partnership's balance sheets immediately after the distribution will be as follows:

	Basis	FMV
Cash	$ 10,000	$ 10,000
Property A	40,000	20,000
Property B	20,000	10,000
	$ 70,000	$ 40,000
Capital, B	$ 30,000	$ 20,000
Capital, C	30,000	20,000
	$ 60,000	$ 40,000

A has recognized a $(10,000) loss on receipt of the distribution. Yet the entire $30,000 pre-distribution built-in loss inherent in the partnership's balance sheets remains. Thus, a subsequent sale by the partnership of properties A and B will yield a combined loss of $(30,000). Partners B and C will now be allocated $(15,000) shares of the loss, rather than $(10,000) as would have been the case had A remained a partner.

If a Section 754 election had been in effect, this problem would be eliminated by Section 734(b). Under Section 734(b), the partnership would be required to reduce its basis in its remaining assets by $10,000 – the difference between its aggregate basis in its assets and the aggregate basis of its remaining partners in their partnership interests.

KNOWLEDGE CHECK

5. Ben was a 20 percent partner in Troutman Partners until his interest was liquidated this month. Ben's tax basis in his partnership interest was $50,000. He received a distribution consisting of $35,000 cash and zero-basis accounts receivable with a face value of $35,000 in complete liquidation of that interest. If the partnership had a Section 754 election in effect, what would be the amount of its basis adjustment under Section 734(b)?

    a. $35,000.
    b. $20,000.
    c. $0.
    d. $(15,000).

INCREASE OR DECREASE IN BASIS OF ASSETS DISTRIBUTED IN COMPLETE LIQUIDATION OF A PARTNER'S INTEREST

Section 734(b) is also triggered when a distribution results in a stepped-up or stepped-down basis in the distributed property in the hands of the distributee, even though no gain or loss is recognized.[7] For example, under Section 732(b), a partner receiving a property distribution in complete liquidation of his or her partnership interest takes a basis in the property received equal to the remaining basis in his or her partnership interest (after reduction for any cash received in the distribution), regardless of the basis the partnership had in the distributed property.

If the partnership's basis in the distributed property differs from this amount, as will generally be the case, the total of the gain recognized by the distributee partner on a subsequent sale of the distributed assets and the gain recognized within the partnership on the sale of undistributed assets will differ from the total gain which would have been recognized if the distributee-partner remained a partner and all assets were sold within the partnership. A Section 734(b) adjustment will avoid this problem. The amount of the adjustment is measured by the difference between the basis of the distributed property to the partnership and its basis in the hands of the recipient partner.[8]

 Example 6-5

The ABC Partnership has the following balance sheets:

	Basis	FMV
Cash	$ 30,000	$ 30,000
Property 1	20,000	20,000
Property 2	40,000	10,000
	$ 90,000	$ 60,000
Capital, A	$ 30,000	$ 20,000
Capital, B	30,000	20,000
Capital, C	30,000	20,000
	$ 90,000	$ 60,000

---

[7] IRC Section 734(b)(1)(B) and (b)(2)(B).

[8] This adjustment to reduce basis does not apply when the distributed property is an interest in another partnership for which the Section 754 election is not in effect [IRC Section 734(b)].

Example 6-5 (continued)

Assume the partnership distributes property 1 to partner B in complete liquidation of her partnership interest. Under Section 731, partner B will recognize no gain or loss on the distribution. Under Section 732, she will take a substitute basis in the property equal to her basis in her partnership interest immediately prior to the distribution (reduced by any cash received in the distribution). Thus, B's basis in property 1 will be $30,000, a step-up of $10,000 in the basis of this asset. The partnership's balance sheets immediately after the distribution will be as follows:

	Basis	FMV
Cash	$ 30,000	$ 30,000
Property 2	40,000	10,000
	$ 70,000	$ 40,000
Capital, A	$ 30,000	$ 20,000
Capital, C	30,000	20,000
	$ 60,000	$ 40,000

Upon a subsequent sale of property 1, B will recognize a $(10,000) loss. Upon a subsequent sale of property 2, the partnership will recognize a $(30,000) loss. Thus, the total loss to be recognized upon sale of the properties has increased by $10,000 as a result of the distribution to B. If a Section 754 election is in effect, Section 734(b) requires the partnership to decrease its basis in remaining assets by $10,000 to reflect the step-up in the basis of property 1 resulting from the d istribution to B. The partnership's post-distribution balance sheet would then appear as follows:

	Basis	FMV
Cash	$ 30,000	$ 30,000
Property 2	30,000	10,000
	$ 60,000	$ 40,000
Capital, A	$ 30,000	$ 20,000
Capital, C	30,000	20,000
	$ 60,000	$ 40,000

KNOWLEDGE CHECK

6. QL Ranches is a general partnership with the following balance sheets:

	Basis	FMV
Cash	30,000	30,000
Property 1	63,000	42,000
Property 2	21,000	78,000
Property 3	36,000	75,000
Total Assets	150,000	225,000
Capital, Lynn	50,000	75,000
Capital, Robert	50,000	75,000
Capital, Jamie	50,000	75,000
Total Capital	150,000	225,000

On December 31, in complete liquidation of his interest, the partnership distributed Property 3 to Robert. None of the partnership's properties constitute inventory or unrealized receivables. If the partnership has a Section 754 election in effect, what will be the amount of the required adjustment to the basis of its assets under Section 734(b)?

    a. $25,000.

    b. $14,000.

    c. $0.

    d. $(14,000).

7. Willow Ridge Partnership distributed property with a tax basis of $50,000 and a fair market value of $60,000 to Richard, a 20 percent partner, in complete liquidation of his interest in the partnership. Richard's basis in his interest prior to receipt of the distribution was $42,000. What is the amount of the resulting Section 734(b) adjustment which must be made if the partnership has a Section 754 election in effect?

    a. $18,000.

    b. $10,000.

    c. $8,000.

    d. $0.

8. In the previous question, what if Richard's basis in his interest had been $62,000, rather than $42,000? Whatwould be the amount of the partnership's Section 734(b) adjustment?

    a. $12,000.

    b. $(2,000).

    c. $0.

    d. $(12,000).

DECREASE IN BASIS OF PARTNERSHIP ASSETS DISTRIBUTED IN PARTIAL LIQUIDATION OF A PARTNER'S INTEREST

Assets distributed to a partner in partial liquidation of his or her partnership interest (as opposed to a complete liquidation of that interest) generally take a carryover basis in his or her hands under Section 732(a). However, if the partnership's basis in the distributed property exceeds the distributee-partner's basis in his or her partnership interest, his or her basis in the distributed property is limited to his or her basis in his or her partnership interest (reduced by any cash received in the distribution). Under Section 732(a)(2), the distributee-partner's basis in distributed property cannot exceed his or her pre-distribution basis in his or her partnership interest.

As a result of this, a low basis partner will often take a stepped-down basis in property received in a non-liquidating distribution or a distribution in partial liquidation of his or her interest. When this happens, the distributee partner will recognize more gain upon a subsequent disposition of the property than the partnership would have recognized upon disposition of the same property. Moreover, because the gain inherent in the partnership's remaining assets remains unchanged, the total amount of gain to be recognized by the partnership and the distributee partner combined upon disposition of the partnership's assets will be greater than if the distribution had not been made and all assets had been sold by the partnership. A Section 754 election will allow the partnership to increase its basis in its remaining assets to alleviate this problem. The basis adjustment required under Section 734(b) in this case is equal to the difference between the basis taken by the distributee-partner in the distributed property and the pre-distribution basis of such property in the partnership's hands.[9] As noted in previous examples, the Section 734(b) adjustment also allows the partnership to maintain the integrity of its balance sheet (tax) and the Schedules K-1 issued to its partners.

Example 6-6

Assume the ABC Partnership has the following balance sheet:

	Basis	FMV
Cash	$ 20,000	$ 20,000
Property 1	30,000	30,000
Property 2	10,000	100,000
	$ 60,000	$ 150,000
Capital, A	$ 20,000	$ 50,000
Capital, B	20,000	50,000
Capital, C	20,000	50,000
	$ 60,000	$ 150,000

---

[9] IRC Section 734(b)(1)(B) and (b)(2)(B).

Example 6-6 (continued)

Assume the partnership distributes property 1 to A in partial liquidation of her partnership interest (reducing her interest from one-third to one-sixth). Although the partnership's basis in property 1 was $30,000, A will take a basis in the property of only $20,000, her pre-distribution basis in her partnership interest. A subsequent sale of property 1 by A will thus trigger a $10,000 gain to her. Sale by the partnership of property 2 will still trigger a $90,000 gain. Thus, the distribution to A has increased the total combined gain to be recognized by the partners by $10,000.

If a Section 754 election is in effect, the partnership will be required under Section 734(b) to increase its basis in remaining assets (property 2) by the step-down in the basis of property 1 taken by A, or $10,000. The partnership's post-distribution balance sheet will be as follows:

	Basis	FMV
Cash	$ 20,000	$ 20,000
Property 2	20,000	100,000
	$ 40,000	$ 120,000
Capital, A	—	$ 20,000
Capital, B	20,000	50,000
Capital, C	20,000	50,000
	$ 40,000	$ 120,000

KNOWLEDGE CHECK

9. Grimace Partners has the following assets.

	Basis	FMV
Property 1	63,000	42,000
Property 2	21,000	78,000
Property 3	36,000	75,000
Total	120,000	195,000

The partnership distributes Property 3 in a non-liquidating distribution to a partner whose tax basis in her partnership interest was $30,000. If the partnership has a Section 754 election in effect, what will be the amount of its basis adjustment under Section 734(b)?

  a. $6,000.
  b. $(6,000).
  c. $39,000.
  d. $0.

Allocating the Adjustment Amount Among Partnership Properties

After the partnership makes a Section 754 election or when a Section 754 election is already in effect for the partnership, the partnership must allocate the amount of the adjustment among its remaining assets. This allocation must be made in a manner that will reduce the difference between the fair market value and the adjusted basis of the partnership properties.[10] How this allocation is made depends on the type of triggering event.

TRANSFERS OF PARTNERSHIP INTERESTS

When a partner transfers an interest in a partnership by sale or bequest, and the partnership has a Section 754 election in effect or agrees to make such an election, Section 743(b) requires that the partnership adjust its basis in its assets to reflect the amount paid for them by the acquiring partner. For this purpose, all assets of the partnership are classified as either

- Capital assets and Section 1231(b) assets (capital gain assets), or
- All other assets (ordinary income assets).[11]

After classifying all partnership assets, the partnership must allocate the basis adjustment first between the two classes of assets and then among the assets within each class. The regulations under Section 755 require that both allocations be based on a hypothetical sale of all partnership assets for their fair values.[12] Allocation of the basis adjustment is then based on the amount of gain or loss that would be allocated to the transferee-partner as a result of the hypothetical sale. Thus, some assets may be allocated negative adjustments and others allocated positive adjustments even though the total adjustment is positive (or negative). Indeed, the regulations make clear that positive and negative adjustments may be made to different assets of the partnership even when the total adjustment under Section 743(b) is zero.[13] Note that the principles of Section 704(c) are applied in making this determination, so that the acquirer of an interest from a contributor-partner is protected from the seller's share of both the partnership's Section 704(b) book gain and his or her Section 704(c) tax gain.

Allocation Between Classes of Property

The adjustment is first made to the ordinary income class of property. The adjustment to this class of property is equal to the amount of income, gain, or loss that would be allocated to the transferee-partner (including Section 704(c) allocations) from the sale of all partnership ordinary income property in the hypothetical sale. The remainder of the Section 743(b) adjustment is then made to capital asset class of partnership properties.

---

[10] IRC Section 755(a)(1).
[11] IRC Section 755(b).
[12] Regulation Section 1.755-1(b)(1)(ii).
[13] Regulation Section 1.755-1(b)(1)(i).

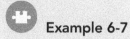

Example 6-7

Assume the JDR Partnership has the following balance sheets:

	Basis	FMV
Cash	$ 20,000	$ 20,000
Inventory	50,000	45,000
Property 1	25,000	75,000
Property 2	85,000	100,000
	$ 180,000	$ 240,000
Capital, J	$ 90,000	$ 120,000
Capital, D	45,000	60,000
Capital, R	45,000	60,000
	$ 180,000	$ 240,000

J has a 50 percent interest in partnership profits, losses, and capital. D and R each have 25 percent interests. However, J's share of the basis of partnership assets is only $90,000. Assume she sells her interest in the partnership to Q for $120,000, recognizing a $30,000 gain. Q takes a $120,000 basis in her partnership interest, but only has a $90,000 share of the inside basis of the partnership's assets. If the partnership has a Section 754 election in effect, it will be required to adjust its basis in its assets; this adjustment is made solely for Q's benefit, to keep her from recognizing gain on the future sale of the partnership's assets in excess of her economic gain (that is, to keep J's gain from being taxed twice).

Assume that the partnership's inventory is not contributed property for purposes of Section 704(c). Further assume that both properties 1 and 2 are capital gain assets, and are also not contributed property under Section 704(c). If JDR sold all its assets in a fully taxable transaction for their fair market values immediately after Q's acquisition of J's partnership interest, Q would be allocated a $30,000 share of the partnership's total gain ($120,000 share of proceeds of the hypothetical sale, less $90,000 share of inside basis). Thus, her total basis adjustment under Section 743(b) would be $30,000. She would be allocated a $(2,500) share of the partnership's ordinary loss from sale of the inventory
(50 percent of the $5,000 loss). Thus, $(2,500) would be allocable to partnership ordinary income property (and reduce its basis with respect to Q) and $32,500 would be allocable to capital gain assets (and increase their basis with respect to Q). Note that this approach effectively allocates any discount (or premium) to the capital asset class.

Allocation of Adjustment Among Assets Within Each Class of Property

Once the adjustment is allocated between the classes of property, the portion allocable to each class must be apportioned among the assets within that class. Generally speaking, this allocation is straightforward. Each asset within the class is allocated a basis adjustment equal to the amount of income, gain, or loss that would be allocated to the transferee-partner if the asset were sold for its fair market value immediately after the partner's acquisition of the partnership interest.[14] If the total adjustment is less than the aggregate amount of gain that would be recognized by the transferee-partner, the deficit is divided among properties in the class by reference to their relative fair market values.[15]

 Example 6-8

Assume the same facts as example 6-7. The total basis adjustment under Section 743(b) is $30,000. Of this amount, negative $2,500 is allocated to the ordinary assets and positive $32,500 to the capital assets. The ordinary income class consists of only one asset, so the entire ($2,500) basis adjustment is allocated to this asset (inventory).

There are two assets in the capital asset class. The sale of properties 1 and 2 by the partnership would generate gains to the partnership of $50,000 and $15,000 respectively. As a 50 percent partner, half of each of these gains would be allocated to Q. Thus, the basis of property 1 will be increased by $25,000 (half of $50,000) and the basis of property 2 by $7,500 (half of $15,000).

In some cases, the amount of the basis adjustment may be less than the gain that would be allocated to the new partner. In such cases, as discussed previously, the shortfall is allocated among partnership properties by reference to their relative fair market values.

---

[14] Regulation Section 1.755-1(b)(3).
[15] Regulation Section 1.755-1(b)(3)(i)(B) and (ii)(B).

KNOWLEDGE CHECK

10. Partnership XYZ has the following balance sheets:

	Basis	FMV
Cash	$ 15,000	$ 15,000
Inventory	48,000	72,000
Property 1	24,000	36,000
Property 2	84,000	90,000
	$ 171,000	$ 213,000
Capital, X	$ 57,000	$ 71,000
Capital, Y	57,000	71,000
Capital, Z	57,000	71,000
	$ 171,000	$ 213,000

X sells her interest in the partnership to W for $71,000, recognizing a $14,000 gain. If the partnership has a Section 754 election in effect, what will be its adjusted basis in the inventory following the acquisition of X's interest by W?

a. $72,000.
b. $56,000.
c. $55,385.
d. $48,000.

Example 6-9

PLT is a general partnership with the following balance sheets:

	Basis	FMV
Cash	$ 15,000	$ 15,000
Property 1	30,000	45,000
Property 2	30,000	90,000
Property 3	75,000	90,000
	$ 150,000	$ 240,000
Capital, P	$ 50,000	$ 80,000
Capital, L	50,000	80,000
Capital, T	50,000	80,000
	$ 150,000	$ 240,000

Example 6-9 (continued)

P, a one-third partner, sells his partnership interest to C for $75,000, recognizing a $25,000 capital gain (his basis in the partnership interest was $50,000). Assuming the partnership has a Section 754 election in effect, it will be entitled to increase the basis of its assets by $25,000 (on behalf of C, the incoming partner). As a one-third partner, P's share of the basis and FMV of partnership assets was as follows:

	Basis	FMV	Gain to C
Property 1	10,000	15,000	$ 5,000
Property 2	10,000	30,000	20,000
Property 3	25,000	30,000	5,000
	$ 45,000	$ 75,000	$ 30,000

Because P sold the interest to C at a discount, the basis adjustment is less than the aggregate gain C will be allocated from sale of the partnership's assets. The $5,000 shortfall will be allocated among the three properties by reference to the relative values of each. Thus, one-fifth (15/75) will be allocated to property 1, and 2/5 each to properties 2 and 3. That is, $1,000 of the shortfall will be allocated to property 1 and $2,000 each to properties 2 and 3. The total basis adjustments to each property will be as follows:

	C's Share of Gain	Allocated Deficit	Net Adjustment
Property 1	$ 5,000	$ (1,000)	$ 4,000
Property 2	20,000	(2,000)	18,000
Property 3	5,000	(2,000)	3,000
	$ 30,000	$ (5,000)	$ 25,000

Thus, the bases of properties 1, 2, and 3 to the partnership will be $34,000, $48,000 and $78,000 respectively. Recall that these adjustments are made for C's benefit, as the new partner. C's share of the basis of each partnership asset will be as follows:

	C's Share of Unadjusted Basis	Basis Adjustment	C's Share, After Adjustment
Property 1	$ 10,000	$ 4,000	$ 14,000
Property 2	10,000	18,000	28,000
Property 3	25,000	3,000	28,000
	$ 45,000	$ 25,000	$ 70,000

INCOME IN RESPECT OF A DECEDENT

When a partnership interest is transferred as a result of the death of a partner, the beneficiary generally takes a stepped-up basis in the interest equal to its fair market value at the date of death (or the alternative valuation date if applicable). To the extent that any portion of the partnership interest constitutes income in respect of a decedent (IRD) under Section 691, however, the basis is not stepped up. Thus, for example, to the extent of the decedent's interest in partnership unrealized receivables, no step-up is allowed. The regulations under Section 755 make clear that no portion of any adjustment allowed under Section 743(b) may be allocated to the transferee-partner's interest in partnership items that constitute IRD.[16]

PARTNERSHIP GOODWILL

If goodwill exists at the time of the transfer and is reflected in the transfer price, it must be included in the allocation of the adjustment.[17] All goodwill must be valued using the residual method (IRC Section 1060, enacted by the Tax Reform Act of 1986). This method specifies that purchase price be allocated

- First to cash and general deposit accounts; then,
- Marketable securities, certificates of deposits, and foreign currency; next,
- Accounts receivable, mark-to-market assets, and certain debt instruments from unrelated borrowers; next,
- Stock in trade and other inventory items; then,
- All other tangible assets; then,
- Tangible and intangible assets other than goodwill; and then,
- The balance to goodwill.

The effect of this requirement is only to specify the methodology for determining the value of goodwill. Once this value is established, goodwill is included in the classification of capital gain assets, and the remainder of the allocation under Section 755 is unchanged.

DISTRIBUTIONS OF PARTNERSHIP PROPERTY

The allocation of an adjustment under Section 734(b) (due to a distribution of partnership property) is different from the allocation of an adjustment under Section 743(b) (due to the transfer of a partnership interest). The allocation of a Section 734(b) adjustment is made to assets of the same character as those that gave rise to the adjustment. As before, all assets of the partnership are classified as either capital gain assets or ordinary income assets.[18] The allocation of the adjustment resulting from a distribution depends on the type of distribution triggering the adjustment.

---

[16] Regulation Section 1.755-1(b)(4).
[17] Regulation Section 1.755-1(a)(2).
[18] IRC Section 755(b).

KNOWLEDGE CHECK

11. Partnership ABC has the following assets:

	Basis	FMV
Cash	$ 15,000	$ 15,000
Inventory	24,000	36,000
Property 1	20,000	50,000
	$ 59,000	$ 101,000

The partnership is required to reduce the basis of its assets by $(18,000) under Section 734(b) as the result of a distribution of capital gain property to a partner. What will be its tax basis in the inventory after the adjustment has been made?

a. $20,000.
b. $24,000.
c. $36,000.
d. $15,000.

Gain or Loss Recognized

Certain distributions (such as a distribution of cash in excess of basis) result in a taxable gain to the distributee partner, and other distributions result in a deductible loss. If the adjustment results from a distribution in which gain or loss was recognized by the distributee partner, the adjustment is allocated only to capital gain assets (as previously defined).[19] Because the distributee partner recognizes capital gain or loss on the distribution, this approach preserves the character of the gain or loss subsequently recognized by the other partners. Within the category of capital gain assets, the adjustment must first be allocated to individual assets with unrealized appreciation (in the case of a positive adjustment) or depreciation (in the case of a negative adjustment) in value, but only to the extent of such unrealized appreciation or depreciation. In the case of a positive adjustment, if the total adjustment exceeds the aggregate unrealized appreciation in the value of partnership capital assets, the excess must be apportioned among all capital assets in proportion to their fair market values.[20]

In the case of negative basis adjustments, if the total negative adjustment exceeds the aggregate unrealized depreciation in value of remaining capital gain assets, the excess is to be allocated among all capital assets in proportion to their remaining adjusted basis.[21]

Finally, the maximum reduction in basis that can be made is to reduce the basis of the remaining capital gain property to zero.[22] If this occurs, or if there is no capital gain property to which the basis adjustment

---

[19] Regulation Section 1.755-1(c)(1).
[20] Regulation Section 1.755-1(c)(2)(i).
[21] Regulation Section 1.755-1(c)(2)(ii).
[22] Regulation Section 1.755-1(c)(3).

can be applied, the adjustment is carried forward and "shall be made when the partnership subsequently acquires property of a like character to which an adjustment can be made."[23]

Example 6-10

Wagner Partners is a general partnership with the following balance sheets:

	Basis	FMV
Cash	$ 95,000	$ 95,000
Property 1	30,000	40,000
Property 2	115,000	75,000
	$ 240,000	$ 210,000
Liabilities	$ 90,000	$ 90,000
Capital, B	50,000	40,000
Capital, K	50,000	40,000
Capital, X	50,000	40,000
	$ 240,000	$ 210,000

Assume that X receives a distribution of $40,000 cash in complete liquidation of her interest in the partnership. Her tax basis in the interest was $80,000 (including her $30,000 share of liabilities). Thus, she recognizes a $(10,000) capital loss on receipt of the liquidating distribution and relief of $30,000 in liabilities.

If the partnership has a Section 754 election in effect, it must reduce its tax basis in remaining assets by $10,000. This adjustment will be made to the partnership's capital and Section 1231 assets (assume that properties 1 and 2 are both capital assets). It is allocated first to assets that have adjusted bases in excess of their values. Here, only property 2 meets this requirement. Thus, the entire adjustment is made to the basis of property 2, and after the adjustment property 2 would have a tax basis of $115,000 – $10,000 = $105,000. If the loss on the distribution had exceeded $40,000 (the depreciation in property 2), the excess would have been allocated between properties 1 and 2 according to their relative basis amounts. If the distribution in complete liquidation had been $70,000, X would have had a recognized gain of $20,000. The adjustment would have been made first to property 1 and then to both properties based on their relative fair market values.

Proposed Regulations: Increases in Basis of Section 1245 Property

Under proposed regulations issued in November 2013, positive adjustments to the basis of Section 1245 property associated with the distribution of property to a partner are ignored in calculating the partnership's subsequent gain or loss realized upon sale of such property.[24] The proposed regulations,

---

[23] Regulation Section 1.755-1(c)(4).
[24] Proposed Regs. Section 1.755-1(c)(2)(iii).

which will not be effective until issued in the Federal Register as final regulations, provide that basis adjustments under Section 734 (for example, as a result of gain recognized by the distributee partner in connection with a cash distribution) will not reduce the amount of ordinary income recognized by the partnership under Section 1245 on the subsequent sale of such property. The proposed regulations clarify, however, that this is the only purpose for which such basis adjustments are ignored. Depreciation or amortization deductions may be claimed with respect to the basis adjustment and such deductions are taken into account in computing the property's recomputed basis. These proposed regulations, if finalized, will increase the complexity of subchapter K and create a potentially significant trap for the unwary.

Change in Basis of Distributed Assets

If the adjustment is the result of a distribution in which the basis of the property distributed was increased or decreased, the adjustment must be made to property of a similar character to the distributed property from which the adjustment arose.[25] Any increase in the basis of property distributed (for example, from a liquidating distribution where the inside basis of distributed property is less than the partner's outside basis) will result in a decrease in the basis of partnership property of the same class as the property whose basis was increased as part of the distribution. Any decrease in the basis of property distributed (for example, from a distribution where the inside basis of distributed property is greater than the partner's outside basis) will result in an increase in the basis of partnership property of the same class as the property whose basis was increased as part of the distribution. This approach attempts to preserve the character of the gain or loss to be recognized by the other partners.

Once the character of the asset is determined, the adjustment should be made in the same manner as described previously. That is, an increase will be made first to appreciated assets to the extent of their appreciation, and any remaining increase will be allocated according to the relative fair market values of the properties in that class of property. Any decrease would first be made to depreciated assets to the extent of their depreciation, and any further decrease would be allocated to property of the same class according to the relative adjusted basis of the properties in that class.

Where an increase or a decrease in the basis of undistributed property cannot be made because the partnership owns no property of the same character, or because the basis of all the property of the same character has been reduced to zero, the adjustment will be made when the partnership subsequently acquires property of a like character to which an adjustment can be made.

---

[25] Regulation Section 1.755-1(b)(1)(i).

Example 6-11

Haines Partners is a general partnership with the following balance sheets:·

	Basis	FMV
Cash	$ 75,000	$ 75,000
Property 1	60,000	40,000
Property 2	30,000	40,000
Property 3	75,000	55,000
	$ 240,000	$ 210,000
Liabilities	$ 90,000	$ 90,000
Capital, A	50,000	40,000
Capital, B	50,000	40,000
Capital, C	50,000	40,000
	$ 240,000	$ 210,000

Assume that C receives a distribution of property 1 in complete liquidation of her interest in the partnership. Her tax basis in the interest was $80,000 (including her $30,000 share of liabilities). Thus, she will take a tax basis of $50,000 in property 1, a decrease of $10,000, and the partnership will be allowed to increase the basis of0 partnership property of a like class. If properties 1 and 3 were both inventory, and property 2 was a capital asset, the entire increase in basis would be allocated to the property of the same class as the distributed property, which in this case would be property 3.

If C received Property 2 in complete liquidation, and Properties 1 and 2 are both capital assets, the basis of Property 2 to C will be $50,000, an increase of $20,000. If the partnership has a Section 754 election in effect, it would be required to reduce the basis of Property 1 by $20,000.

12. Bar-X Partners has the following assets.

	Basis	FMV
Cash	30,000	30,000
Property 1	63,000	42,000
Property 2	21,000	78,000
Property 3	36,000	75,000
Total	150,000	225,000

The partnership is obligated to reduce the basis of its assets (assume they are all capital assets) under Section 734(b) by $10,000. To which asset(s) will the basis adjustment be allocated?

a. Property 1.
b. Property 2.
c. Property 3.
d. All three properties.

13. The ABC Partnership has the following assets:

	Basis	FMV
Cash	$ 60,000	$ 60,000
Property 1	20,000	20,000
Property 2	10,000	40,000
	$ 90,000	$ 120,000

The partnership is required to make a positive basis adjustment under Section 734(b) in the amount of $10,000. Whatwill be the partnership's tax basis in Property 2 after the basis adjustment is made?

a. $10,000.
b. $15,000.
c. $20,000.
d. $40,000.

SECTION 751(B) DISTRIBUTIONS

A Section 751 (b) distribution is one that results in a disproportionate distribution of "hot" assets (unrealized receivables and inventory items that have substantially appreciated in value). As discussed in the preceding chapter, a Section 751(b) distribution is treated as part-sale and part-distribution. Practitioners should be careful to apply the provisions of Section 734(b) only to the distribution portion of the transaction when Section 751(b) applies.

MAKING THE SECTION 754 ELECTION

The election to make the optional basis adjustments allowed by Sections 734(b) and 743(b) must be made in a timely partnership return filed in the year in which the distribution or transfer occurred or in a preceding year.[26] The election must be signed by one of the partners and must include

- the name and address of the partnership; and
- a declaration that the partnership elects, under Section 754, to apply the provisions of Sections 734(b) and 743(b).

If a Section 754 election is not filed in a timely manner, the taxpayer may request an extension of time to make the election. Once made, an election under Section 754 is effective until revoked.

In any year in which a partnership adjusts the basis of property under Section 734(b), the partnership must attach a statement to its return showing the computation of the adjustment and the assets to which the adjustment has been allocated.[27]

A partnership wishing to revoke a Section 754 election must obtain the permission of the District Director for the IRS District in which the partnership is required to file its return (26 CFR Section1.754-1(c)). The request must be filed within 30 days of the close of the partnership year for which the revocation will be effective, must set forth the grounds on which revocation is sought, and must be signed by a partner. Situations that may be considered valid justifications for revoking the election are

- A change in the nature of the partnership business.
- A substantial increase in the assets of the partnership.

RELIEF WHEN ELECTION NOT MADE

When a partner obtains a partnership interest by transfer from another partner, he or she may not be able to force the partnership to make a Section 754 election even though it would be beneficial to the transferee-partner for the election to be made. In that instance, the transferee partner may be able to obtain some relief if

- The partner obtains all or part of the partnership interest by sale or exchange, or upon the death of a partner;
- Within two years of such transfer a distribution of assets from the partnership is made to the transferee partner; and
- The partnership did not make an optional basis adjustment upon the original transfer.[28]

In this circumstance, the distributee partner can elect to determine the basis of the distributed assets in his or her hands as if the basis adjustment under Section 743(b) had been made when the transfer originally occurred.

---

[26] Regulation Section 1.754-1(b).
[27] Regulation Section 1.734-1(d).
[28] IRC Section 732(d).

A partner wishing to make the election under Section 732(d) does so by attaching to his or her tax return a statement

- Stating that he or she is making an election under Section 732(d),
- Showing the computation of the special basis adjustment for the property distributed using the allocation rules under Section 755, and
- Showing the assets to which the adjustment has been allocated.[29]

If the distribution includes any property subject to the allowance for depreciation, depletion, or amortization, the election must be in the tax return for the year of the distribution. Otherwise, it must be made in the tax return for the first year in which the basis of the distributed property is pertinent in determining his or her income tax liability.[30]

The adjustment amount and the assets to which it is allocated are determined as of the date of the transfer. No adjustment is made for additional depletion or depreciation which would have been claimed if the Section 743(b) election had been made because no deduction was allowable for such amounts.[31] If the property received in the distribution is not the same property which would have had a basis adjustment under Section 743(b), the basis adjustment under Section 743(d) can be applied to any like property received in the distribution so long as the transferee has relinquished his or her interest in the original basis adjustment property (whether or not the partnership still owns that property).[32]

A partner is required to apply the special basis rule of Section 732(d) to any distribution (whether or not within two years of his or her acquisition) if

- He or she acquired any part of his or her interest in the partnership by transfer when a Section 754 election was not in effect;
- At the date of his or her acquisition the fair market value of all partnership property (other than money) exceeded 110 percent of its tax basis;
- A distribution in liquidation immediately after the acquisition would have resulted in a shift of basis [determined under Section 732(c)] from property not subject to an allowance for depreciation, depletion, or amortization to property subject to such an allowance; and
- A basis adjustment under Section 743(b) would change the basis of the property actually distributed.[33]

---

[29] Regulation Section 1.732-1(d)(3).
[30] Regulation Section 1.732-1(d)(2).
[31] Regulation Section 1.732-1(d)(1)(iv).
[32] Regulation Section 1.732-1(d)(1)(v).
[33] Regulation Section 1.732-1(d)(4).

KNOWLEDGE CHECK

14. Joe inherited a 20 percent interest in a real estate partnership from his grandmother. The partnership did not have a Section 754 election in effect, and opted not to make one. One year later, the partnership distributed appreciated property to Joe in a non-liquidating distribution. What will be Joe's tax basis in the property received from the partnership?

    a. Its fair market value as of the date of Joe's grandmother's death.
    b. The basis the partnership would have had in the property if a Section 754 election had been in effect at the date of his grandmother's death.
    c. Joe will take a carryover basis in the property received equal to the partnership's basis in such property.
    d. Joe will take a tax basis in the property received equal to his tax basis in the partnership interest just prior to receipt of the distribution.

Chapter 7

SALE OF AN INTEREST IN A PARTNERSHIP OR LLC

LEARNING OBJECTIVES

After completing this chapter, you should be able to do the following:

- Determine the tax consequences associated with the sale of a partner's or member's interest in a partnership or LLC.
- Determine the amount of a partner's gain from sale of a partnership interest which must be recharacterized as ordinary income under Section 751(a).
- Recognize how using the installment method to account for the sale of a partnership interest will affect how the partner will report his or her gain on the sale.
- Recognize when the sale of an interest in a partnership will trigger a technical termination of the partnership.
- Determine the tax basis and holding period of assets owned by the partnership following a technical termination.
- Determine the tax consequences associated with subsequent dispositions of built-in gain or loss assets following a technical termination.

General Tax Consequences Associated With Sale

The general tax consequences of the sale of an interest in a partnership or an LLC are relatively straightforward. The general rule under Section 741 holds that the interest itself is a capital asset, much like stock in a corporation. Accordingly, under the general rule, the partner or LLC member will recognize a capital gain or loss in an amount equal to the difference between the amount realized on the sale and the basis in the interest. Determination of whether this gain is long- or short-term is based on the partner's holding period in the partnership interest, and not on the partnership or LLC's holding period for its assets.

 Example 7-1

J is a one-third partner in JDR Partners, a general partnership engaged in the real estate development business. She has been a partner for eight years. Her tax basis in her partnership interest is $100,000. In October, she sold this interest to D for $175,000. Ignoring the potential application of Section 751(a), J will recognize a $75,000 long-term capital gain on the sale, taxable at a maximum rate of 15 percent or 20 percent (depending upon J's income, and possibly subject to an additional 3.8 percent tax).

EFFECT OF LIABILITIES

When the entity has liabilities, those liabilities are allocated among the partners or members and are included in their tax basis. The purchaser's assumption of the selling partner's share of partnership or LLC liabilities must also be included in the amount realized from sale or disposition of the interest. In effect, responsibility for this portion of the entity's liabilities has been shifted to the buyer, albeit indirectly, and increases the economic benefits received by the seller from the exchange. Because a partner's share of partnership liabilities is added to both basis and the amount realized, the net effect of liabilities on gain or loss from a sale will generally be zero.

 Example 7-2

A is a one-fourth partner in Alpha Partners.

His basis in his partnership interest is $125,000, consisting of his $50,000 net contribution to capital and his $75,000 share of partnership liabilities.

A plans to sell his interest in the partnership to an unrelated buyer for $200,000 cash.

The total amount realized from the sale will be $275,000 – the $200,000 cash proceeds plus the $75,000 share of partnership debt assumed by the buyer.

Thus, he will recognize a $150,000 gain on the transaction ($275,000 amount realized less his $125,000 basis). Under Section 741, if the partnership has no "hot" assets, his gain will be classified as a capital gain.

RECEIPT OF PROPERTY OTHER THAN CASH

The like-kind exchange rules of Section 1031 do not apply to the exchange of interests in partnerships or LLCs. Thus, any property other than money received by the selling partner in exchange for his or her interest in the partnership interest is included at fair market value in the amount realized from sale.

 Example 7-3

L, a 20 percent partner in Windmill Partners, sold his interest in the partnership to C.

His basis in his partnership interest was $350,000, consisting of his $150,000 capital balance and his $200,000 share of partnership liabilities.

L received a cash payment of $125,000, and a tract of real estate with a tax basis of $175,000 and a fair market value of $275,000.

The real estate was not encumbered by debt of any kind.

C also assumed responsibility for L's share of partnership liabilities.

The total amount realized by L on the sale to C is $600,000, consisting of the $125,000 cash payment, the $275,000 fair market value of the real estate, and the $200,000 relief of indebtedness.

As noted, L's tax basis in the partnership interest is $350,000, so he will recognize a capital gain of $250,000 on the exchange with C.

Note that where the seller receives a promissory note from the buyer, the installment method may be used to report the gain under Section 453. Where the partnership owns depreciable property that would be subject to depreciation recapture under Sections 1245 or 1250, application of the installment method is somewhat complicated.

KNOWLEDGE CHECK

1. J is a one-third partner in JDR Partners, a general partnership engaged in the real estate development business. She has been a partner for eight years. Her tax basis in her partnership interest is $100,000, consisting of her $30,000 capital account and her $70,000 share of partnership liabilities. In October, she sold this interest to D for $115,000 cash. D assumed responsibility for J's share of partnership debt. Assume that the partnership has no "hot" assets. How much gain will J recognize as a result of the sale?

    a. $0.
    b. $15,000.
    c. $85,000.
    d. $70,000.

HOLDING PERIOD OF PARTNERSHIP INTEREST

Practitioners should be aware of Regulations Section 1.1223-3, governing the determination of the holding period of partnership interests. The regulations provide that in cases where a partner acquired his or her interest in the partnership in more than one transaction, the holding period for the partnership interest must be divided to reflect the different acquisition dates.[1] Moreover, the regulations imply that each contribution of cash or property made to the partnership is to be treated as a separate transaction.

 Example 7-4

R contributed $25,000 cash and a tract of real property with a tax basis of $40,000 and a fair market value of $75,000 to the QLR Partnership in exchange for a one-third interest.

R purchased the real property three years ago and has made no improvements to it since that time.

Under Section 722, R's tax basis in his partnership interest is $65,000. For purposes of determining his holding period, however, the partnership interest is treated as having been acquired at two different times. The portion of the interest obtained in exchange for the cash contribution is treated as having been acquired on the date of the contribution to the partnership, while the portion obtained in exchange for the contribution of real property will have a holding period dating back to his acquisition of the realty (three years).

For purposes of determining the portion of the partnership interest attributable to the cash contribution, the focus is on the fair value of the cash and property contributed to the partnership.

The property was valued at $75,000 at the date of the contribution. Combined with the $25,000 cash contribution, the value of the partnership interest at the date R joined the partnership was $100,000.

One-fourth (25/100) of this interest is deemed to have been acquired for cash as of the date of the contribution. Three-fourths (75/100) is deemed to have been acquired in exchange for property; the holding period of this portion includes the holding period of the property used to acquire it.

Thus, R's holding period for 3/4 of the partnership interest is three years. If R sells the partnership interest for its $100,000 fair market value within 12 months, he will recognize a $35,000 capital gain, of which one-fourth, or $8,750, will be short-term capital gain, and the remainder, $26,250, will be long-term capital gain.[2]

Warning: Note the inequity in example 7-4. Although the entire gain from sale of the partnership interest is attributable to the real estate contributed by the partner, one-fourth of this gain is classified as short-term capital gain (and thus is not eligible for the preferential 15 percent or 20 percent maximum tax rate). This is a significant trap for the unwary.

---

[1] Regulations Section 1.1223-3(b)(1).
[2] See Regulations Section 1.1223-3(f), Example 1.

KNOWLEDGE CHECK

2. Six months ago, Eddie contributed $50,000 cash and a tract of real estate valued at $200,000 to Munster Productions, Ltd., a limited liability company that has elected to be treated as a partnership for federal tax purposes, in exchange for a 25 percent interest in profits and capital. Eddie's tax basis in the real estate, purchased five years ago, was $135,000. This month, Eddie sold his interest in the partnership for $300,000. How much long-term capital gain will Eddie recognize as a result of the sale?

   a. $0.
   b. $50,000.
   c. $92,000.
   d. $115,000.

Similar dangers await partners or LLC members who sell their interests within twelve months of making a capital contribution to the partnership or LLC. The regulations treat each capital contribution by a partner as a separate transaction requiring division of the partnership (or LLC) interest.

 Example 7-5

K is a 20 percent partner in MoonStruck, Limited, an LLC which has elected to be taxed as a partnership.

He joined the company four years ago making an initial capital contribution of $50,000.

This year, when the company decided to begin construction of a large new apartment complex, each of the investors was required to contribute another $100,000 in capital.

Just prior to the capital contribution, the balance in K's capital account was $150,000.

Six months after making the additional capital contribution, K sold his interest in the entity to another investor, recognizing a $300,000 gain on the sale.

The $100,000 capital contribution made earlier in the year represented 40 percent of K's interest in the entity. Thus, 40 percent of his gain, or $120,000, will be classified as a short-term capital gain. The remaining 60 percent will be treated as a long-term capital gain (assuming that Section 751(a) does not apply).[3]

Warning: Again, example 7-5 illustrates how the provisions of the regulations under Section 1223 can result in harsh and illogical consequences for unsuspecting partners or LLC members. It is extremely important that tax advisers review all changes in partner or member capital balances over the past 12 months when advising clients about the tax consequences of planned sales.

---

[3] See Regulations Section 1.1223-3(f), Example 4.

"Hot" Assets and Section 751(a)

"HOT" ASSETS UNDER SECTION 751(A)

The tax consequences are slightly more complicated if the partnership has "hot" assets, as defined in Section 751. For purposes of Section 751(a), "hot" assets are defined as "unreali2ed receivables of the partnership"4 or "inventory items of the partnership."5 Thus, these assets are essentially those that would generate ordinary income to the partnership or LLC if sold at their fair market values. Where the partnership or LLC has unrealized receivables or inventory, sale of an interest in the entity will result in some or all of the selling partner's gain being classified as ordinary income, rather than capital gain. In some rather extreme cases, the result may be ordinary income in an amount larger than the total gain realized on the sale, accompanied by a capital loss. Tax advisers need to be particularly careful to explain this potential outcome to clients who may be adversely affected by it.

Unrealized Receivables

Unrealized receivables include the right to payment for goods delivered (or to be delivered) or for services rendered (or to be rendered) to the extent that such payments would trigger ordinary income to the partnership or LLC when collected.6 Thus, accounts receivable of a cash method partnership is an example of unrealized receivables. However, the term unrealized receivables includes much more than a cash method partnership's accounts receivable. Under Section 751(c), the following items are also treated as unrealized receivables:

- Mining property as defined in Section 617(f)(2)
- DISC stock [Section 992(a)]
- Section 1245 property to the extent that a sale at FMV would generate recapture income
- Stock in certain foreign corporations described in Section 1248
- Section 1250 property to the extent that a sale at FMV would generate recapture income
- Certain farm land described in Section 1252(a)
- Certain franchises, trademarks, or trade names referred to in Section 1253(a)
- Certain oil, gas, or geothermal property which would be subject to recapture under Sections 617(d)(1), 995(c), 1254(a) or one of the other provisions described previously, if sold by the partnership at FMV
- The ordinary income portion of market discount bonds as defined by Section 1278
- The ordinary income portion of other short-term obligations as defined in Section 1283

The most commonly encountered item of unrealized receivables is the recapture element of Section 1245 property.

---

4 IRC Section 751(a)(1).
5 IRC Sec. 751(a)(2). Note that for purposes of Section 751(b), inventory is treated as a "hot" asset only if it has "substantially appreciated," as defined in Section 751(d)(3). Substantial appreciation is not required for partnership inventory to trigger the provisions of Section 751(a).
6 IRC Section 751(c).

Inventory Items

For purposes of Section 751(a), inventory items include the following:

- Stock in trade or other property of a kind normally included in inventory, or property held primarily for sale to customers in the ordinary course of business
- Any other property which, on sale, would be classified as property other than a capital asset or Section 1231 property
- Any other property which, if held by the selling partner directly, would be property described in any of the previous three categories.[7]

RULES OF APPLICATION

Mechanically, the application of Section 751(a) is uncomplicated. To the extent that the amount realized from the sale of the partnership or LLC interest is attributable to the selling partner's share of partnership or LLC unrealized receivables or substantially appreciated inventory, it is treated as realized from the sale of ordinary income assets. Accordingly, the selling partner or member will recognize ordinary income in the same amount as would be allocated to such partner under Sections 704(b) and (c) had the partnership or LLC sold all its "hot" assets for fair market value immediately prior to sale of the partnership interest by the selling partner or member. The difference between the total gain recognized by the partner or member on sale of the interest and the ordinary income (or loss) recognized under Section 751(a) is classified as a capital gain or loss.

KNOWLEDGE CHECK

3. Cloudcroft Partners has the following assets as of the end of September:

	Basis	FMV
Cash	$15,000	$15,000
Stock portfolio	50,000	100,000
Inventory	60,000	190,000
Real estate (Section 1231 property)	125,000	195,000
	$250,000	$500,000

What is the total value of the partnership's "hot" assets for purposes of Section 751(a)?

a. $0.
b. $190,000.
c. $290,000.
d. $500,000.

[7] IRC Section 751(d)(3).

Example 7-6

Alto, Ltd., a limited liability company classified as a partnership for federal income tax purposes, had the following balance sheets as of the end of September:

	Basis	FMV
Cash	$15,000	$15,000
Inventory	39,000	90,000
Capital asset 1	56,000	125,000
Capital asset 2	100,000	160,000
	$210,000	$390,000
Capital, D	$70,000	$130,000
Capital, E	70,000	130,000
Capital, F	70,000	130,000
	$210,000	$390,000

On October 1, D sold her one-third interest in Alto to G for its $130,000 fair market value. Her tax basis in her Alto investment is $70,000. Thus, she must recognize a net gain on the sale of $60,000.

However, because Alto has appreciated inventory, a portion of this gain will be classified as ordinary income, rather than capital gain. Had the company sold its inventory for its full $90,000 fair market value, D would have been allocated $17,000 ordinary income (one-third of the total).

Thus, $17,000 of D's gain on the sale will be treated as ordinary income for tax purposes. The remainder of D's gain, $43,000 ($60,000 total gain less $17,000 ordinary income) will be classified as capital gain.

In some cases, the ordinary income triggered by sale of a partnership interest may exceed the total gain recognized on the sale. In such cases, the excess will be offset with a capital loss to the seller.

Example 7-7

Blue Hound Partners had the following balance sheets as of the end of September:

	Basis	FMV
Cash	$15,000	$15,000
Accounts Receivable	0	45,000
Equipment (original cost 150,000)	45,000	105,000
Capital assets	180,000	120,000
	$240,000	$285,000
Capital, O	$80,000	$95,000
Capital, P	80,000	95,000
Capital, B	80,000	95,000
	$240,000	$285,000

Example 7-7 (continued)

On October 1, O sold his one-third interest in the partnership to an unrelated buyer for its $95,000 fair market value. O's tax basis in his partnership interest was $80,000.

Thus, he realized a net gain on the sale of $15,000. Under Section 751(a), however, he must recognize as ordinary income his share of the income that would be recognized by the partnership if it sold (collected) the accounts receivable and Section 1245 property (equipment) just prior to sale of his partnership interest.

The total gain inherent in these assets is $105,000; O's share of this would be $35,000. Thus, he will recognize $35,000 in ordinary income from sale of his interest. Because his total gain was only $15,000, he will also recognize a $(20,000) capital loss.

KNOWLEDGE CHECK

4. Oakwood Partners had the following balance sheets as of the end of September:

	Basis	FMV
Cash	$15,000	$15,000
Accounts Receivable	0	60,000
Equipment (original cost 150,000)	45,000	90,000
Capital assets	150,000	120,000
	$210,000	$285,000

The partnership has no debt. JD is a one-third partner with an equal one-third interest in each of the partnership's assets. If she sells her interest in the partnership for its $95,000 fair market value, how much ordinary income will she recognize under Section 751(a)?

    a. $20,000.
    b. $25,000.
    c. $35,000.
    d. $50,000.

STATEMENT MUST BE ATTACHED TO RETURN

For any year in which a partner or LLC member sells his or her interest in a partnership or LLC that owns Section 751 property as of the date of the sale, the partner or member must attach a statement to his or her tax return setting forth separately the following information:[8]

- The date of the sale or exchange
- The amount of ordinary income recognized under Section 751(a)
- The amount of capital gain or loss recognized on the sale

---

[8] Regulations Section 1.751-1(a)(3).

Collectibles and Unrecaptured Section 1250 Gain

Like partnership "hot" assets, the existence of collectibles and properties with unrecaptured Section 1250 gain within the partnership can convert what would otherwise be long term capital gain on the sale of a partnership interest into collectibles gain (subject to a maximum tax rate of 28 percent) or unrecaptured Section 1250 gain (subject to a maximum tax rate of 25 percent). Both of these types of income are subject to the 3.8 percent surtax on the net investment income of higher-income taxpayers.

COLLECTIBLES GAIN

When an interest in a partnership held for more than one year is sold or exchanged, the transferor must recognize collectibles gain in the amount of net gain (but not net loss) that would be allocated to that partner if the partnership sold all of its collectibles for cash at their fair market value immediately before the transfer of the interest in the partnership. In general, the term "collectibles" includes works of art, rugs or antiques, precious metals or gems, stamps or coins, and alcoholic beverages. Net collectibles gains are subject to the same tax rates as ordinary income, except that the tax rate on these gains can be no more than 28 percent. Note that the treatment as collectibles gain in this case depends only on the partner's holding period in the partnership interest, and not the partnership's holding period in the collectibles. If only a part of the partner's interest has a long-term holding period, or only part of the exchange of the partnership interest is taxable, only a ratable portion of the partner's share of the collectibles gain will be recognized by the partner. The collectibles gain will reduce the long term capital gain recognized by the partner on the sale of the interest, and might in fact create or increase a residual long term capital loss on the sale.

Example 7-8

The Artique partnership holds paintings worth $300,000, with a basis of $200,000.

Andy, a 25 percent partner in Artique, sells his partnership interest for $400,000. Its basis to him was $250,000, and his overall gain on the sale is $150,000.

Assuming that none of the gain from the hypothetical sale of the paintings would be specially allocated, and Andy's holding period in his partnership interest is entirely long term, he will recognize a collectibles gain of $25,000 (25 percent of $100,000).

The other $125,000 of gain he recognizes would be long-term capital gain. If his holding period in his partnership interest had been only 50 percent long term, he would recognize a short-term capital gain of $75,000, a collectibles gain of $12,500 (50 percent of $25,000), and a long-term capital gain of $62,500 ($75,000 – $12,500).

If his entire holding period was long term, but his basis was $390,000, his overall gain would be $10,000, his collectibles gain would again be $25,000, and his residual long-term capital loss would be $(15,000).

UNRECAPTURED SECTION 1250 GAIN

Generally speaking, unrecaptured Section 1250 gain is the depreciation that has been taken on real property, less the depreciation that would be recaptured as ordinary income if the asset were sold. However, unrecaptured Section 1250 gain cannot exceed the gain recognized on the sale of the asset, less the depreciation recaptured as ordinary income. Unrecaptured Section 1250 gains are subject to the same tax rates as ordinary income, except that the tax rate on these gains can be no more than 25 percent. As with collectibles gains, unrecaptured Section 1250 gains only come into play when a partner sells a partnership interest for which her holding period was long-term. When an interest in a partnership held for more than one year is sold or exchanged, the transferor is required to recognize the unrecaptured Section 1250 gain that would be allocated to that partner if the partnership sold all of its Section 1250 property at their fair market values immediately before the transfer of the interest in the partnership. If a portion of the holding period of the partnership interest is not long-term, or if the exchange of the interest was not fully taxable, only a pro rata portion of the partner's share of the unrecaptured 1250 gain will have to be recognized. As with collectibles gains, unrecaptured Section 1250 gains will reduce the long-term capital gain recognized by the partner on the sale of the interest, and this reduction can create or increase a residual long-term capital loss on the sale.

Installment Sales

The installment sale rules of Section 453 are applicable to the sale of an interest in a partnership or LLC unless the selling partner or member elects to recognize the entire gain in the year of sale. Under Section 453(a), as long as one payment (or more) is received in a tax year after the year of sale, the installment method can be used by the seller to report his or her gain. (The installment sale method does not apply when the seller realizes a loss on the transaction.)

Under Sections 453(b)(2) and 453(i)(2), however, the installment method may not be used to report gain from the sale

- Of personal property "of a kind which is required to be included in the inventory of the taxpayer if on hand at the close of the taxable year," nor
- To the extent of the amount which would be treated as ordinary income under Section 1245 or 1250 (or so much of Section 751 as relates to Section 1245 or 1250).

Thus, the issue facing a partner or an LLC member who sells his or her interest in the entity for cash and an installment note is how to classify the sale. The IRS's position, explained in Revenue Ruling 89-108,[9] is as follows:

> "Under Section 453 of the Code, the income from the sale of a partnership interest may not be reported under the installment method to the extent it represents income attributable to the partnership's ... inventory ... which would not be eligible for the installment sale treatment if sold directly."

In addition, there is authority to the effect that a sale of a partnership interest is not eligible for installment sale treatment to the extent of the selling partner's share of unrealized receivables from services rendered.[10] As indicated previously, sale of a partnership interest would not be eligible for installment sale treatment to the extent of the selling partner's share of Section 1245 and Section 1250 recapture.[11]

 Example 7-9

Johnson is a 20 percent partner in Wildcat Drillers, LP. The partnership has total assets with a tax basis of $600,000 and a fair market value of $1,000,000.

Included in this total is depreciable equipment with a tax basis of $250,000 and a fair market value of $300,000. The difference between the basis and value of this equipment is entirely attributable to excess depreciation deductions claimed in prior years. The partnership has no other inventory or unrealized receivables and has no debt.

Assume that Johnson sells his 20 percent interest in the partnership for its $200,000 value, receiving a cash payment of $50,000 plus a five-year $150,000 note receivable.

---

[9] 1989-2 CB 100 (Jan. 01, 1989).

[10] CCA 200722027, *Lori M. Mingo, et vir. v. Commissioner*, TC Memo 2013-149.

[11] Section 453(i)(2).

Example 7-9 (continued)

Further, assume that Johnson's tax basis in the interest is $120,000 (equal to his share of the partnership's inside basis in its assets).

He will recognize a total gain of $80,000, of which $10,000 (his share of the partnership's Section 1245 recapture on the equipment) will be characterized as ordinary income and will be recognized in the year of sale.

The $70,000 remainder will be characterized as long-term capital gain. Under the installment method, he will recognize 25 percent ($50,000/$200,000) of the remaining $70,000 of long-term capital gain in the year of sale. The remaining 75 percent of his taxable gain will be reported over the next five years as he receives payments on the note receivable.

Thus, in the year of sale, he will recognize $10,000 ordinary income and $17,500 ($70,000/$200,000 = 35 percent Gross Profit percent × $50,000 cash received) capital gain. The remainder of his capital gain can be reported on the installment method.

KNOWLEDGE CHECK

5. White Star, Ltd. is a limited liability company that has elected to be treated as a partnership for federal income tax purposes. Edward has a 20 percent interest in White Star profits, losses, and capital. The company had the following assets (and no liabilities) as of the end of December:

	Basis	FMV
Cash	$25,000	$25,000
Accounts Receivable	0	60,000
Equipment (original cost 150,000)	45,000	95,000
Capital assets	200,000	300,000
	$270,000	$480,000

Edward sold his entire 20 percent interest in the company to an unrelated buyer for $16,000 cash, and a five-year, 10 percent note in the amount of $80,000. Edward recognized a $60,000 taxable gain on the sale, which he plans to report under the installment method. What portion of Edward's gain is not eligible to be reported using the installment method and, therefore, must be recognized in the year of sale?

 a. $10,000.
 b. $12,000.
 c. $22,000.
 d. $60,000.

Net Investment Income Tax

Code Section 1411 imposes a net investment income tax equal to 3.8 percent of a taxpayer's net investment income. Determining whether this tax applies to the net gain recognized by a partner or LLC member upon the sale of an interest in a partnership or LLC depends on both the nature of the partner's or member's investment in the partnership or LLC and upon the type of activity(ies) conducted by the partnership or LLC. In general, the net investment income tax applies to net gain from the sale of an interest in a passive activity, regardless of the character of the gain ordinary or capital). In contrast, the net gain (or loss) recognized on the sale of an interest in a partnership or LLC in which the partner or member materially participated, or which was otherwise not classified as a passive activity under Section 469, will generally not be subject to the net investment income tax, even if all or part of the gain is classified as capital.[12] Of course, to the extent that the gain is attributable to the appreciation of financial instruments or commodities held by the partnership or LLC, then such portion of the gain will be subject to the net investment income tax.[13]

---

[12] Code Section 1411(c)(1)(A)(iii).
[13] Code Section 1411(c)(4)(A).

Sale of an Active (Non-passive) Interest in a Partnership or LLC

Under Code Section 1411, the net investment income tax applies to portfolio income, other gross income from a trade or business which constitutes a passive activity to the taxpayer, and net gain from the sale of assets used in a passive activity or in the activity of selling financial instruments and/or commodities. If a taxpayer sells an interest in a partnership or LLC which is not classified as a passive activity with respect to the taxpayer, only that portion of the net gain from the sale that is attributable to Section 1411 property held by the partnership will be subject to the net investment income tax.

Section 1411 property is property held by the partnership or LLC that, if sold by the entity, would result in net gain or loss subject to the net investment income tax.[14] Such property includes the following:

- Portfolio assets, including investments in commodities, held by the partnership
- Collectibles held by the partnership
- Assets owned by the partnership that are used in a trade or business that is passive with respect to the taxpayer

Example 7-10

A, a 50 percent general partner in ABC Partnership, sold her partnership interest to D, an unrelated buyer, for $460,000 cash. A's tax basis in her partnership interest was $215,000. The partnership owned the following assets at the date of the sale:

	Basis	FMV
Cash	$30,000	$30,000
Accounts receivable	0	90,000
Investment in collectibles	80,000	120,000
Section 1245 property (original cost $300,000)	120,000	180,000
Section 1231 property	200,000	500,000
Total Assets	$430,000	$920,000

---

[14] Proposed Regs. Section 1.1411-7(a)(2)(iv).

Example 7-10 (continued)

ABC partnership is engaged in a trade or business activity, and A's investment in the partnership is not a passive investment under Section 469. A will recognize $245,000 gain on the sale of her interest in the partnership. Assume that A is subject to a marginal income tax rate of 35 percent. The gain on sale of her partnership interest will be taxed as follows:

	Ordinary Income	Collectibles Gain	Capital Gain
Recognized gain	$45,000	$20,000	$180,000
Tax rate	35%	28%	20%
Section 1411 tax	0	3.8%	0
Combined tax rate	35%	31.8%	20%
Tax	$15,750	$6,360	$36,000

Because the partnership interest is not a passive activity with respect to A, only that portion of A's gain that is attributable to the partnership's Section 1411 property is subject to the net investment income tax. The investment in collectibles is the only Section 1411 property owned by the partnership. Thus, although the majority of A's gain is capital in nature, only $20,000 of the gain will be subject to the Section 1411 tax. A will owe an additional $58,110 in income taxes as a result of the sale (assuming no offsetting losses from other transactions).

Sale of a Passive Interest in a Partnership or LLC

Where the partner's interest in a partnership is classified as a passive activity under Code Section 469, the net gain recognized by such a partner from the sale of the partnership interest will be subject to the net investment income tax. This is true regardless of the character of the partner's gain on sale of the interest. Under Code Section. 1411(c)(1)(A)(iii), net investment income includes gain from the sale of property not held or used in an active (not passive) trade or business.

Example 7-11

Assume the same facts as in example 7-10, except that A was a 50 percent limited partner in ABC Partnership. Because A is a limited partner, the partnership investment is a passive activity with respect to A, and her entire gain will be subject to the net investment income tax. Assuming that A is subject to a marginal income tax rate of 35 percent, her gain from sale of her partnership interest will be taxed as follows:

	Ordinary Income	Collectibles Gain	Capital Gain
Recognized gain	$45,000	$20,000	$180,000
Tax rate	35%	28%	20%
Section 1411 tax	3.8%	3.8%	3.8%
Combined tax rate	38.8%	31.8%	23.8%
Tax	$17,460	$6,360	$42,840

Because the partnership interest is a passive activity with respect to A, the entire net gain recognized on sale of the interest will be subject to the investment income tax, even that portion of the gain that is classified as ordinary income under Section 751(a). A will owe an additional $66,660 in income taxes as a result of the sale (assuming no offsetting losses from other transactions).

Potential for Termination of the Partnership

TECHNICAL TERMINATIONS UNDER SECTION 708

Section 708(b)(1)(B) of the Internal Revenue Code triggers a deemed termination of a partnership or an LLC if "within a 12-month period there is a sale or exchange of 50 percent or more of the total interest in partnership capital and profits." The regulations under Section 708 make it clear that a so-called "technical termination" does not require that the prohibited transfer of 50 percent or more of the interests in the partnership occur in a single sale or exchange transaction. A series of unrelated sales or exchanges which, together, result in the transfer of at least a 50 percent interest in the partnership or LLC within a 12-month period will trigger a technical termination (strictly for tax purposes).

CONSEQUENCES

Treasury Regulations Section 1.708-1 provides that upon a technical termination of the partnership,

- The old partnership is deemed to have contributed all of its assets and liabilities to a new partnership in exchange for an interest in the new partnership; and
- The old partnership is then deemed to have liquidated, distributing its interests in the new partnership to the purchasing partner and the other remaining partners in proportion to their interests in the old partnership.

The regulations further provide that the taxable year of the old partnership closes on the date of the sale or exchange which triggered the technical termination.

Administrative Costs

What this means for the partnership and its remaining partners depends on the characteristics of the old partnership prior to the technical termination. In general, the primary costs are administrative, resulting in the following potential costs:

- The partnership must file two tax returns for the year of the termination – a final short-year return for the old partnership, and an "initial" short-year return for the new partnership. (The partnership's federal identification number does not change.)
- The old partnership's taxable year, method of accounting, and other elections do not carry over to the new partnership, which must make new elections of its own.
- Excess deduction carryovers under Section 704(d) may expire because the remaining partners will not be able to generate tax basis in their interests in the old partnership, from which such deductions or losses were generated.[15]

---

[15] See for example *Sennett v. Commissioner*, 80 TC 825 (aff d CA-9, 85-1 USTC ¶9153), in which a taxpayer was not allowed to deduct Section 704(d) carryforwards upon his withdrawal from the partnership even though he made payments to the partnership essentially restoring his deficit capital balances to zero. Such payments would presumably have given him additional basis in his partnership interest, but he was no longer a partner.

Although losses previously disallowed under Section 704(d) may not survive the technical termination, carryforwards under Sections 465 and 469 (at-risk and passive activity loss carryforwards) will survive, as they are specific to the underlying activity conducted by the partnership rather than to the partnership itself.

Tax Basis and Holding Period of Assets

Other characteristics of the old partnership carry over to the new partnership. For example, as noted previously, the new partnership retains the employer identification number of the old partnership. Moreover, under Section 721, the new partnership's tax basis in all property deemed contributed to it by the old partnership retains the same tax basis as such property had in the hands of the old partnership. Under Section 722, the holding period of all assets also remains the same as in the hands of the old partnership.

It is important to note that if the old partnership had a Section 754 election in effect (or chooses to make one), this election will remain in effect for the purpose of allowing the purchasing partner in the termination transaction to claim a basis adjustment under Section 743(b). However, the old partnership's Section 754 election will not apply to subsequent taxable years of the new partnership (other than the initial taxable year of such partnership, and only with respect to the purchasing partner who entered the partnership in the transaction that resulted in the technical termination).

 Example 7-12

On September 1, A, a 50 percent partner in ABC Partnership, sold her partnership interest to D, an unrelated buyer.

The sale terminated ABC Partnership under Section 708(b)(1)(B). ABC, a calendar-year partnership, had a Section 754 election in effect at the date of the sale. ABC will file its final tax return reporting its income for the period January 1 – September 1.

New partnership BCD will take ABC's tax basis in its assets, stepped-up (or down) to reflect the Section 743(b) adjustment for D's benefit.

Assume that BCD does not make a Section 754 election on either its initial short-year return for the period beginning September1 or on a subsequent return. In the year following D's purchase of A's interest in the old ABC partnership, C decides to sell her 25 percent interest in BCD to partner B. Unless BCD makes an election under Section 754 in the year of C's sale, B will not be entitled to a basis adjustment under Section 743(b) because ABC's old Section 754 election does not carry over to new partnership BCD.

In many cases, partners may choose to have the old partnership make a Section 754 election on its final return, rather than having the new partnership make the election with its initial return. This way, the incoming partner receives the benefits of basis adjustments under Section 743(b) without restricting the flexibility of the new partnership in subsequent transactions.

Regulations Section 1.704-4(a)(4)(ii) provide that Section 704(c) built-in gains and losses of the old partnership carry over to the new partnership. Built-in gains will not be increased as a result of the termination of the old partnership and formation of the new one, even if the property of the old partnership has increased in value. That is, the contribution of property by the old partnership to the new one does not create built-in gain or loss under the provisions of Sections 704(c) or 737. Only Section 704(c) gains or losses inherent in the old partnership's balance sheet as of the date of the termination carry over to the new partnership. The incoming partner, however, does step into the shoes of the selling partner with respect to Section 704(c). Thus, in many cases, it may be especially important that the incoming partner be protected by having either the old or new partnership make an election under Section 754.

Example 7-13

Wilson Properties, a calendar-year general partnership, has the following balance sheets at August 30:

	Tax Basis	Book Value
Cash	$15,000	$15,000
Property 1	75,000	225,000
Property 2	100,000	100,000
	$190,000	340,000
Capital, J	$20,000	$170,000
Capital, D	85,000	85,000
Capital, R	85,000	85,000
	$190,000	$340,000

Property 1 was contributed by partner J and the $150,000 built-in gain inherent in that property will be allocable to partner J under Section 704(c) when realized. On August 30, property 1 was valued at $300,000, and property 2 was valued at $200,000. J, a 50 percent partner, sold her interest in the partnership to Q for $257,500 cash.

The sale of J's interest to Q will trigger a technical termination of Wilson Properties. Old Wilson Properties will be deemed to have transferred all its assets to new Wilson Properties in exchange for a partnership interest therein. Old Wilson Properties then terminates, distributing the interests in new Wilson Properties to partners Q, D and R. The aggregate tax basis of new Wilson Properties' assets remains $190,000, the same as before the technical termination. Although property 1 has appreciated by another $75,000 over its Section 704(b) book value, the Section 704(c) gain inherent in this property remains $150,000 and will be allocated to new partner Q when realized by the partnership (whether through sale, depreciation, and so forth). Property 2 has also appreciated in value relative to its Section 704(b) book value; however, none of this appreciation is subject to Section 704(c). The deemed contribution of this property by old Wilson Properties to new Wilson Properties is not treated as a contribution of appreciated property to a partnership for purposes of Section 704(c).

KNOWLEDGE CHECK

6. Mountain West is a partnership in the real estate development business. The company, which uses the calendar-year, had the following assets (and no liabilities) as of the end of June when Linda sold her 30 percent interest in partnership capital and profits.

	Basis	FMV
Cash	$25,000	$25,000
Unimproved Realty	150,000	250,000
Improved Realty (cost 450,000)	300,000	600,000
Other Assets	125,000	325,000
	$600,000	$1,200,000

On October 31, another partner, Carol, sold her 25 percent interest in capital and profits. Carol was not the partner who purchased Linda's interest. Which of the following statements is true?

   a. The partnership will be deemed to terminate upon sale of Carol's interest, and the $600,000 built-in gain inherent in its balance sheet will be recognized on the old partnership's last tax return as if all its assets had been sold for fair market value.

   b. The partnership will be deemed to terminate upon sale of Carol's interest, and the old partnership will be required to file a partnership return for the period of January 1 – October 31.

   c. The partnership will be deemed to terminate as of October 31, and any "hot" assets held by the partnership will be deemed to have been sold as of that date.

   d. The partnership will recognize built-in gain to the extent of the sale of Linda's 30 percent interest at the time her interest was sold.

7. Which of the following characteristics does not transfer from the old partnership to the new one following a technical termination under Section 708(b)(1)(B)?

   a. The old partnership's federal identification number.
   b. Tax elections made by the old partnership.
   c. Built-in gains inherent in partnership assets subject to Section 704(c).
   d. The book and tax capital accounts of the continuing partners.

WHAT CONSTITUTES A SALE UNDER SECTION 708?

It is important to note that a technical termination is triggered whenever at least 50 percent of the aggregate interests in profits and capital are transferred within any 12-month period. The sales or exchanges do not have to occur within a single taxable year to trigger these provisions. They do, however, have to represent different interests in the partnership. For example, the regulations provide that if a partner A sells a 30 percent interest in capital and profits to new partner F, and new partner F subsequently sells that same 30 percent interest to partner M, the two sales taken together constitute the sale of a 30 percent interest in partnership capital and profits (rather than 60 percent).

KNOWLEDGE CHECK

8. Mabel sold a 30 percent interest in the capital and profits of a partnership to Burl on November 1, 2006. On February 1, 2007, Burl sold this interest to Mario. Assume no other transfers of an interest in this partnership. Which of the following statements is true?

    a. Burl's sale of the interest will trigger a technical termination of the partnership under Section 708(b)(1)(B).

    b. If Burl had sold the interest to Mario before year-end, it would have triggered a technical termination of the partnership, but because the two transactions occurred in separate taxable years, the provisions of Section 708(b)(1)(B) are not triggered.

    c. Burl's sale of the interest to Mario will trigger a technical termination unless Mario is related to either Burl or Mabel.

    d. The sale of the same interest twice only counts as one transfer and does not trigger a technical termination.

Regulations Section 1.708-1(b)(2) clarifies that a sale or exchange does not have to occur outside the existing group of partners to trigger a termination – sale to another partner is treated as a sale or exchange. In contrast, liquidation of a partner's interest in exchange for a distribution of cash or property is not treated as a sale or exchange, nor is admission of a new partner to the partnership in exchange for a contribution of property under Section 721.

Sale of an interest in an upper-tier partnership (a partnership owning an interest in another partnership) is not treated as a disposition of an interest in the profits and capital of a lower-tier partnership (a partnership an interest in which is owned by the upper-tier partnership) unless such sale terminates the upper-tier partnership. If the upper tier partnership is terminated as a result of the sale or exchange of an interest therein, the upper-tier partnership is treated as having sold or exchanged its entire interest in the capital and profits of the lower-tier partnership. Thus, for example, sale of a 50 percent interest in a partnership that holds a 30 percent interest in another partnership will result in the deemed sale or exchange of a 30 percent interest in the lower-tier partnership (as the upper-tier partnership transfers its interest in the lower-tier partnership to a new upper-tier partnership).

Although the regulations explicitly provide that the transfer of a partnership interest by gift, bequest, or inheritance is not treated as a sale or exchange of that interest, this result may be partially overridden if the partnership holds debt. Assumption by the donee of the donor's share of partnership debt in connection with a gift may be recharacterized as a partial sale of the donated interest.[16] Other transactions that may constitute a sale include

- Taxable and tax-free exchanges of a partnership interest,
- Contribution of a partnership interest to a corporation[17] or to another partnership,[18] and
- Distribution of a partnership interest from a corporation or from another partnership.[19]

---

[16] See, for example, Rev. Rul. 93-80, 1993-2 CB 239, in which abandonment of an interest in a partnership with outstanding indebtedness is partially recharacterized a portion of that partnership interest as a sale.

[17] See Rev. Rul. 81-38, 1981-1 CB 386.

[18] See Ltr. Rul. 8929003, 8229034.

[19] Section 761(e).

Knowledge Check

9. Pete exchanged his 50 percent interest (capital and profits) in Roth Partners for a 30 percent interest in Edelburgh Partnership. Which of the following statements is true?

    a. If the two partnerships are engaged in the same type of business, the exchange may be treated as a nontaxable Section 1031 exchange.

    b. The exchange will terminate Roth Partners under Section 708(b)(1)(B).

    c. The exchange will terminate Edelburgh Partnership under Section 708(b)(1)(B).

    d. Roth Partners will not terminate because a termination of 50 percent or less of a partnership's interest will not cause a technical termination of the partnership.

Partnership Agreement: Restrictions on Sale of Interest

Because of the administrative costs and other potential consequences to the partners, it is not uncommon for a partnership or LLC agreement to include restrictions on the sale or transfer of interests by a partner or member. An example of such a provision is as follows:

"Notwithstanding any other provision of this Agreement, no Limited Partner may assign or otherwise transfer all or any part of its interest in the Partnership, and no attempted or purported assignment or transfer of such interest shall be effective, unless after giving effect thereto, the aggregate of all the assignments or transfers by the Partners of interests in the Partnership within the 12 month period ending on the proposed date of such assignment or transfer would not equal or exceed 50 percent of the total interests of the Partners in the capital or profits of the Partnership, and such assignment or transfer would not otherwise terminate the Partnership for the purposes of Section 708 of the Code."

Note that a sale that violates such an anti-assignment provision in the partnership agreement may still be counted as a sale for purposes of Section 708(b)(1)(B) unless the partnership can demonstrate that the sale was nullified as a result of the contractual prohibition imposed by the partnership agreement.

Consequences to the Purchaser

Under Section 742, the buyer will take a tax basis in the purchased interest equal to the amount paid for it. However, because the partnership or LLC is not directly involved in the transaction, in the absence of a Section 754 election, the buyer's capital balance on the partnership's books and records will not reflect the amount he or she paid for the interest. Instead, the capital balance of the seller will transfer over to the buyer. This creates the potential that the seller's share of the appreciation or depreciation inherent in partnership or LLC assets prior to the sale will be taxed to the buyer in a subsequent year, even though the buyer presumably paid fair market value for his or her share of these assets.

 Example 7-14

Q is a one-third owner of RQJ Ltd., a limited liability company taxed as a partnership for federal income tax purposes.

Her capital balance in RQJ is $165,000, and her share of the LLC's liabilities is $135,000. Her tax basis in her LLC interest is $300,000, and that is also her share of the basis of the partnership assets.

In October, she sold this interest to D for $250,000 cash. D assumed responsibility for her share of the LLC's debts. Thus, the total selling price for the LLC interest is $385,000.

Assuming the LLC has no "hot" assets, Q will recognize an $85,000 capital gain on the sale. D will take a tax basis of $385,000 in the newly acquired interest. Her capital account in the LLC's books and records, however, will remain $165,000.

Likewise, unless the LLC has a Section 754 election in effect (or chooses to make one), D's share of RQJ's inside basis will be $300,000, carried over from Q.

KNOWLEDGE CHECK

10. Jenkins Partnership had the following assets just prior to a technical termination triggered by sale of a 75 percent interest in partnership capital and profits:

	Basis	FMV
Cash	$25,000	$25,000
Unimproved Realty	150,000	250,000
Improved Realty (cost $450,000)	300,000	600,000
Other Assets	125,000	325,000
	$600,000	$1,200,000

    What will be the new Jenkins Partnership's tax basis in its assets?

    a. $600,000.

    b. $900,000.

    c. $1,200,000.

    d. $150,000.

As discussed in chapter 6, the Code allows a partnership or LLC to alleviate the potential tax burden subsequently borne by the buyer in such situations. If the partnership has a Section 754 election in effect, or chooses to make one, the incoming partner will be entitled to adjust his or her share of the basis of partnership assets to reflect the price paid for them.

KNOWLEDGE CHECK

11. Assume the same facts as the previous question. Further assume that Jenkins Partnership had no Section 704(c) assets prior to the termination. Which of the following statements is true?

    a. The technical termination will cause appreciated assets to be treated as Section 704(c) assets following their transfer to the new Jenkins Partnership.

    b. The technical termination will not cause appreciated assets to be treated as Section 704(c) assets following their transfer to the new Jenkins Partnership unless those assets were already subject to the provisions of Section 704(c).

    c. If any of the assets of the old Jenkins partnership constituted Section 704(c) property, they will be revalued for purposes of applying Section 704(c) to the new Jenkins Partnership.

    d. None of the previous statements is true.

TAX GLOSSARY

401(k) Plan – A qualified retirement plan to which contributions from salary are made from pre-tax dollars.

Accelerated Depreciation – Computation of depreciation to provide greater deductions in earlier years of equipment and other business or investment property.

Accounting Method – Rules applied in determining when and how to report income and expenses on tax returns.

Accrual Method – Method of accounting that reports income when it is earned, disregarding when it may be received, and expense when incurred, disregarding when it is actually paid.

Acquisition Debt – Mortgage taken to buy, hold, or substantially improve main or second home that serves as security.

Active Participation – Rental real estate activity involving property management at a level that permits deduction of losses.

Adjusted Basis – Basis in property increased by some expenses (for example, by capital improvements) or decreased by some tax benefit (for example, by depreciation).

Adjusted Gross Income (AGI) – Gross income minus above-the-line deductions (such as deductions other than itemized deductions, the standard deduction, and personal and dependency exemptions).

Alimony – Payments for the support or maintenance of one's spouse pursuant to a judicial decree or written agreement related to divorce or separation.

Alternative Minimum Tax (AMT) – System comparing the tax results with and without the benefit of tax preference items for the purpose of preventing tax avoidance.

Amortization – Write-off of an intangible asset's cost over a number of years.

Applicable Federal Rate (AFR) – An interest rate determined by reference to the average market yield on U.S. government obligations. Used in Sec. 7872 to determine the treatment of loans with below-market interest rates.

At-Risk Rules – Limits on tax losses to business activities in which an individual taxpayer has an economic stake.

Backup Withholding – Withholding for federal taxes on certain types of income (such as interest or dividend payments) by a payor that has not received required taxpayer identification number (TIN) information.

Bad Debt – Uncollectible debt deductible as an ordinary loss if associated with a business and otherwise deductible as short-term capital loss.

Basis – Amount determined by a taxpayer's investment in property for purposes of determining gain or loss on the sale of property or in computing depreciation.

Cafeteria Plan – Written plan allowing employees to choose among two or more benefits (consisting of cash and qualified benefits) and to pay for the benefits with pretax dollars. Must conform to Sec. 125 requirements.

Capital Asset – Investments (such as stocks, bonds, and mutual funds) and personal property (such as home).

Capital Gain/ Loss – Profit (net of losses) on the sale or exchange of a capital asset or Sec. 1231 property, subject to favorable tax rates, and loss on such sales or exchanges (net of gains) deductible against $3,000 of ordinary income.

Capitalization – Addition of cost or expense to the basis of property.

Carryovers (Carryforwards) and Carrybacks – Tax deductions and credits not fully used in one year are chargeable against prior or future tax years to reduce taxable income or taxes payable.

Conservation Reserve Program (CRP) – A voluntary program for soil, water, and wildlife conservation, wetland establishment and restoration and reforestation, administered by the U.S. Department of Agriculture.

Credit – Amount subtracted from income tax liability.

Deduction – Expense subtracted in computing adjusted gross income.

Defined Benefit Plan – Qualified retirement plan basing annual contributions on targeted benefit amounts.

Defined Contribution Plan – Qualified retirement plan with annual contributions based on a percentage of compensation.

Depletion – Deduction for the extent a natural resource is used.

Depreciation – Proportionate deduction based on the cost of business or investment property with a useful life (or recovery period) greater than one year.

Earned Income – Wages, bonuses, vacation pay, and other remuneration, including self-employment income, for services rendered.

Earned Income Credit – Refundable credit available to low-income individuals.

Employee Stock Ownership Plan (ESOP) – Defined contribution plan that is a stock bonus plan or a combined stock bonus and money purchase plan designed to invest primarily in qualifying employer securities.

Estimated Tax – Quarterly payments of income tax liability by individuals, corporations, trusts, and estates.

Exemption – A deduction against net income based on taxpayer status (such as single, head of household, married filing jointly or separately, trusts, and estates).

Fair Market Value – The price that would be agreed upon by a willing seller and willing buyer, established by markets for publicly-traded stocks, or determined by appraisal.

Fiscal Year – A 12-month taxable period ending on any date other than December 31.

Foreign Tax – Income tax paid to a foreign country and deductible or creditable, at the taxpayer's election, against U.S. income tax.

Gift – Transfer of money or property without expectation of anything in return, and excludable from income by the recipient. A gift may still be affected by the unified estate and gift transfer tax applicable to the gift's maker.

Goodwill – A business asset, intangible in nature, adding a value beyond the business's tangible assets.

Gross Income – Income from any and all sources, after any exclusions and before any deductions are taken into consideration.

Half-Year Convention – A depreciation rule assuming property other than real estate is placed in service in the middle of the tax year.

Head-of-Household – An unmarried individual who provides and maintains a household for a qualifying dependent and therefore is subject to distinct tax rates.

Health Savings Account (HSA) – A trust operated exclusively for purposes of paying qualified medical expenses of the account beneficiary and thus providing for deductible contributions, tax-deferred earnings, and exclusion of tax on any monies withdrawn for medical purposes.

Holding Period – The period of time a taxpayer holds onto property, therefore affecting tax treatment on its disposition.

Imputed Interest – Income deemed attributable to deferred-payment transfers, such as below-market loans, for which no interest or unrealistically low interest is charged.

Incentive Stock Option (ISO) – An option to purchase stock in connection with an individual's employment, which defers tax liability until all of the stock acquired by means of the option is sold or exchanged.

Income in Respect of a Decedent (IRD) – Income earned by a person, but not paid until after his or her death.

Independent Contractor – A self-employed individual whose work method or time is not controlled by an employer.

Indexing – Adjustments in deductions, credits, exemptions and exclusions, plan contributions, AGI limits, and so on, to reflect annual inflation figures.

Individual Retirement Account (IRA) – Tax-exempt trust created or organized in the U.S. for the exclusive benefit of an individual or the individual's beneficiaries.

Information Returns– Statements of income and other items recognizable for tax purposes provided to the IRS and the taxpayer. Form W-2 and forms in the 1099 series, as well as Schedules K-1, are the prominent examples.

Installment Method– Tax accounting method for reporting gain on a sale over the period of tax years during which payments are made, such as, over the payment period specified in an installment sale agreement.

Intangible Property– Items such as patents, copyrights, and goodwill.

Inventory – Goods held for sale to customers, including materials used in the production of those goods.

Involuntary Conversion – A forced disposition (for example, casualty, theft, condemnation) for which deferral of gain may be available.

Jeopardy – For tax purposes, a determination that payment of a tax deficiency may be assessed immediately as the most viable means of ensuring its payment.

Keogh Plan – A qualified retirement plan available to self-employed persons.

Key Employee – Officers, employees, and officers defined by the Internal Revenue Code for purposes of determining whether a plan is "top heavy."

Kiddie Tax – Application of parents' maximum tax rate to unearned income of their child under age 19. Full-time students under 24 are also subject to the kiddie tax.

Lien – A charge upon property after a tax assessment has been made and until tax liability is satisfied.

Like-Kind Exchange – Tax-free exchange of business or investment property for property that is similar or related in service or use.

Listed Property – Items subject to special restrictions on depreciation (for example, cars, computers, cell phones).

Lump-Sum Distribution – Distribution of an individual's entire interest in a qualified retirement plan within one tax year.

Marginal Tax Rate – The highest tax bracket applicable to an individual's income.

Material Participation – The measurement of an individual's involvement in business operations for purposes of the passive activity loss rules.

Mid-month Convention – Assumption, for purposes of computing depreciation, that all real property is placed in service in the middle of the month.

Mid-quarter Convention – Assumption, for purposes of computing depreciation, that all property other than real property is placed in service in the middle of the quarter, when the basis of property placed in service in the final quarter exceeds a statutory percentage of the basis of all property placed in service during the year.

Minimum Distribution – A retirement plan distribution, based on life expectancies, that an individual must take after age 70 ½ in order to avoid tax penalties.

Minimum Funding Requirements – Associated with defined benefit plans and certain other plans, such as money purchase plans, assuring the plan has enough assets to satisfy its current and anticipated liabilities.

Miscellaneous Itemized Deduction – Deductions for certain expenses (for example, unreimbursed employee expenses) limited to only the amount by which they exceed 2% of adjusted gross income.

Money Purchase Plan – Defined contribution plan in which the contributions by the employer are mandatory and established other than by reference to the employer's profits.

Net Operating Loss (NOL) – A business or casualty loss for which amounts exceeding the allowable deduction in the current tax year may be carried back two years to reduce previous tax liability and forward 20 years to cover any remaining unused loss deduction.

Nonresident Alien – An individual who is neither a citizen nor a resident of the United States. Nonresidents are taxed on U.S. source income.

Original Issue Discount (OID) – The excess of face value over issue price set by a purchase agreement.

Passive Activity Loss (PAL) – Losses allowable only to the extent of income derived each year (such as by means of carryover) from rental property or business activities in which the taxpayer does not materially participate.

Passive Foreign Investment Company (PFIC) – A foreign based corporation subject to strict tax rules which covers the treatment of investments in Sections 1291 through 1297.

Pass-Through Entities – Partnerships, LLCs, LLPs, S corporations, and trusts and estates whose income or loss is reported by the partner, member, shareholder, or beneficiary.

Personal Holding Company (PHC) – A corporation, usually closely-held, that exists to hold investments such as stocks, bonds, or personal service contracts and to time distributions of income in a manner that limits the owner(s) tax liability.

Qualified Subchapter S Trust (QSST) – A trust that qualifies specific requirements for eligibility as an S corporation shareholder.

Real Estate Investment Trust (REIT) – A form of investment in which a trust holds real estate or mortgages and distributes income, in whole or in part, to the beneficiaries (such as investors).

Real Estate Mortgage Investment Conduit (REMIC) – Treated as a partnership, investors purchase interests in this entity which holds a fixed pool of mortgages.

Realized Gain or Loss – The difference between property's basis and the amount received upon its sale or exchange.

Recapture – The amount of a prior deduction or credit recognized as income or affecting its characterization (capital gain vs. ordinary income) when the property giving rise to the deduction or credit is disposed of.

Recognized Gain or Loss – The amount of realized gain or loss that must be included in taxable income.

Regulated Investment Company (RIC) – A corporation serving as a mutual fund that acts as investment agents for shareholders and customarily dealing in government and corporate securities.

Reorganization – Restructuring of corporations under specific Internal Revenue Code rules so as to result in nonrecognition of gain.

Resident Alien – An individual who is a permanent resident, has substantial presence, or, under specific election rules is taxed as a U.S. citizen.

Roth IRA – Form of individual retirement account that produces, subject to holding period requirements, nontaxable earnings.

S Corporation – A corporation that, upon satisfying requirements concerning its ownership, may elect to act as a pass-through entity.

Saver's Credit – Term commonly used to describe Sec. 25B credit for qualified contributions to a retirement plan or via elective deferrals.

Sec. 1231 Property – Depreciable business property eligible for capital gains treatment.

Sec. 1244 Stock – Closely held stock whose sale may produce an ordinary, rather than capital, loss (subject to caps).

Split-Dollar Life Insurance – Arrangement between an employer and employee under which the life insurance policy benefits are contractually split, and the costs (premiums) are also split.

Statutory Employee – An insurance agent or other specified worker who is subject to social security taxes on wages but eligible to claim deductions available to the self-employed.

Stock Bonus Plan – A plan established and maintained to provide benefits similar to those of a profit-sharing plan, except the benefits must be distributable in stock of the employer company.

Tax Preference Items – Tax benefits deemed includable for purposes of the alternative minimum tax.

Tax Shelter – A tax-favored investment, typically in the form of a partnership or joint venture, that is subject to scrutiny as tax-avoidance device.

Tentative Tax – Income tax liability before taking into account certain credits, and AMT liability over the regular tax liability.

Transportation Expense – The cost of transportation from one point to another.

Travel Expense – Transportation, meals, and lodging costs incurred away from home and for trade or business purposes.

Unearned Income – Income from investments (such as interest, dividends, and capital gains).

Uniform Capitalization Rules (UNICAP) – Rules requiring capitalization of property used in a business or income-producing activity (such as items used in producing inventory) and to certain property acquired for resale.

Unrelated Business Income (UBIT) – Exempt organization income produced by activities beyond the organzation's exempt purposes and therefore taxable.

Wash Sale – Sale of securities preceded or followed within 30 days by a purchase of substantially identical securities. Recognition of any loss on the sale is disallowed.

INDEX

ADVANCED TAX STRATEGIES FOR LLCS AND PARTNERSHIPS

BY LARRY TUNNELL, PH.D., CPA;
ROBERT RICKETTS, PH.D., CPA

Solutions

DTT GS-0417-0A

The AICPA offers a free, daily, e-mailed newsletter covering the day's top business and financial articles as well as video content, research and analysis concerning CPAs and those who work with the accounting profession. Visit the CPA Letter Daily news box on the www.aicpa.org home page to sign up. You can opt out at any time, and only the AICPA can use your e-mail address or personal information.

Have a technical accounting or auditing question? So did 23,000 other professionals who contacted the AICPA's accounting and auditing Technical Hotline last year. The objectives of the hotline are to enhance members' knowledge and application of professional judgment by providing free, prompt, high-quality technical assistance by phone concerning issues related to: accounting principles and financial reporting; auditing, attestation, compilation and review standards. The team extends this technical assistance to representatives of governmental units. The hotline can be reached at 1-877-242-7212.

SOLUTIONS

CHAPTER 1

Solutions to Knowledge Check Questions

1.

    a. Correct. J's capital account is reduced by her allocable share of partnership losses and expenses, whether or not she can deduct them.

    b. Incorrect. Even though J cannot deduct her share of the partnership's rental real estate loss, it still reduces her capital balance

    c. Incorrect. The ($800) share of partnership nondeductible expenses must be subtracted from J's capital balance.

    d. Incorrect. J's capital account is reduced by her allocable share of charitable contributions and nondeductible expenses.

2.

    a. Incorrect. The adjustment to L's capital account is based on the value of the property distributed, rather than on the pre-distribution balance in that account.

    b. Correct. L's capital account must be reduced by the fair market value of the property distributed to her.

    c. Incorrect. This is the tax basis of the distributed property.

    d. Incorrect. This is the book gain that is split 50/50 and added to capital accounts. In a nonliquidating distribution, L's capital account must be reduced by the fair market value of the property distributed to her.

3.

    a. Incorrect. Claire's capital account must be adjusted to reflect her share of partnership income and distributions received since inception of the partnership.

    b. Correct. Under Section 704(b), each partner is entitled to receive the amount in his or her book capital account upon liquidation of the partnership or of their interest therein.

    c. Incorrect. This figure omits Claire's original contribution to partnership capital.

    d. Incorrect. Claire will be entitled to receive the balance in her book capital account upon liquidation of the partnership. Her book capital account must be reduced by the $30,000 of distributions made to Claire.

4.

   a.   Incorrect. Wendy's share of the partnership loss does not reduce the balance in her capital account to zero.

   b.   Incorrect. Wendy's share of the partnership's loss is only $90,000 (25 percent).

   c.   Correct. Wendy's share of the partnership's losses is only $90,000, reducing her capital account to $110,000.

   d.   Incorrect. Wendy will be entitled to receive the balance in her book capital account upon liquidation of the partnership. Her book capital account will be reduced by $90,000, her share of the losses.

5.

   a.   Incorrect. As a limited partner, the balance in K's capital account cannot be reduced below zero. Thus, the total allocation of loss and/ or deduction to her cannot exceed $30,000.

   b.   Incorrect. The partnership must prorate the $30,000 negative allocation to K between the rental loss and the charitable contributions.

   c.   Correct. The total allocation to K is limited to $30,000, consisting of 3/ 4 of each item allocated to her.

   d.   Incorrect. The total allocation to K is limited to $30,000 (her total contributions to the partnership), consisting of 3/ 4 of each item allocated to her.

6.

   a.   Incorrect. S will be entitled to receive at least the balance in her capital account.

   b.   Incorrect. Under a balancing provision, none of the loss on sale of the lease will be allocated to S.

   c.   Incorrect. The partnership recognizes a loss on sale of the leasehold. It would have to recognize a gain for S to receive more than the $100,000 pre-sale balance in her capital account.

   d.   Correct. Under the balancing allocation provision of the agreement, the entire $50,000 loss on sale of the leasehold can be allocated to G. Thus, S's capital balance will be unaffected by the loss on sale of the leasehold.

7.

   a.   Incorrect. The allocation increases, rather than diminishes, the after-tax economic consequences to partner B.

   b.   Correct. The allocation reduces A's tax liability outside the partnership, but reduces her economic interest in the partnership by more than it reduces her tax liability. Thus, the net effect is a reduction in A's after-tax economic consequences. (Note that the regulations assume there will be no future capital gain because the Sec. 704(b) value of the partnership's assets is presumed to equal their fair values).

   c.   Incorrect. The regulations assume there will be no future capital gain because the Sec. 704(b) value of the partnership's assets is presumed to equal their fair values. Thus, the allocation does not violate the transitory allocations test.

   d.   Incorrect. The allocation does not increase B's tax liability outside the partnership.

8.

   a.   Incorrect. E is entitled to receive the balance in her capital account upon liquidation of the partnership.

   b.   Incorrect. H is obligated to pay $250,000 to the partnership so that E can receive the full balance of her capital account upon liquidation of the partnership.

   c.   Correct. E will be entitled to receive the balance in her capital account on liquidation of the partnership.

   d.   Incorrect. This is the balance in partner H's capital account.

9.

   a.   Incorrect. G's capital balance may fall below zero.

   b.   Incorrect. Since L's capital balance may not fall below zero, L's share of the loss in excess of ($50,000) must be reallocated to G.

   c.   Correct. G will be allocated 20 percent of the loss, plus that portion of L's share of the loss in excess of ($50,000).

   d.   Incorrect. G will be allocated 20 percent of the loss, plus that portion of L's share of the loss in excess of ($50,000). L is allowed allocation of up to $50,000 of the loss.

10.

   a.   Correct. The depreciation allocation to RR does not reduce his capital account below zero and will therefore be recognized in its entirety.

   b.   Incorrect. Depreciation will be reallocated to QL, and away from RR, only to the extent that the original allocation creates or increases a deficit in RR's capital balance in excess of his share of partnership minimum gain.

   c.   Incorrect. None of the depreciation will be reallocated to QL this year.

   d.   Incorrect. No portion of the first year's depreciation will be reallocated to QL. All of the depreciation is allocated to RR, not 80 percent of it.

11.

   a.   Incorrect. Depreciation will constitute a nonrecourse deduction to the extent that it increases the excess of the outstanding balance of the nonrecourse debt over the tax basis of the property.

   b.   Correct. The basis of the machinery will be $240,000, which is $30,000 less than the outstanding balance of the nonrecourse loan.

   c.   Incorrect. The depreciation is a nonrecourse deduction only to the extent it reduces the basis of the property below the balance of the nonrecourse note.

   d.   Incorrect. Depreciation reduces the basis of the machinery to $240,000; the balance of the nonrecourse mortgage is $270,000, and the difference is a nonrecourse deduction. The gross income of the partnership is irrelevant to this calculation.

CHAPTER 2

Solutions to Knowledge Check Questions

1.

    a. Incorrect. Bill cannot shift the built-in gain to his partner(s).

    b. Incorrect. Only the pre-contribution gain is allocable wholly to Bill.

    c. Incorrect. Bill must also share in the gain in excess of the built-in gain.

    d. Correct. Bill will be allocated the entire $17,000 built-in gain inherent at the date of contribution, plus half of the $8,000 in post-contribution appreciation.

2.

    a. Incorrect. Section 704(c) applies only to the pre-contribution built-in gain inherent in the property contributed by Ellen.

    b. Correct. Ellen's partner will be allocated only his or her one-half share of the gain ($3,000) attributable to post-contribution appreciation in value of the property contributed by Ellen.

    c. Incorrect. Ellen's partner will only be allocated half of the post-contribution gain.

    d. Incorrect. Ellen will be allocated all of the pre-contribution gain and half of the post-contribution gain. The remainder will be allocated to her partner(s).

3.

    a. Incorrect. The pre-contribution "built-in" gain must be allocated wholly to Clara.

    b. Incorrect. Clara must report all of the pre-contribution gain and one-fourth of the post-contribution gain.

    c. Correct. Clara will be allocated all of the built-in gain inherent in the property at the date of contribution, plus one-fourth of the gain attributable to the post-contribution appreciation in value of the property for a total of $100,000.

    d. Incorrect. The portion of the gain attributable to post-contribution appreciation in value is shared by all the partners, not just the contributor (Clara).

4.

    a. Incorrect. In addition to the pre-contribution gain, Q must share in the gain attributable to the post-contribution appreciation in the contributed property.

    b. Incorrect. The pre-contribution "built-in" gain must be allocated solely to Q.

    c. Correct. The entire $150 pre-contribution gain, plus ½ of the $200 post-contribution gain must be allocated to Q for a total of $250.

    d. Incorrect. Q will be allocated only half of the gain attributable to post-contribution appreciation in the property.

5.

    a. Incorrect. This is one-third of *book* depreciation. Tax depreciation is only $30.

    b. Incorrect. Depreciation allocations are subject to the provisions of Section 704(c).

    c. Correct. Y and Z will be entitled to the same depreciation for tax that they are allocated for book, $12 each. X will be entitled to whatever amount of tax depreciation ($6) is left after the allocations to Y and Z.

    d. Incorrect. The other partners, Y and Z, will be allocated tax depreciation equal to their shares of book depreciation, not the other way around.

6.

  a. Incorrect. Tax depreciation exceeds the amount of book depreciation allocable to the other partners. Thus, A will receive an allocation of tax depreciation.

  b. Incorrect. Tax depreciation is first allocated to the other partners. A is entitled only to the residual left after the non-contributors have received full shares.

  c. Incorrect. Section 704(c) will limit A's share of tax depreciation.

  d. Correct. Partners B and C will each be entitled to $8,000 of depreciation expense for book and tax. A will be allocated the remaining tax depreciation of $2,000.

7.

  a. Incorrect. Under the traditional method, total depreciation allocations cannot exceed the aggregate amount of tax depreciation claimed by the partnership.

  b. Correct. After Ann's partner is allocated a share of tax depreciation equal to her share of book depreciation, there will be no tax depreciation left for Ann.

  c. Incorrect. Section 704(c) will limit the allocation of tax depreciation to Ann.

  d. Incorrect. This is Ann's share of *book* depreciation.

8.

  a. Incorrect. Book depreciation does not have to equal tax depreciation.

  b. Incorrect. Book depreciation must be computed at the same rate as tax depreciation.

  c. Correct. Tax depreciation in Y3 will equal $15,360, or 40 percent ($15,360/ $38,400) of the tax basis of the property at the date of contribution. Thus, book depreciation of $24,000 must equal 40 percent of the value of the property at the date of contribution.

  d. Incorrect. Book depreciation as a percentage of the *value* of the property at the date of contribution must equal tax depreciation as a percentage of the tax basis of the property at that date. This figure is based on the cost of the property rather than its value at the date of contribution.

9.

  a. Correct. After allocation of depreciation expense to partner B, no tax depreciation will be left to be allocated to A.

  b. Incorrect. Section 704(c) requires allocation of all the depreciation to partner B.

  c. Incorrect. This is the amount to be allocated to partner B.

  d. Incorrect. This is A's share of *book* depreciation.

10.

  a. Correct. All the gain will be allocated to M under Section 704(c).

  b. Incorrect. Section 704(c) will require that all gain be allocated to partner M.

  c. Incorrect. This is the amount of gain that will be allocated to partner M.

  d. Incorrect. This is the built-in gain inherent in the land, and would ordinarily be allocated to partner M, rather than P.

11.

    a. Incorrect. Under the remedial allocations method, P (as the noncontributing partner) will receive the same allocation for both tax and book purposes.

    b. Incorrect. This allocation ignores Section 704(c).

    c. Correct. The partnership realizes a ($25,000) book loss and a $15,000 tax gain. As the noncontributing partner, P will be allocated a ($12,500) loss for tax purposes, and M will be allocated a $27,500 tax gain.

    d. Incorrect. Under the remedial allocations method, P is entitled to deduct her share of post-contribution loss in the value of the property. P will not recognize any gain.

CHAPTER 3

Solutions to Knowledge Check Questions

1.

    a. Incorrect. R's share of the partnership's debt is treated as a contribution of money to the partnership.

    b. Correct. R's basis in the partnership is $100.

    c. Incorrect. This is the value of the property less the liability. Value is not relevant in a nontaxable transaction.

    d. Incorrect. R must also account for the transfer of debt.

2.

    a. Incorrect. A's share of partnership liabilities will increase her basis in the partnership interest.

    b. Incorrect. In computing basis in her partnership interest, A must account for both the liabilities she transfers to the partnership, and for her share of the partnership's liabilities.

    c. Correct. A's $250,000 share of partnership debt is treated as a contribution of money to the partnership under Section 752(a). A's basis is $50,000.

    d. Incorrect. Negative basis is not allowed. A's basis in her partnership interest will be equal to the basis of the property she contributed, less the debt encumbering that property, plus her share of partnership debt.

3.

    a. Incorrect. Under Section 752(b), a decrease in a partner's share of partnership liabilities is treated as a cash distribution from the partnership to the partner.

    b. Correct. The decrease in A's share of partnership liabilities ($83,333) will exceed A's basis in her partnership interest ($50,000), triggering recognition of gain under Section 731(a).

    c. Incorrect. This is the decrease in A's share of partnership liabilities in connection with the admission of C to the partnership. However, her basis in the interest was $50,000 prior to C's admission.

    d. Incorrect. C's cash contribution does not result in a gain to A. A will recognze gain equal to the excess of the deemed Section 752 distribution ($83,333) over the tax basis of her partnership interest.

4.

    a.   Correct. C's assumption of responsibility for the mortgage on property 2 exceeds her pre-liquidation share of partnership liabilities and the distribution will be nontaxable.

    b.   Incorrect. The built-in gain inherent in property 2 at the date of the liquidation is not triggered by the distribution.

    c.   Incorrect. C's assumption of the partnership's liability (mortgage on property 2) is greater than her relief from her share of the partnership's liabilities, so the net assumption of liabilities is treated as a cash contribution by C to the partnership and the transaction remains nontaxable.

    d.   Incorrect. C did not receive cash in excess of basis, so the transaction is nontaxable.

5.

    a.   Incorrect. Nonrecourse indebtedness generally does not increase the amount at risk.

    b.   Incorrect. Real estate debt will not always increase the amount at risk. For example, where a partnership purchases real estate using seller-financing the seller-financing will not increase the partners' amounts at risk.

    c.   Incorrect. The allocation of non-qualified nonrecourse liabilities to a general partner does not increase such partner's amount at risk under Section 465.

    d.   Correct. The amount at risk is increased only by a partner's or LLC member's share of *qualified* liabilities.

6.

    a.   Correct. A constructive liquidation analyses how the partners would share the partnership's liabilities in a worst-case scenario.

    b.   Incorrect. The partners cannot allocate partnership liabilities in the partnership agreement. Liabilities are allocated in accordance with the economic risks borne by the partners.

    c.   Incorrect. This process would indicate how much each partner would receive upon liquidation of the partnership, but sheds no light on how partnership liabilities should be allocated.

    d.   Incorrect. A constructive liquidation analyzes the consequences in a hypothetical worst-case scenario in order to determine how the partners would share responsibility for the partnership's liabilities.

7.

    a.   Correct. The regulations are based on the theoretical framework established in Section 704(b).

    b.   Incorrect. The regulations look to the economic obligations each partner would have (if any) in the hypothetical event that all the partnership's assets become worthless.

    c.   Incorrect. The tax capital accounts do not reflect the partners' economic arrangements with the partnership.

    d.   Incorrect. The liquidation is hypothetical, but is based on actual capital accounts.

8.

    a.   Incorrect. This is the allocation to the *limited* partners. Q is the general partner.

    b.   Correct. Q, the only general partner, will be allocated 100 percent of the partnership's recourse loan of $1,500,000.

    c.   Incorrect. Recourse indebtedness generally cannot be allocated to limited partners.

    d.   Incorrect. The limited partners generally cannot share in recourse debts.

9.

a. Incorrect. This is the portion of the loan that will be allocated to the limited partners.

b. Incorrect. S's guarantee of the loan will cause it to be characteri2ed as a recourse loan.

c. Correct. Due to S's guarantee, the loan is a recourse loan, allocable entirely to S, the only general partner.

d. Incorrect. This answer assumes that the limited partners will bear risk of loss for the loan to the extent of their capital contributions to the partnership. Under the regulations, no portion of a recourse loan can be allocated to the limited partners.

10.

a. Correct. Because of Q's disproportionate share of the risk of partnership losses, she will be allocated all of the partnership's recourse debt.

b. Incorrect. Recourse debts are not allocated in accordance with the partners' loss-sharing ratios, but in accordance with the results of a hypothetical constructive liquidation.

c. Incorrect. The partnership's recourse liability will be disproportionately allocated to Q to reflect her greater individual share of the risk of partnership losses.

d. Incorrect. This would be the reduction in L's capital account in the event of a hypothetical constructive liquidation, but L would still have a positive capital account balance. Since L's hypothetical capital account balance is positive L would not be allocated any of the recourse debt.

11.

a. Incorrect. The partnership's recourse liability will be disproportionately allocated to D to reflect her greater individual share of the risk of partnership losses.

b. Incorrect. Since the partners share in partnership losses differently, they will share responsibility for the partnership's recourse liabilities differently.

c. Correct. In a hypothetical constructive liquidation, D would be allocated $600,000 of the partnership's $1,000,000 loss on sale of the shopping center. This allocation would leave her with a $450,000 deficit in her capital account, which she would have to restore to enable the partnership to repay its recourse lender.

d. Incorrect. Although the debt is disproportionately allocated to D, a constructive liquidation would leave E with some personal responsibility for repayment as well.

12.

a. Incorrect. A constructive liquidation would leave B with a small amount of personal responsibility for repayment of the partnership's debt.

b. Incorrect. B's share of the debt will be less than her share of partnership losses.

c. Incorrect. B's share of partnership recourse liabilities must be determined by reference to the partners' obligations in a hypothetical constructive liquidation.

d. Correct. In a constructive liquidation, B would be allocated $150,000 of the partnership's $600,000 loss on the shopping center, reducing her capital account to negative $50,000. Thus, she would bear responsibility for $50,000 of the partnership's recourse debt.

CHAPTER 4

Solutions to Knowledge Check Questions

1.

    a. Incorrect. The guarantee of interest on the note will cause some or all of the note to be recharacterized as a recourse loan.

    b. Incorrect. Only that amount equal to the present value of the interest guaranteed by C will be recharacterized as a recourse loan.

    c. Incorrect. The note is recharacterized to the extent of the present value, rather than the face value, of the interest on the note.

    d. Correct. The lender will have recourse against C in the event that the partnership defaults on the interest due on the loan.

2.

    a. Incorrect. The pledge is recognized even though it is contingent.

    b. Correct. The regulations look to the value of the pledged property as of the date it was pledged to secure the loan.

    c. Incorrect. The amount of the loan recharacterized as recourse debt will be fixed as of the date the loan is made to the partnership.

    d. Incorrect. Since E has pledged real estate against the loan, she bears personal risk of loss and some or all of the liability will be recharacterized as recourse.

3.

    a. Incorrect. The *de minimis* rule focuses on the magnitude of the lender's investment in the partnership, rather than the nature of that interest.

    b. Incorrect. If related to a partner, the lender will be deemed related to the partnership.

    c. Correct. A qualified nonrecourse loan obtained from a partner or related person is *not* recharacterized as recourse debt if the lender has an interest in "each item of partnership income, gain, loss, deduction, or credit" of 10 percent or less for *every taxable year* that the partner is a member of the partnership.

    d. Incorrect. The *de minimis* rule is triggered if the lender has less than a 10 percent interest in each item of partnership income, gain, loss, deduction, and credit.

4.

    a. Incorrect. Minimum gain is not equal to the excess of FMV over book value.

    b. Correct. The minimum gain is equal to the excess of the debt balance ($850,000) over the basis of the property ($800,000).

    c. Incorrect. The nonrecourse debt exceeds the basis of the property, so the partnership has a minimum gain.

    d. Incorrect. The minimum gain is equal to the excess of the debt balance ($850,000) over the basis of the property ($800,000).

5.

    a.   Correct. The total minimum gain is $150,000, of which $50,000 is tax minimum gain and the remainder is book minimum gain.

    b.   Incorrect. The book minimum gain is determined by reference to the principal balance of the outstanding debt, rather than the fair market value of the property.

    c.   Incorrect. The total minimum gain must be divided between book and tax.

    d.   Incorrect. Minimum gain is based on the difference between tax basis or book value and the outstanding principal balance of the nonrecourse loan.

6.

    a.   Incorrect. The partner's share of partnership book minimum gain is a factor to be considered in allocating partnership nonrecourse liabilities.

    b.   Correct. Partner loss-sharing ratios are not relevant in allocating partnership nonrecourse liabilities.

    c.   Incorrect. The partner's share of partnership profits is a factor to be considered in allocating partnership nonrecourse liabilities.

    d.   Incorrect. The partner's share of partnership tax minimum gain is a factor to be considered in allocating partnership nonrecourse liabilities.

7.

    a.   Incorrect. This is J's capital balance.

    b.   Incorrect. The partners' loss sharing ratios are ignored in allocating nonrecourse liabilities.

    c.   Incorrect. The nonrecourse liability is allocated in accordance with the partners' interests in partnership profits (that is, minimum gain, Section 704(c) minimum gain, and other gain).

    d.   Correct. The partnership has no minimum gain, so the nonrecourse liability will be allocated 50:50 between the two partners, in accordance with their interests in partnership profits.

8.

    a.   Incorrect. This is the minimum gain.

    b.   Incorrect. This ignores the allocation of the minimum gain.

    c.   Incorrect. The partners will share the partnership's nonrecourse liability in accordance with their shares of partnership minimum gain, to the extent thereof, and then in accordance with their shares of partnership "regular" profits.

    d.   Correct. The partnership's minimum gain is $120,000, shared by the partners $24,000 to J and $96,000 to D. J will also be allocated 50 percent of the partnership's remaining $3,280,000 nonrecourse liability.

9.

    a.   Incorrect. This ignores the allocation of the minimum gain.

    b.   Incorrect. Walter's share of partnership minimum gain is 25 percent.

    c.   Correct. Walter's share of the nonrecourse debt is equal to 25 percent of the minimum gain ($15,000), plus 10 percent of the remaining balance of the mortgage ($85,000).

    d.   Incorrect. Walter's share of the debt is determined in two steps, rather than one, and is not equal to 25 percent of the entire amount.

10.

    a.   Incorrect. Interest expense is another significant partnership item.

    b.   Incorrect. Gain on sale of property is another significant partnership item.

    c.   Incorrect. Cancellation of debt income is another significant partnership item.

    d.   Correct. All of the above are other significant partnership items.

11.

    a.   Incorrect. The depreciation reduces the basis of the encumbered property to a level below the outstanding principal balance of the nonrecourse debt.

    b.   Correct. Depreciation expense reduces the book value (and tax basis) of the machinery to $400,000, which is $50,000 less than the outstanding balance of the nonrecourse mortgage.

    c.   Incorrect. Depreciation is not allocated *pro rata* between nonrecourse and financing. Instead, it is all presumed to be financed by equity, or recourse debt, until such time as the book value of the encumbered property falls below the outstanding balance of the nonrecourse debt.

    d.   Incorrect. Depreciation is a nonrecourse deduction only to the extent that it reduces the basis of the encumbered property below the outstanding balance of the nonrecourse mortgage.

12.

    a.   Incorrect. The liability is a Section 1.752-7 liability and should be ignored until such time as it is paid or G transfers her interest in the partnership.

    b.   Correct. Under Regs. Section 1.752-7, the liability will be ignored until such time as it is paid or G transfers her interest in the partnership. Thus, the transfer of cash by G is not offset by the transfer of the contingent liability.

    c.   Incorrect. The liability is ignored until the G sells her interest in the partnership or the partnership pays the liability. Thus, G's share does not increase her tax basis in the partnership interest.

    d.   Incorrect. The liability is ignored under Section 1.752-7, but the cash transfer increases G's basis in the partnership interest.

13.

    a.   Incorrect. In determining her gain on the sale, G must reduce her tax basis in the partnership interest by the remaining contingent liability, which is presumably $5 million.

    b.   Correct. Since the liability has not been satisfied, G must reduce her tax basis in the partnership interest by the remaining amount of the contingent liability in measuring the gain on sale.

    c.   Incorrect. G's tax basis in the partnership interest is reduced by the amount of the contingent liability prior to the sale.

    d.   Incorrect. G's tax basis is $1 million after subtracting the contingent liability. Sale for $6 million will therefore trigger a $5 million gain.

CHAPTER 5

Solutions to Knowledge Check Questions

1.
   a. Correct. Jamie does not recognize gain on receipt of a distribution other than cash.
   b. Incorrect. Jamie does not recognize gain on receipt of property, and the fair market value of the property received does not impact her basis in the partnership.
   c. Incorrect. Although the fair market value of the property received exceeds Jamie's basis in the partnership interest by $12,000, there is no gain recognized because it is a non-cash distribution.
   d. Incorrect. $4,000 is the difference between Jamie's partnership basis and tax basis of the property received. There would be no recognition of gain to that extent. Answer choice "a", indicating zero gain on the transaction is correct because no cash was received in the transaction.

2.
   a. Correct. Lynn's tax basis in property 1 cannot exceed her basis in the partnership interest immediately before receipt of the distribution.
   b. Incorrect. Although the property's tax basis is $30,000, Lynn cannot receive this tax basis. Her tax basis in the property received is limited to her tax basis of her partnership interest.
   c. Incorrect. The fair market value of the property received does not convey to her basis in the property. Lynn's tax basis in the property will be $23,000, the maximum basis she can have in this set of circumstances.
   d. Incorrect. Lynn's tax basis in property 1 is limited to her $23,000 basis in the partnership, regardless of the fact that the partnership's basis in the property is $30,000.

3.
   a. Incorrect. Perry must first reduce his tax basis in the partnership interest by the cash received before accounting for the property received.
   b. Incorrect. Perry's basis in property 1 cannot exceed his basis in the partnership interest immediately prior to receiving the distribution of property 1.
   c. Incorrect. The fair market value of the property received does not become Perry's basis in the property. His basis in the property will be limited to his basis in the partnership interest, after it is reduced by the cash received.
   d. Correct. The cash distribution reduces Perry's tax basis in his partnership interest to $8,000. This becomes his tax basis in property 1.

4.
   a. Correct. The reduction of Carlos' share of partnership liabilities is treated as a cash distribution, reducing his basis in the partnership interest to $15,000. This becomes his basis in property 1.
   b. Incorrect. The reduction of Carlos' share of partnership liabilities is treated as a cash distribution, his remaining $15,000 basis in the partnership becomes his tax basis in the property received.
   c. Incorrect. Carlos takes a substitute basis in property 1.
   d. Incorrect. Carlos would not receive the partnership's tax basis in the property. The reduction of Carlos' share of partnership liabilities is treated as a cash distribution, reducing his basis in the partnership interest to $15,000. This becomes his basis in property 1.

5.

    a.   Correct. Since Amy did not receive cash in excess of her basis in the partnership interest, she is not required to recognize gain on the distribution.

    b.   Incorrect. This distribution is taxable only to the extent that Amy received cash in excess of her basis in her partnership interest.

    c.   Incorrect. This is the aggregate appreciation in the value of the properties. It would be recognized by the partnership, not Amy, if this were a taxable transaction.

    d.   Incorrect. The distribution of property to a partner is generally a nontaxable transaction.

6.

    a.   Correct. Amy's basis in the properties is limited to her tax basis in the partnership interest immediately prior to the distribution.

    b.   Incorrect. Amy has insufficient basis in her partnership interest to absorb the full tax bases of the properties to the partnership.

    c.   Incorrect. Amy's basis in the properties received is determined by reference to their bases in the partnership's hands, rather than their fair market values.

    d.   Incorrect. Amy will take a carryover basis in the properties, limited in the aggregate to her tax basis in her partnership interest.

7.

    a.   Incorrect. Amy's basis in the distributed properties is equal to their basis in the partnership's hands, limited to her basis in the partnership interest prior to the distribution. Although she will "step down" the basis of property 2 due to this limitation, it will not be stepped all the way down to FMV in this case.

    b.   Correct. Since property 2 is the only property whose basis exceeded its FMV, and since the excess was larger than the total step-down to be taken by Amy, the entire step-down of $6,000 will be allocated to property 2.

    c.   Incorrect. The basis of property 2 will be reduced to reflect the step-down in basis required under Section 732.

    d.   Incorrect. Amy will allocate the entire step-down in basis to property 2.

8.

    a.   Incorrect. The step-down is not allocated equally between the two properties.

    b.   Correct. Since neither property has declined in value (that is, both properties have FMVs in excess of their basis), the basis reduction must be allocated between the two by reference to their relative basis to the partnership. 20/ 50 of the reduction will therefore be allocated to the second tract.

    c.   Incorrect. The step-down is allocated between the two properties by reference to their relative basis to the partnership, rather than their relative fair market values.

    d.   Incorrect. Keith will reduce the basis of both properties to reflect the difference between his basis in the partnership interest and the aggregate basis, to the partnership, of the distributed properties.

9.

    a.   Incorrect. R's basis in the partnership interest exceeds the tax basis of the cash and ordinary income property received in the distribution.

    b.   Correct. The step-down in basis of $8,000 is allocated entirely to the capital asset in this case.

    c.   Incorrect. R will take a reduced tax basis in the capital asset.

    d.   Incorrect. The distribution is not taxable, so R will not take a fair market value basis in the capital asset received from the partnership.

10.

    a.   Incorrect. This is Z's realized loss, but he cannot deduct it until he sells or otherwise disposes of the capital asset.

    b.   Incorrect. This is the excess of the tax basis of the property received over its FMV. Z cannot deduct this loss.

    c.   Correct. Since Z received property other than cash, receivables, or inventory, he cannot recognize a loss under Section 731(a)(2).

    d.   Incorrect. Z recognizes no loss on the distribution.

11.

    a.   Incorrect. Jamie is not required to step down the basis of any of the assets received.

    b.   Correct. Jamie cannot increase the basis of ordinary income assets received in a distribution from the partnership.

    c.   Incorrect. Jamie must take a carryover basis in ordinary income assets received in a partnership distribution.

    d.   Incorrect. Jamie will take a carryover basis in the receivables.

12.

    a.   Incorrect. The basis increase in the capital assets is allocated first to those assets whose FMV exceeds their tax basis.

    b.   Incorrect. The entire step-up in basis will be allocated to capital asset 2.

    c.   Correct. Because capital asset 1 has a basis equal to its FMV, it will not be allocated any portion of the basis increase.

    d.   Incorrect. Because capital asset 1 has a basis equal to its FMV, the entire basis increase will be allocated to capital asset 2.

13.

    a.   Incorrect. The basis increase in the capital assets is allocated first to those assets whose FMV exceeds their tax basis.

    b.   Correct. Because capital asset 1 has a basis equal to its FMV, the entire basis increase will be allocated to capital asset 2.

    c.   Incorrect. This is the FMV of capital asset 2.

    d.   Incorrect. The entire basis increase will be allocated to capital asset 2 and none of the increase will be allocated to capital asset 1.

CHAPTER 6

Solutions to Knowledge Check Questions

1.

    a.   Correct. In the absence of a Section 754 election, the LLC will not be able to adjust its basis in its assets. Gary's share of the inside basis of LLC assets will equal 25 percent, or $90,000.

    b.   Incorrect. Absent a Section 754 election, the LLC will not be allowed to increase its basis in its assets to reflect the price Gary paid for them.

    c.   Incorrect. This is the total basis of the partnership's assets.

    d.   Incorrect. This is the value of the partnership's assets.

2.

    a.   Incorrect. Since a Section 754 election is in effect, the LLC must adjust its basis in its remaining assets to reflect the amount paid by the acquiring member for his interest in those assets.

    b.   Correct. The amount of the basis adjustment under Section 743(b) is generally equal to the gain recognized by the selling member.

    c.   Incorrect. This is the selling partner's tax basis in the partnership interest.

    d.   Incorrect. This is the fair market value of the transferred partnership interest.

3.

    a.   Incorrect. The basis of this property must be increased to protect the buyer from recognizing gain that the seller effectively recognized upon sale of the interest.

    b.   Correct. The basis of this asset is increased by the amount of gain that would have been recognized by the transferee partner if the asset had been sold for its fair market value immediately after the purchase of the interest in the LLC.

    c.   Incorrect. Only the buyer's *share* of the appreciation in the property is added to the LLC's basis in the property.

    d.   Incorrect. The basis of this asset is increased by the buyer's share of the appreciation inherent in the property.

4.

    a.   Incorrect. This is D's basis in the newly acquired interest.

    b.   Incorrect. This is the seller's share of the basis of LLC assets.

    c.   Correct. D will recognize a $15,000 gain on the distribution. The partnership will be entitled to adjust its basis in its assets by a like amount.

    d.   Incorrect. Because D recognizes a gain on the distribution, the partnership—if it has a Section 754 election in effect – must increase its basis in its remaining assets under Section 734(b).

5.

    a.   Incorrect. This is the difference between the basis (zero) and the face value of the receivables.

    b.   Incorrect. This is the difference between the value of the assets received and Ben's tax basis in his partnership interest.

    c.   Incorrect. Ben will recognize a loss on the transaction, and the partnership will be required to adjust its basis in its assets by the same amount.

    d.   Correct. Ben will recognize a ($15,000) loss on receipt of the liquidating distribution, and the partnership will be required to reduce its basis in its remaining assets by this amount.

6.

    a.   Incorrect. Since the property distribution does not trigger gain to Robert, the difference between his basis in the interest and the FMV of the distributed property is not relevant in determining the amount of the basis adjustment.

    b.   Incorrect. Robert took a stepped-up basis in property 3, so the partnership will have to make a negative adjustment to the basis of its remaining assets.

    c.   Incorrect. Because Robert took a different basis in property 3 from the partnership, it will be required to adjust the basis of its remaining assets.

    d.   Correct. The basis adjustment is the inverse of the step-up in basis taken by Robert in property 3.

7.

    a.   Incorrect. The Section 734(b) adjustment is equal to the difference between the partnership's basis in the distributed property and Richard's basis in that property

    b.   Incorrect. This is the difference between the basis and fair market value of the distributed property.

    c.   Correct. The Section 734(b) adjustment is $8,000 if the partnership has a Section 754 election in effect.

    d.   Incorrect. Robert takes a different basis in the property than the partnership had in that property, so the partnership must adjust the basis of its remaining assets.

8.

    a.   Incorrect. Richard will now take a higher basis in the distributed property than the partnership had, so the partnership must *reduce* its basis in remaining assets.

    b.   Incorrect. The basis adjustment is calculated by comparing Richard's basis in the property with the partnership's *basis* in such property prior to the distribution.

    c.   Incorrect. The partnership must reduce its basis in its remaining assets to reflect the step-up in basis taken by Richard in the distributed property.

    d.   Correct. The partnership must reduce its basis in its remaining assets by $12,000.

9.

    a.   Correct. The distributee-partner will take a stepped-down basis in property 3 of only $30,000, entitling the partnership to increase the basis of its other assets by $6,000.

    b.   Incorrect. To protect the partners, the partnership must increase its tax basis in its remaining assets.

    c.   Incorrect. This is the difference between the basis and FMV of the distributed property.

    d.   Incorrect. Because the distributee-partner took a different basis in the asset than the partnership had, and the partnership had a Section 754 election in effect, the partnership is allowed to adjust its basis in its remaining properties.

10.

   a.   Incorrect. The property does not get stepped up all the way to fair market value.

   b.   Correct. The total basis adjustment is $14,000. Of this amount, $8,000 will be allocated to the inventory, reflecting the amount W paid for his share of this asset ($24,000 = 72,000 × ⅓) over his pre-adjustment share of the partnership's basis in this asset ($16,000 = 48,000 × ⅓).

   c.   Incorrect. The basis adjustment is not allocated in proportion to the pre-adjustment basis of partnership assets.

   d.   Incorrect. The basis of the inventory is adjusted upward to reflect the amount paid by the buyer for his share of this asset.

11.

   a.   Incorrect. The basis of ordinary income property is not reduced as a result of a Section 734(b) adjustment.

   b.   Correct. The negative Section 734(b) adjustment can be made only to property 1.

   c.   Incorrect. The basis adjustment is negative.

   d.   Incorrect. The basis of ordinary income property is not reduced as a result of a Section 734(b) adjustment.

12.

   a.   Correct. The negative adjustment is allocated first to the properties whose tax basis exceeds their fair market value.

   b.   Incorrect. Only property 1 has a tax basis in excess of its fair market value.

   c.   Incorrect. The negative adjustment is allocated first to assets with a tax basis in excess of fair market value.

   d.   Incorrect. The decline in value of property 1 is greater than the required basis reduction.

13.

   a.   Incorrect. The basis adjustment will be allocated to property 2.

   b.   Incorrect. No portion of the basis adjustment is allocated to property 1.

   c.   Correct. Because the basis and fair market value of property 1 are equal, the entire basis adjustment will be allocated to property 2.

   d.   Incorrect. The property does not get stepped up all the way to fair market value.

14.

   a.   Incorrect. The partnership does not increase its basis in its assets to their fair market values upon the death of a partner.

   b.   Correct. Under Section 732(d), Joe can elect to determine the basis of the distributed assets in his hands as if the basis adjustment under Section 743(b) had been made.

   c.   Incorrect. See Section 732(d).

   d.   Incorrect. Joe determines his basis in the distributed property as if a Section 754 election had been in effect at the date of his grandmother's death.

CHAPTER 7

Solutions to Knowledge Check Questions

1.
   a. Incorrect. J will recognize gain on sale of her partnership interest to an outside buyer.
   b. Incorrect. D's assumption of J's share of partnership liabilities is included in the selling proceeds.
   c. Correct. The selling price is $185,000. Subtracting the basis of $100,000 leaves an $85,000 gain.
   d. Incorrect. The selling price of the partnership interest is $185,000 and its basis is $100,000.

2.
   a. Incorrect. The sale is a fully taxable transaction.
   b. Incorrect. Eddie's tax basis in the partnership interest is not equal to the fair market value of the property contributed to the partnership in exchange for that interest.
   c. Correct. Eddie's LLC interest will be divided into two pieces – one piece with a holding period of six months (20 percent) and a second piece with a holding period of five years and six months (80 percent).
   d. Incorrect. One-fifth ($50/250) of Eddie's interest in the LLC will be treated as a short-term capital asset.

3.
   a. Incorrect. The inventory is a "hot" asset under Section 751 (a).
   b. Correct. Inventory is a "hot" asset under Section 751 (a).
   c. Incorrect. The stock portfolio is not a "hot" asset.
   d. Incorrect. Only the inventory is a "hot" asset.

4.
   a. Incorrect. The accounts receivable is not the only "hot" asset owned by the partnership.
   b. Incorrect. JD must recognize ordinary income in the amount that would have been allocated to her had the partnership sold all its Section 751 (a) assets for fair market value.
   c. Correct. Both the accounts receivable and equipment are "hot" assets.
   d. Incorrect. JD must be allocated a share of both the value and the basis of the "hot" assets.

5.
   a. Correct. To the extent Edward's gain is attributable to Section 1245 recapture income, it may not be reported on the installment method.
   b. Incorrect. The portion of the gain attributable to the unrealized receivables may be reported on the installment method.
   c. Incorrect. The portion of the gain attributable to the unrealized receivables may be reported on the installment method.
   d. Incorrect. The installment method may be used to report gain from the sale of an interest in a partnership or an LLC as long as one or more payments are received after the close of the taxable year in which the sale occurred.

6.

    a.   Incorrect. The termination does not trigger a built-in gain being recognized.

    b.   Correct. Sale of 50 percent or more of the interests in profits and capital will trigger a technical termination of the partnership.

    c.   Incorrect. The termination does not trigger a deemed sale of partnership assets.

    d.   Incorrect. Sale of 30 percent of the interest in profits and capital of the partnership will not trigger recognition of 30 percent of built-in gain existing at the time of the sale.

7.

    a.   Incorrect. The new partnership continues to use the old partnership's EIN.

    b.   Correct. The new partnership must make new elections.

    c.   Incorrect. Section 704(c) gains inherent in partnership assets retain their character in the new partnership.

    d.   Incorrect. The book and tax capital accounts of the continuing partners carry over to the new partnership.

8.

    a.   Incorrect. Sale of the same interest twice only counts as one transfer.

    b.   Incorrect. These two transfers involve the same interest and therefore only a 30 percent interest in the partnership is deemed to have been sold for purposes of Section 708(b)(1)(B).

    c.   Incorrect. It does not matter whether Mario is a related party.

    d.   Correct. The sale of the same interest twice only counts as one transfer. Burl's sale will not trigger a technical termination of the partnership.

9.

    a.   Incorrect. Partnership interests cannot be exchanged tax-free under Section 1031.

    b.   Correct. The exchange of a 50 percent interest in profits and capital in a taxable transaction will trigger a technical termination under Section 708(b)(1)(B).

    c.   Incorrect. The exchange does not constitute a sale of an interest in 50 percent or more of the profits and capital in Edelburgh Partnership.

    d.   Incorrect. The exchange of a 50 percent interest in profits and capital in a taxable transaction will trigger a technical termination under Section 708(b)(1)(B).

10.

    a.   Correct. The tax basis of the "old" partnership's assets carries over to the "new" partnership.

    b.   Incorrect. Assets are not deemed sold in connection with a technical termination and the partnership's tax basis does not change.

    c.   Incorrect. The "new" partnership takes the same basis in its assets as the "old" partnership had.

    d.   Incorrect. The "new" partnership does not step-down the basis of its assets.

11.

    a. Incorrect. Transfer of appreciated assets to the "new" partnership in a Section 708(b)(1)(B) termination is ignored for purposes of Section 704(c).

    b. Correct. Regulations Section 1.704-4(a)(4)(ii) provide that Section 704(c) built-in gains and losses of the "old" partnership carry over to the "new" partnership.

    c. Incorrect. Only that portion of the value of Section 704(c) property that was originally subject to the provisions of Section 704(c) will continue to be subject to those provisions in the "new" partnership.

    d. Incorrect. Regulations Section 1.704-4(a)(4)(ii) provide that Section 704(c) built-in gains and losses of the "old" partnership carry over to the "new" partnership.

Learn More

AICPA CPE

Thank you for selecting AICPA as your continuing professional education provider. We have a diverse offering of CPE courses to help you expand your skillset and develop your competencies. Choose from hundreds of different titles spanning the major subject matter areas relevant to CPAs and CGMAs, including:

- Governmental & Not-for-Profit accounting, auditing, and updates
- Internal control and fraud
- Audits of Employee Benefit Plans and 401(k) plans
- Individual and corporate tax updates
- A vast array of courses in other areas of accounting & auditing, controllership, management, consulting, taxation, and more!

Get your CPE when and where you want

- Self-study training options that includes on-demand, webcasts, and text formats with superior quality and a broad portfolio of topics, including bundled products like –
  - ➢ CPExpress for immediate access to hundreds of one and two-credit hour online courses for just-in-time learning at a price that is right
  - ➢ Annual Webcast Pass offering live Q&A with experts and unlimited access to the scheduled lineup, all at an incredible discount.
- Staff training programs for audit, tax and preparation, compilation and review
- Certificate programs offering comprehensive curriculums developed by practicing experts to build fundamental core competencies in specialized topics
- National conferences presented by recognized experts
- Affordable AICPA courses on-site at your organization – visit **aicpalearning.org/on-site** for more information.
- Seminars sponsored by your state society and led by top instructors. For a complete list, visit **aicpalearning.org/publicseminar**.

Take control of your career development

The AICPA | CIMA Competency and Learning website at **https://competency.aicpa.org** brings together a variety of learning resources and a self-assessment tool, enabling tracking and reporting of progress toward learning goals.

Visit the AICPA store at cpa2biz.com/CPE to browse our CPE selections.

Just-in-time learning at your fingertips 24/7

Where can you get <u>unlimited online access</u> to 900+ credit hours (650+ CPE courses) for one low annual subscription fee?

CPExpress, the AICPA's comprehensive bundle of online continuing professional education courses for CPAs, offers you immediate access to hundreds of one and two-credit hour courses. You can choose from a full spectrum of subject areas and knowledge levels to select the specific topic you need when you need it for just-in-time learning.

Access hundreds of courses for one low annual subscription price!

How can CPExpress help you?

- ✓ Start and finish most CPE courses in as little as 1 to 2 hours with 24/7 access so you can fit CPE into a busy schedule

- ✓ Quickly brush up or get a brief overview on hundreds of topics when you need it

- ✓ Create and customize your personal online course catalog for quick access with hot topics at your fingertips

- ✓ Print CPE certificates on demand to document your training – never miss a CPE reporting deadline!

- ✓ Receive free Quarterly updates – Tax, Accounting & Auditing, SEC, Governmental and Not-For-Profit

Quantity Purchases for Firm or Corporate Accounts

If you have 10 or more employees who require training, the Firm Access option allows you to purchase multiple seats. Plus, you can designate an administrator who will be able to monitor the training progress of each staff member. To learn more about firm access and group pricing, visit aicpalearning.org/cpexpress or call 800.634.6780.

To subscribe, visit **cpa2biz.com/cpexpress**

Why AICPA?

Think of All the Great Reasons to Join the AICPA.

CAREER ADVOCACY SUPPORT
On behalf of the profession and public interest on the federal, state and local level.

PROFESSIONAL & PERSONAL DISCOUNTS
Save on travel, technology, office supplies, shipping and more.

ELEVATE YOUR CAREER
Five specialized credentials and designations (ABV®, CFF®, CITP®, PFS™ and CGMA®) enhance your value to clients and employers.

HELPING THE BEST AND THE BRIGHTEST
AICPA scholarships provide more than $350,000[1] to top accounting students.

GROW YOUR KNOWLEDGE
Discounted CPE on webcasts, self-study or on-demand courses & more than 60 specialized conferences & workshops.

PROFESSIONAL GUIDANCE YOU CAN COUNT ON
Technical hotlines & practice resources, including Ethics Hotline, Business & Industry Resource Center and the Financial Reporting Resource Center.

KEEPING YOU UP TO DATE
With news and publications from respected sources such as the Journal of Accountancy.

MAKING MEMBERS HAPPY
We maintain a 94%+ membership renewal rate.

FOUNDED ON INTEGRITY
Representing the profession for more than 125 years.

RELATIONSHIPS THAT COUNT
Over 400,000 Members in 145 Countries

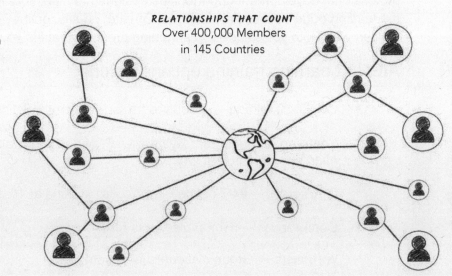

TO JOIN, VISIT:
aicpa.org/join or call 888.777.7077.